W9-ACD-721

Black Writers of the Thirties

Black Writers
of the
Thirties

James O. Young

Louisiana State University Press / Baton Rouge

Dale H. Gramley Library
SALEM COLLEGE
Winston-Salem, N. C. 27108

PS
153
N5
Y6
1973

ISBN 0–8071–0060–9
Library of Congress Catalog Card Number 72–96402
Copyright © 1973 by Louisiana State University Press
All rights reserved
Manufactured in the United States of America
Printed by Heritage Printers, Inc.,
Charlotte, North Carolina
Designed by Albert R. Crochet

For Angela, my wife,
and Timothy and Andrew, my sons

Contents

Preface

In 1929, President Robert Russa Moton of Tuskegee Institute published *What the Negro Thinks,* fully confident that he had recorded the "typical . . . thoughts that go through the minds of Negroes in all parts of the country," regardless of their social, economic, or intellectual backgrounds. His ambitious project was predicated upon the widely held assumption that "the Negro" really existed. In the present study I have attempted to avoid Moton's simplistic generalization. Rather, I have tried to examine the ideas in the published works of black American writers in a variety of political, economic, social, and cultural contexts during the Great Depression of the 1930s. In doing so, I have discovered little of the unanimity which Moton was probably desirous of finding.

Most scholars who have studied the intellectual history of black America have been attracted to the Washington-Du Bois feud, or to the flamboyant Harlem Renaissance of the 1920s, or, more recently, to the role of writers in the contemporary Negro revolution. They have largely ignored the history of black writers during the depression era. This period, however, saw the rise to prominence of a new generation of men and women whose orientation toward the problems and culture of black America often departed substantially from that of the older generation.

Probably the most important basis for the differences between the older and the younger generations resided in the fact that the older men were "race men." A "race man," as Horace Cayton has described him in his autobiography, was "an individual who was proud of his race and always tried to uphold it whether it was good or bad, right or wrong." These older men had been fighting the race's battles for decades. Whether in the face of nationwide depression or the ultimate crisis of war, they tended to look at all problems and possible solutions from the perspective of race, because race had been the single most influential factor in their lives. Many of them were convinced that the problems of race were the most significant problems facing the nation, and, indeed, the whole world. It was impossible for them to be objective about anything concerning the race. Many, such as the historian Carter Woodson, were romantic black nationalists. All of the race men, in varying degrees, expressed what younger writers condemned as "race chauvinism."

A second factor which separated the older men from the younger generation was the fact that, with the notable exception of James Weldon Johnson, the values of the older men were largely those of nineteenth-century middle-class society. They thought in terms of thrift, hard work, sacrifice, respectability, and individual enterprise. Their literary tastes inclined towards genteel romanticism. These values often forced them to be embarrassed by, or to deny the reality of, much of the black man's experience in this country. For, ironically, much of their so-called chauvinism was designed to demonstrate to white America that there was no valid reason that respectable black Americans should not be integrated into the mainstream of society.

Most of the younger writers who came on the scene during, or immediately before, the depression era tended to have a broader perspective than the race men. The dramatic impact of the economic crisis led many of them to believe that the forces, and particularly the economic forces, which affected all men were equal to, if not more important than, race in the lives of black Americans.

This was particularly true of the academic radicals who sometimes ignored race almost altogether, while creative writers, never losing sight of the reality or pervasiveness of race, tried to dramatize the black experience in all of its complexity.

Many of these younger writers charged that the older generation of race men had given black Americans an excessively provincial view. Because Negroes were predominantly of the working classes, they thought that many of their problems were really the problems of labor, not necessarily of race. Hence, while many of the older men were calling upon Afro-Americans to organize among themselves, the young writers often publicized the idea that black workers should ally themselves with white workers in a united front. Several black poets somewhat romantically celebrated this proposal as if it was already a reality.

Some of the younger writers discussed in this study were university-trained social scientists who attempted to carry the objectivity of their discipline into their understanding of race and the problems of race. Among the younger intellectuals they were the most intolerant of what they ridiculed as the emotional "black chauvinism" of the race men. Unfortunately, they also tried to impose rather optimistic social theories upon harsh social realities.

The young creative writers also turned away from the romantic glorification of so-called racial traits and "respectable" race heroes to attempt realistic interpretations of the lives of black men. In so doing they brought into view much of the ugliness which the older race men had tenaciously kept from the public eye for fear that it would reinforce the larger society's conception of Negro inferiority. But instead of exposing the black man's inferiority, the most talented among them demonstrated the ultimate universality of all human experience, whether black or white.

No attempt is being made here to set up a simple dichotomy between the thinking of the older race men and the young radicals. In some instances their views merged. For example, almost all black writers, whether they supported President Roosevelt or not, were generally critical of the affect of the New Deal on the status of black Americans. Also, though they concerned themselves with the same issues, most black writers did not consistently side with either the older race men or the young radicals. Men like William Pickens and A. Philip Randolph offered their own alternative positions.

Finally, I must comment on my criteria for selecting writers. Selection was, of necessity, based upon subjective judgments. I doubt that there is any way to scientifically quantify the relative importance of these men. In the preparation of this study I carefully perused the writings of more than one hundred significant writers. I finally selected those who enjoyed the widest reputation —those who appeared in print most frequently and whose names were most commonly mentioned in Afro-American periodicals and weeklies. Further, while not ignoring communism as an influence or an issue, I have not given much attention to Communist writers whose viewpoints were merely a puppetlike repetition of the current Party line. That has been analyzed elsewhere. I have been concerned with how a gifted writer such as Richard Wright, who often deviated from the line, grappled with its discipline in an effort to maintain his individual identity.

I am deeply indebted to a number of people for their advice and encouragement during the preparation of this study. The original draft was prepared as a doctoral dissertation in history at the University of Southern California under the direction of Joseph Boskin and Howard S. Miller. Professor Boskin, currently of Boston University, first introduced me to the fascinating realm of Afro-American history, and it was upon his suggestion that I undertook the present study. His influence upon my thinking has been enormous. To Professor Miller, currently of the University of Missouri at St. Louis, I am equally grateful. If this book is intelligible, his extensive criticisms are responsible, and his sense of humor often prevented an overly serious student from descending into a state of melancholia. Professors Dean Flower, of Smith College, and Stephen Moore, of the University of Southern California, both carefully read the entire manuscript and offered intelligent criticism. Professors Frank Mitchell and John Schutz, both of the University of Southern California, extended helpful advice on numerous occasions. Former fellow students, Joseph Joyce and Ronald Ross, also made pertinent suggestions. The research for this study was facilitated by the staffs of a number of libraries. Special thanks go to the staffs of the Arthur Schomburg Collection of Negro Literature and History, a branch of the New York Public Library; the Fifth Avenue branch of the New York Public Library; the University of Southern California Library; the University of California at Los Angeles Research Library; the Bancroft Library at the University of California; and the Los Angeles Public Library. Financial assistance during the preparation of this book was generously provided by a National Defense Education Act Title IV Fellowship and a John Randolph Haynes and Dora Haynes Foundation Fellowship. To those people responsible for providing and awarding these grants I am immensely indebted. I also wish to thank Mr. Charles East, Mr. Leslie Phillabaum, and Ms. Beverly Jarrett of the Louisiana State University Press, for their assistance in the preparation of the book for publication.

Finally, it is really impossible to adequately express the depth of gratitude which I feel toward those three people whose love and forbearance were my main sources of inspiration. To Angela, my wife, and to Timothy and Andrew, my sons, this book is dedicated.

Los Angeles, California
March, 1973

Black Writers of the Thirties

1

Aged Race
Men

Late in August, 1933, the National Association for the Advancement of Colored People (NAACP) called together many of black America's intellectual elite to discuss the problems of the race in light of the depression. The magnitude of the crisis was such that the older race leaders felt it incumbent upon them "to bring together and into sympathetic understanding, Youth and Age interested in the Negro problem."[1]

The Amenia conference of 1933, held at the palatial Hudson River estate of NAACP president Joel Spingarn, brought scant sympathy and less understanding. For three days, the young intellectuals, such as Ralph Bunche, E. Franklin Frazier, and Abram Harris, denounced the tactics and ideologies of their elders. They charged that the ideas of long-time leaders like W. E. B. Du Bois

1. W. E. B. Du Bois, "Youth and Age at Amenia," *Crisis*, XL (November, 1933), 226. For an interesting account of the Amenia conference, and one which differs somewhat in its emphases from that offered in this chapter, see Raymond Wolters, *Negroes and the Great Depression* (Westport, Conn.: Greenwood Publishing Corp., 1970), 219–29. Wolters bases his analysis principally upon internal evidence and points out that the young radicals saw the value of intraracial unity, whereas the present study, based upon published materials, emphasizes the fact that the young radicals did not publicize this aspect of their thinking. For other discussions of the Amenia conference, see S. P. Fullinwider, *The Mind and Mood of Black America: Twentieth-Century Thought* (Homewood, Ill.: Dorsey Press, 1969), 175–77; and for discussions of Du Bois's role in the conference and the events surrounding it, see Francis L. Broderick, *W. E. B. Du Bois: Negro Leader in a Time of Crisis* (Stanford: Stanford University Press, 1959), 150–79; and Elliott M. Rudwick, *W. E. B. Du Bois: A Study in Minority Group Leadership* (Philadelphia: University of Pennsylvania Press, 1961), 265–85.

and James Weldon Johnson were irrelevant. They were "race men" —men who looked at all problems and solutions with a racial perspective. In their provincialism, the older men had overlooked the obvious relationships between the Negro's problems and the larger issues confronting the nation. The manifesto which these young men published after the conference was thought by some to be the beginning of a second Niagara Movement.[2] Indeed, the document had great symbolic value because it indicated just how far they had moved away from the older men.

Besides repudiating the provinciality of the older generation, they went on to attack their old-style liberalism. While their elders had generally continued to place their faith in the struggle for civil rights within the capitalistic system, many of the young men, like so many other intellectuals during the 1930s, were convinced that industrial capitalism had failed. Hence, the primary problem for black Americans was not civil rights or even racism, but rather the exploitation of labor by private capital. The older leadership, they charged, had practically ignored the basic economic needs of the black masses. Negroes must, they thought, achieve economic power first of all. This would be impossible under the present economic system. So they posited three possible alternatives: to follow European models and substitute either fascism or communism, or to rebuild in the direction of a socialized democracy. Since they believed that fascism would most certainly "crystalize the Negro's position at the bottom of the social structure," and that communism would demand a monumental transformation in the psychology of both white and black workers in the United States, they advocated reform over revolution.[3]

2. Ralph Bunche, "The Programs, Ideologies, Tactics and Achievements of Negro Betterment and Interracial Organizations," memorandum for the Carnegie-Myrdal Study (MS in the Schomburg Collection of the New York Public Library), II, 209; "Current Events of Importance in Negro Education," *Journal of Negro Education*, II (October, 1933), 516. For a definition of a "race man," see Horace Cayton's autobiography, *Long Old Road* (New York: Trident Press, 1965), 250.

3. "Current Events of Importance," 516–17.

They thought that the older, liberal methods of agitation for civil rights would not bring about such reform. The only viable method was for the white and black workers to unite and force the necessary legislation because "the welfare of white and black labor is one and inseparable." The "problem" for these young radicals, unlike their elders, was essentially class, not race. They optimistically assumed that with the creation of a true class consciousness among all American workers, racial antagonism would almost automatically disappear. To bring about such a change in attitude, they called for a mass labor movement, embracing skilled and unskilled, black and white workers. Such a movement might eventually become a separate labor party, but for the present it would exert pressure on the two already-existing parties for wide-ranging social legislation such as old age pensions, unemployment insurance, and the regulation of child and female labor.

Thus, the younger radical intellectuals saw the solution of the race's problems within the solution of the problems of the laboring classes in a depression-ridden America. In their published writings throughout the 1930s they would continue to advocate the unity of all workers in hopes that they might be forged into a political and economic force which would demand the creation of a socialized society. They acknowledged that black Americans were faced with certain specific problems; and in private some of them, such as Frazier, called for internal unity, but this idea was not publicized by them.[4] In their published writings at least, they generally tended to disregard the importance of race. Indeed, they gave the appearance of seeking to escape from it. It was this position on the importance of race which, perhaps more than any other single factor, made communication difficult, if not impossible, between the radical young intellectuals and the older race men for the rest of the decade.

W. E. B. Du Bois, who bore the brunt of much of the criticism at

4. Wolters, *Negroes and the Great Depression*, 224–25.

the conference because of the racial orientation of his thinking, was disappointed by this failure of communication. He found the young men intelligent, even inspiring, but also impetuous. "Their difficulty," he wrote, "was mainly the difficulty of all youth. Inspired and swept on by its vision, it does not know or rightly interpret the past and is apt to be too hurried to carefully study the present."[5] Du Bois believed that the young radicals were naïvely optimistic in their faith in class unity as a panacea for race relations. They had ignored the tragic history of racial relations in the twentieth century—a history in which Du Bois and many of the older race men had been deeply involved, and a history which Du Bois thought gave black men little cause for optimism.

But the race leader most critical of youth at Amenia was not even present at the conference. The septuagenarian, Dean Kelly Miller of Howard University, was insulted because "the leadership of the elders was waved aside with condescending deference." His disturbance also stemmed from his interpretation of the Amenia conference as something of a turning point. "Up to the time of the second Amenia conference," he noted, "reliance for the hope of the race was placed in the Constitution, philanthropy, and religion. The appeal was made to the conscience of the nation and to the sense of justice and fair play of the American people." But, now, sadly, the "young elite" had chosen their model from Moscow. "The gospel of benevolence is supplanted by the gospel of guts"[6] wrote Miller. The old dean was no doubt fearful that the economics of the Amenia radicals would alienate those pious and philanthropic capitalists who had heretofore been uppermost among the Negro's benefactors.

Finally Miller, like most of the older generation, was incredulous

5. Du Bois, "Youth and Age at Amenia," 226.
6. Kelly Miller, "The Young Negro Brain Trust," Norfolk *Journal and Guide*, September 23, 1933.

at the naïveté of the "self-styled young intellectuals" in their advocacy of white and black labor solidarity as the basic solution. He thought that this showed a surprising lack of knowledge of the psychology of race prejudice. After all, it was the white workers who formed the mobs which lynched black workers. Miller offered the brash young men a bit of fatherly advice: "Do not be too hasty in removing the ancient land marks which the fathers have set."[7]

Reared on a backcountry South Carolina farm during Reconstruction and a Howard graduate, class of 1886, Miller had spent most of his career at his alma mater as a faculty member and administrator. His was a voice that was heard widely in Afro-America throughout the 1920s and 1930s. His newspaper columns, syndicated in Afro-American weeklies all over the nation, carried his message to a far wider audience than that reached by the Amenia radicals.

Intellectually, Miller never forgot those values which he learned on the farm and the mid-nineteenth-century middle-class values which he imbibed as an undergraduate at Howard. A self-styled "ameliorist,"[8] he continued to believe that the best hope for the race was "the Constitution, philanthropy, and Christianity." Such views inspired the younger radicals to dub Miller an "intellectual mossback."[9] Perhaps more than any other figure, he was the antithesis of the Amenia radicals whom he had mistakenly lumped in the same class with avowed Communists.[10]

Much of Miller's attack upon the young "radicals" was also an attack upon his aggressive junior colleagues at Howard University. Before his retirement in 1934, he had been the sociology instructor at Howard, even though he was not formally trained in the disci-

7. *Ibid.*
8. "The Negro Radical Exposed by Kelly Miller," Pittsburgh *Courier*, September 15, 1934.
9. George Streator, "Letter to the Editor: Kelly Miller a Mossback?" New York *Amsterdam News*, September 22, 1934.
10. "Kelly Miller Says—," Chicago *Defender*, June 8, 1935.

pline. His teaching method consisted of platitudinous lectures on self-help and character building.[11] When Mordecai Johnson assumed the presidency of Howard in 1928, however, he brought in young, well-trained professionals like Ralph Bunche, Sterling Brown, Abram Harris, and finally, Miller's replacement as head of the sociology department, E. Franklin Frazier. There was immediate and often bitter conflict between Miller and the older faculty, on the one side, and Johnson and the young faculty on the other.[12] According to one young critic, Miller felt threatened because "the young faculty . . . not only know more about Miller's field than Miller ever knew, but in addition have never bothered to join hands with him in trying to get ignorant."[13]

Indeed, there was more than a little anti-intellectualism in Miller's assaults on the well-educated young radicals: "As a whole, they are inebriated with the first effects of a little learning which has always been a dangerous thing." In addition to the threat of their "little learning," he saw great danger arising from the fact that "they tend to be purely agnostic and pagan."[14] He truly believed that their radical economic theories and irreverence were threats to the future of the race.

Miller thought that the impractical, theoretical orientation of the young radicals prevented them from seeing the reality of the Negro's situation in America. Unlike them, he always saw the Negro's fundamental problem in terms of the color line. Also, unlike his youthful detractors, he was not optimistic about its destruction; it was always for him a "far off, divine event." Until then, the Negro, like the patient Job, must simply mark time and suffer affliction.

11. Fullinwider, *Mind and Mood of Black America*, 97.
12. See "Kelly Miller Says H. U. Prexy Presided Over One Session of Red Conference," Baltimore *Afro-American*, June 1, 1935.
13. Streator, "Kelly Miller a Mossback?"
14. "The Negro Radical Exposed by Kelly Miller," and Kelly Miller, "The Reorganization of the Higher Education of the Negro in Light of Changing Conditions," *Journal of Negro Education*, V (July, 1936), 491.

Faith and patience would win in the end, while "hope for relief through disruptive agitation is merely the optimism of the fool." Only a change of heart among the all-powerful whites would erase the color line. "After all has been said and done," he concluded, "the race must learn to endure that which it cannot cure."[15]

Miller's plea for docility sometimes appeared to be motivated by an acceptance of the inferiority of the black man. Although, as a race man, he would have avoided making such comments before a white audience, he frequently criticized the race in his columns in the Afro-American press. "It is well that the Negro with his obvious imperfections of character has not been able to acquire any considerable amount of wealth," he wrote, for "he would waste it in riotous living."[16] The whites ruled the "lesser breeds" because they were "the most dynamic and progressive of all of the children of men."[17]

If Miller believed that black Americans were essentially incapable of improving their social status, he did not believe that economic advance was impossible. However, unlike the young radicals, he did not look to the urban proletariat for salvation. Instead, he and a number of other southern race men, such as Gordon Blaine Hancock, Benjamin F. Hubert, and P. B. Young, looked back to the "eternally sound" advice of Booker T. Washington, who insisted that the small farm was the site of the Negro's economic salvation.[18]

15. Kelly Miller, "Is the Color Line Crumbling?" *Opportunity*, VII (September, 1929), 292; his "Should Black Turn Red?" *Opportunity*, XI (November, 1933), 330; and his "I'm Not in the Schuyler Bracket . . . Du Bois Misrepresents My Position," Pittsburgh *Courier*, April 14, 1934.

16. Kelly Miller, "The Deceitfulness of Wealth," Norfolk *Journal and Guide*, September 2, 1933. For other examples see Kelly Miller, "Is Black Turning Red?" Louisiana *Weekly*, April 11, 1936; and Kelly Miller, "The Jew in Account with the Negro," New York *Amsterdam News*, March 30, 1935.

17. Kelly Miller, "The Negro in Europe," New York *Amsterdam News*, December 18, 1929.

18. "Kelly Miller Commends Editorial on Backward Movement to the Farm," New York *Age*, September 16, 1933. See also Raymond Gavins, "Gordon Blaine Hancock: Southern Black Leader in a Time of Crisis, 1920–1954" (Ph.D. dissertation,

The Negro, thought Miller, was not yet ready for the mechanization and urban environment of the twentieth century. Rather, his future must depend upon earning a subsistence in the rural South. "The Negro is not only a peasant but a tropical folk. He is not adapted to cold climate nor crowded city life, not yet to manufactury."[19] He predicted that it would take at least another full generation of "farm discipline" to prepare the Negro race for industrial life.

Miller was heartened because the whites were abandoning the farms in large numbers in order to move into the city: "Every time the white man abandons a farm . . . I would like to see a Negro take it up." Reassuringly, he said, "Give any Negro forty acres and a mule, and he can succeed in raising a crop of cotton." Thus, the Negro could succeed as a small individual farm proprietor where the white man—"the most dynamic and progressive of all the children of men"—had already admitted defeat. All the Negro had to do was to "over-work and under-live the more arrogant majority."[20] Despite all the scientific studies which deprecated the Negro's rural life,[21] Miller was confident of the efficacy of his plan; after all, he himself had risen up from the farm.[22] Younger critics were cynical of Miller's motives. "Kelly Miller," wrote George Streator, "is also a partisan of the hoe—for other men's children."[23] And Du Bois, who often traded sharp words with Miller, suggested that he would

University of Virginia, 1970), 101–104. Hancock was a professor of economics and sociology at Virginia Union University and a leader of the Commission on Interracial Cooperation. Hubert was the president of Georgia State Industrial College, and Young was the editor of the Norfolk *Journal and Guide*.

19. "Kelly Miller Views Farm Life," Norfolk *Journal and Guide*, January 7, 1933.

20. Kelly Miller, "Back to the Farm," Norfolk *Journal and Guide*, December 31, 1932; his "King Cotton and His Black Subjects," Boston *Chronicle*, September 19, 1931; and his "The Farm—The Negro's Best Chance," *Opportunity*, XIII (January, 1935), 24. This article is the most complete statement by Miller on the subject.

21. See for example Charles S. Johnson's *The Shadow of the Plantation* (Chicago: University of Chicago Press, 1934).

22. Kelly Miller, "The American Negro Should Secure a Firm Grip on the Soil," Washington *Tribune*, October 19, 1933.

23. George Streator, "In Search of Leadership," *Race*, I (Winter, 1935–36), 20.

like to see a few of the advocates of the "Back to the Land" movement "sentenced to the Georgia farming belt with blackened faces
for six good long months." "After that," he concluded, "we're ready
to argue with them cheerfully and to the point."[24]

For Miller, the farm offered not only economic salvation, but also
the preservation of those values which he held so dear. In fact, he
contended that most of those who had already been ruined by the
city could not survive the rigors of agrarian life: "They are so ef-
feminated in mind and body by urban influences that they do not
possess the virility, the stubbornness of spirit, the hardihood of
purpose," to be of any value should they decide to return. Thus, he
did not advocate "Back to the Land" so much as "Stay on the
Land."[25] Although Miller continued to champion this program
throughout the decade, nothing ever came of it. Former black
sharecroppers and tenant farmers continued their city-bound
migration.[26]

In general, Miller countered the position of most articulate
blacks, who by 1934 were becoming increasingly skeptical of the
New Deal because of its ineffectiveness in dealing with the problems of black Americans.[27] Miller ardently approved of the New
Deal's approach to the economic problems of the country, particularly its defense of the free-enterprise system. In a fashion which
was typical of him, he praised President Roosevelt because "the
times demand liberal conservatism and conservative liberalism."
Happily, he concluded, "in Roosevelt these qualities meet." In
regard to the black man's position in American society, Miller eulo-
gized what he called the president's leadership in the "moral recovery" of the nation: "President Roosevelt, using the moral authority

24. W. E. B. Du Bois, "As the Crow Flies," *Crisis*, XL (September, 1933), 197.
25. Miller, "The Farm—The Negro's Best Chance"; his "The Negro's Economic
Plight," New York *Amsterdam News*, October 4, 1933.
26. Gavins, "Gordon Blaine Hancock," 103–104; August Meier and Elliott M.
Rudwick, *From Plantation to Ghetto: An Interpretive History of American Negroes*
(New York: Hill & Wang, 1966), 210–11.
27. Wolters, *Negroes and the Great Depression*, 219.

Dale H. Gramley Library
SALEM COLLEGE
Winston-Salem, N. C. 27108

of his high office, has appealed for the mobilization of the conscience of the nation to roll away this national reproach."[28] Unlike
most black writers, Miller remained uncritical of the president and
the New Deal throughout the depression years.[29] However, as the
possibility of war increased in 1939, he, like most of the race men,
advised black Americans not to give blind support to the administration: "Sad experience proves that if the Negro forgets his grievances while the war is on the American people will ignore them
when the war is over."[30]

Besides his economic and social conservatism, there was another
issue upon which Miller was at an opposite pole from the younger
radicals. Although he at first joined the chorus which condemned
Du Bois when, in 1934, he presented a scheme that would accept
the reality of segregation and then put that reality to work for the
Negro,[31] Miller generally shared Du Bois's new attitude. The rural
communities which he hoped to see established were to be segregated,[32] and he even went so far as to praise the value of segregated
education later in the decade.[33] Eventually, he even admitted, "Du
Bois has now arrived at the position which I held ten years ago."[34]

While the young radicals could not pin the label of "black chauvinist" as much on Miller as they could on Du Bois, the dean
occasionally equaled Du Bois's ecstasy when contemplating the

28. "Time for the Radical Has Not Yet Come Claims Kelly Miller," Philadelphia
Tribune, November 17, 1932; and his "The White Man's Burden," New York *Amsterdam News*, January 24, 1934.

29. For examples of Miller's praise of the New Deal, see "The New Deal at Cam-
paign Time," New York *Amsterdam News*, August 25, 1934; "Roosevelt and the
Negro to the Present," Boston *Chronicle*, December 9, 1933; "Kelly Miller Dis-
cusses the Election, and Lauds the New Dealer's Program," Washington *Tribune*,
November 10, 1934; and "Why the Negro Should Vote for President Roosevelt,"
Boston *Chronicle*, September 26, 1936.

30. Norfolk *Journal and Guide*, October 28, 1939, as quoted in Gavins, "Gordon
Blaine Hancock," 136.

31. Kelly Miller, "Does the NAACP Reverse Itself on Segregation?" Baltimore
Afro-American, February 10, 1934.

32. Miller, "The Farm—The Negro's Best Chance."

33. Miller, "Reorganization of Higher Education of the Negro," 491.

34. Miller, "I'm Not in the Schuyler Bracket."

potential glories of a separate Negro nation. Miller was skeptical of the practicality of a scheme popular in the early 1930s to create a separate forty-ninth state for the Negro, but he was decidedly receptive to the ideal behind it—"a land somewhere where he may express his racial soul to his heart's content." Miller was realistic enough to admit that the Negro would probably never be able to separate physically from the rest of society, but this did not rule out the possibility that the black nation "may take the form of a more spiritual and cultural imperium in imperio."[35] Such black nationalist sentiments the younger intellectuals found intolerable.

Unlike Miller, the noted historian Carter Godwin Woodson did not indulge in open combat with the younger radical intellectuals; his criticisms were launched by way of implication. But he was almost as distant from them as was the aged dean. Like Miller and all of the older generation, Woodson considered race the fundamental problem in contemporary society. However, his thinking blatantly manifested more of what the younger generation condemned as "black chauvinism" than most of the other older intellectuals. Again, like many of the older men, Woodson sought economic salvation during the depression through small-scale individual race enterprise. And for the keys to success in such enterprises, Woodson also looked back to the teachings of Booker T. Washington—frugality, cleanliness, industry, and "uprightness."[36] Interestingly enough, in the end these mid-nineteenth-century middle-class values undercut his black nationalism.

Woodson was born on a small farm in 1875, the son of former slaves. With uncommon stubbornness, he worked his way up from the coal mines of West Virginia to a Harvard Ph.D. in 1912. In 1915, he founded the Association for the Study of Negro Life and History and its organ, the *Journal of Negro History*. Best known as the fore-

35. Kelly Miller, "The Forty-Ninth State," Norfolk *Journal and Guide*, July 28, 1932.
36. See Carter Woodson, "Holding the Negro Between Him and the Fire," New York *Age*, December 30, 1933.

most Negro historian of the era,[37] he also exerted considerable influence during the early 1930s as a polemicist in the Afro-American press.

"The race" dominated Woodson's thought. All of his efforts were concentrated upon glorifying the race in the past and uplifting it in the present. Yet, as much as he concentrated on it, his own definition remained quite ambiguous. Often he romantically assumed its existence in universal terms, as when he bragged that the Africans were "our brethren in black."[38] However, the lack of race solidarity among Afro-Americans generally led him to despair that "there is no Negro race in America. We have here in a sequestered vale simply everything the white man shoves aside."[39] As often as he was forced to concede this and although social scientists in the 1930s could not even agree on a definition of race,[40] he still wanted to believe in the universal brotherhood of the black race and he worked feverishly to make it a reality. For Woodson, "the race" was an ideal to which all Afro-Americans owed unquestioning allegiance. Until such allegiance became a reality, there could be no progress—economic, political, or social—for American Negroes.

In order to bring this about, Woodson constantly urged Afro-Americans to unify their thought and actions behind race institutions and business enterprises.[41] He always deprecated anything which undermined race loyalty. On one occasion he even went to the extreme of asking Negroes to stop hating other Negroes: "Why waste time hating a Negro who can do you very little harm when

37. See Lawrence D. Reddick, "A New Interpretation for Negro History," *Journal of Negro History*, XXII (January, 1937), 21.

38. Carter Woodson, "Writer Says Moral Code of Africans Higher Than Ours," Chicago *Defender*, February 8, 1936.

39. "We As a Race Agree on Nothing, Says Woodson," Chicago *Defender*, December 14, 1935.

40. See Brewton Berry's analysis of twenty different opinions on this subject, "The Concept of Race in Sociology Textbooks," *Social Forces*, XVIII (1940), 411.

41. See Carter Woodson's "The United Negro Church Seems to Be Inevitable," New York *Amsterdam News*, August 12, 1931; "Comparison of Negroes in America and West Indies," New York *Amsterdam News*, October 28, 1931; and "If I Were Living in Atlanta," Pittsburgh *Courier*, December 3, 1932.

you have around enemies daily taking counsel as to how they may
... impose upon you sufficient disabilities to exterminate you altogether?"[42] By implication, such a statement required that Negroes
should hate their white oppressors.

"The main problem in the uplift of the American Negro," asserted Woodson, "is to change his attitude toward himself."[43] The
principal cause of intraracial disharmony was what he termed the
"miseducation of the Negro." Miseducation was the process by
which the dominant white society bred self-contempt in the Negro.
Woodson maintained that attempting to change the opinion of the
white majority toward the Negro would be a waste of time so long
as the black man continued to despise himself. Nor could the race
unite until it was bound together by pride in a common heritage
and culture.

The Harvard-trained historian believed that the most flagrant
instance of "miseducation" manifested itself in the black intelligentsia's estrangement from the rest of the race. The schools were
turning out "mentally incapacitated misfits," incapable of living in
the world into which society relegated them. They were indoctri-
nated with the values, aspirations and prejudices of white society,
instead of being informed about themselves and the world in which
they must necessarily live. Thus, for Woodson, the well-educated
Negro intellectual became a dangerous tool of the race's oppressors. Insulated by his training and values, he could not "fall in love
with his own people and begin to sacrifice for their uplift."[44] Young
men like Harvard-trained Ralph Bunche, and E. Franklin Frazier
who had a doctorate from the University of Chicago, were presum-

42. Carter Woodson, "What Negro Do You Hate?" Norfolk *Journal and Guide*,
July 25, 1936. Woodson called for the "silencing" of Negro theologians because their
arguments created disunity among black Christians, in "World Often Confused by
Theologians," Philadelphia *Tribune*, October 1, 1931.

43. Carter Woodson, "Purchasing the Badge," Louisiana *Weekly*, November 25,
1933.

44. Carter Woodson, "Renewed Interest to Mark Negro History Week Observation," Norfolk *Journal and Guide*, January 19, 1935; and his "The 'Miseducation' of
the Negro in Economics," New York *Amsterdam News*, June 3, 1931.

ably unfit to lead the race. They did not "think black" enough to suit Woodson.

Indeed, Woodson claimed that the Negro who dropped out of school after learning the "fundamentals" was most fortunate. He was not shrouded in self-hate and thus might be willing to make the sacrifices necessary in the service of the race. He noted that "practically all of the successful Negroes in this country are those who never learned this prejudice 'scientifically' because they entered upon their life's work without formal education."[45] Significantly, most of Woodson's "successful" Negroes were men who had built up their own business enterprises—the petit bourgeoisie. These were men whom the Amenia radicals condemned for their utter selfishness—parasites whose race loyalty was strictly financial.

Woodson called for a new type of education for the Negro, and although he would never admit it, it was based upon a tacit acceptance of segregation. His new system, principally designed for segregated black schools, would provide for all of the fundamentals and then go on to instill pride in the African and Afro-American heritage and culture. This would help create that unity of thought which Woodson conceived as indispensable to the organization of the race from within. In addition to this, it would teach the Negro "practical" economic lessons which would permit him to prosper in a segregated society even in times of depression.

In his preoccupation with race Woodson seldom addressed himself directly to the economic problems of the depression and very rarely commented on the New Deal, but he was vitally concerned with the "miseducation" of the Negro in economics. Too often Negroes made their purchases in white-owned establishments merely because they could save more money than in black-owned stores. The masses must be willing to make sacrifices. Thus Woodson sup-

45. Carter Woodson, "The Miseducation of the Negro," *Crisis*, XXXVIII (August, 1931), 266. For the most complete presentation of Woodson's thoughts on "miseducation," see his *The Miseducation of the Negro* (Washington, D.C.: The Associated Publishers, Inc., 1933).

ported a program similar to Gordon Blaine Hancock's "Double Duty Dollar" scheme; dealing with black merchants would help black business to prosper and provide jobs for black people. Another of the "practical" economic lessons which Woodson taught was that there was possible economic salvation if the highly educated Negro could ignore the unrealistic aspirations imposed upon him by white society. He must be willing "to run ice wagons, push banana carts, keep peanut stands, and peddle wares from door to door." Presumably this small-scale individual enterprise would lead to larger opportunities.[46] The importance of Woodson's economic education, apart from its seeming ignorance of conditions during the 1930s, was that it encouraged the black masses to organize along race, and not class, lines. However, within the race his program was designed to re-create a class system based upon the dominant society's model. Consciously or not, Woodson was a spokesman for the Negro bourgeoisie.

Woodson's new educational system would be staffed by qualified black teachers uncontaminated by the "propaganda" of the "traducers and oppressors." He did not completely rule out the value of sympathetic white teachers on a temporary basis, but he believed that in the end the black man must rely entirely upon himself in all matters. He did not trust white people—even liberals. In cooperative efforts with white liberals, too often "the Negroes do the 'coing' and the whites do the 'operating.' "[47]

Woodson had a penchant for blaming the white man for all of the black man's moral weaknesses. He often portrayed the African as a morally perfect child of nature.[48] It was not until he came

46. Woodson, "The 'Miseducation' of the Negro in Economics." His infrequent comments on FDR were usually favorable; see "The Emancipation of the Negro Voter," Washington *Tribune*, March 17, 1937. For a discussion of Hancock's "Double Duty Dollar" proposal, see Gavins, "Gordon Blaine Hancock," 104–106.

47. Carter Woodson, "Negro Educators Needed," New York *Amsterdam News*, March 11, 1931.

48. See for example, Carter Woodson, *The African Background Outlined* (Washington, D.C.: The Association for the Study of Negro Life and History, 1935), 150, 156.

under the influence of the white man that he fell from grace. Thus, Woodson commented typically that "it is difficult to keep the whites out of Negro denizens of vice, where unfortunately the Negroes learn to imitate the whites in their weaknesses."[49] The Negro, without "weaknesses" of his own, was "spoiled" when exposed to whites.

And yet, at the same time, Woodson blamed Afro-Americans themselves for much of their plight. Woodson's "black chauvinism" did not mix well with his mid-nineteenth-century middle-class values. He frequently published brief biographical accounts of "successful" Negroes of the past in his newspaper columns. Almost without exception, he told of the thrifty, industrious, self-reliant, and "clean-living" men who rose from the depths to the heights on their own merits.[50] These articles were supposed to create racial pride and "educate" the masses on how to achieve success. However, by implication, he was inferring that if these men "made it," others had no valid excuse for failing. In essence, Woodson was perpetuating the cast-off Horatio Alger myth of nineteenth-century "white" society. Indeed, he believed that the only way Negroes could ever achieve the "respect" of the rest of society was by being "just as clean, just as industrious, just as thrifty, and just as upright as any others in the community." He admitted that too often Negroes were noisy, lazy, vicious, and filthy. "As I grow older," he concluded, "I become inclined to think that we do get what we deserve."[51] Thus, Woodson blamed the white man for the Negro's moral failures, but at the same time he blamed the Negro for not

49. Carter Woodson, "Finding the Negro Community and Working in It," New York Age, November 21, 1931. See also his "The Union of Churches Considered Utopian," Louisiana Weekly, September 19, 1931; and "The Difficulty of Learning from the Depression," Chicago Defender, April 16, 1932.

50. See especially Carter Woodson, "Forgotten Negroes," Louisiana Weekly, February 24, 1934.

51. Carter Woodson, "Do We Get What We Deserve?" New York Age, March 12, 1932.

imitating the "respectable" white virtues. It was a conflict which Woodson was incapable of resolving.

In addition to criticizing the race for ignoring the eternal verities, Woodson, the promulgator of race pride, was often embarrassed by certain race creations which he considered deviations from respectability. He became most violent on the subject of jazz: "It is said that the Negro created jazz. If he did so he should be ashamed of it." It was not "real music"; it was much too "exotic." Its effect upon members of the race was detrimental to advancement: "Persons who are concerned with social progress, then, must take steps to restrict jazz and stamp it out as an evil." Indeed, in a statement incredible even for Woodson, he praised Adolph Hitler for setting a precedent by throwing all jazz performers out of Germany. Woodson claimed that there was nothing racial in this action. "Self-respecting Negroes are welcome in Germany. Hitler set a noble example in trying to preserve the good in civilization. Would to God that he had the power . . . to round up all jazz promoters and performers of both races . . . and execute them as criminals."[52] Thus, in the end, Woodson's "black chauvinism" was primarily concerned with the "respectable" accomplishments of black people. He did not accept the real expressions of the black masses— such as jazz or emotional religion. Woodson employed a dated, white yardstick in measuring "the good in civilization." Significantly, he never applied the concept of "miseducation" to himself. In many ways, his brand of "black chauvinism" was designed to make black Americans "acceptable" to white middle-class society.

It was popular in 1934 to castigate W. E. B. Du Bois and his new program of conceding the reality of segregation and then exploiting it to the fullest extent. Although Woodson could scarcely be considered an ardent integrationist, he joined the chorus in opposi-

52. "Jazz Demoralizing, Creators Should Be Ashamed—Woodson," Philadelphia *Tribune*, October 12, 1933.

tion to the Du Bois plan. He publicly proclaimed that he would not make another contribution to the NAACP until "they clear themselves of this stigma." Like most of Du Bois's detractors, Woodson assumed that the editor of the *Crisis* was consciously advocating segregation. Perhaps he did not take the trouble to actually read Du Bois's plan, for in the same article Woodson demonstrated that in essence he agreed with him. He praised Booker T. Washington for being not a segregationist, but a realist: "Like any other sensible person, if it is forced upon us, we must make the most of it."[53] The description could have fit Du Bois.

Like most of the other older intellectuals, Du Bois continued throughout the depression to consider race the most significant issue in the world. But unlike Miller and Woodson, whose opinions remained almost unaffected by the traumas of the depression, Du Bois underwent a substantial transformation in his conception of the solutions to the race's problems. During the late 1920s and early 1930s, Du Bois shifted his emphasis from political rights to economic power, and from a militant antisegregation stance to an acceptance of the unchanging reality of segregation. Like the young radicals, Du Bois had come to believe that the primary goal of black men in the United States should be the acquisition of economic power. But unlike them, he believed that this power could be gained only through black solidarity. His experiences as a race leader throughout the first three decades of the twentieth century had left him disillusioned with the idea of any manner of black-white unity, be it with the working class, with New Deal liberals, or with Communist party radicals. Although he mildly supported Roosevelt even as late as 1940, he practically ignored the New Deal in his published writings. He believed it was a waste of effort to

53. Carter Woodson, "Why Some Negroes Advocate Segregation," Louisiana *Weekly*, April 21, 1934. For a further discussion of the dynamics of Woodson's blending of the seemingly contradictory ideas of race chauvinism and assimilationism, see Vincent Harding, "Beyond Chaos: Black History and the Search for the New Land," Black Paper No. 2 (Atlanta: Institute of the Black World, 1970), 6–7.

either defend or attack the New Deal because ultimately it either could not or would not solve the problems of racism.[54] Because of the changes in his thinking, Du Bois suffered more criticism than any other Afro-American intellectual during the decade. His older colleagues thought he had betrayed the tried and true methods, and for the young "radicals," Du Bois became the personification of "black chauvinism."[55]

Throughout most of his career as editor of the *Crisis*, Du Bois had militantly agitated for the Negro's political rights and against all forms of segregation. On the eve of the depression he maintained that "political power is the beginning of all permanent reform and the only hope for maintaining gains."[56] By 1933, however, after lamenting the failure of black men to gain the rights of citizenship, he concluded that "our greatest failure is inability to earn a decent living."[57] Again, in 1929, aware of the fact that "it is impossible by any scientific measurement to divide men into races, and even to prove there are separate races" he was still of the opinion that *"the logical end of racial segregation is Caste, Hate and*

54. See Du Bois, "As the Crow Flies," New York *Amsterdam News*, August 10, 1940; John B. Kirby, "The Roosevelt Administration and Blacks: An Ambivalent Legacy," in Barton J. Bernstein and Allen J. Matusow (eds.), *Twentieth Century America: Recent Interpretations* (2nd ed. rev.; New York: Harcourt Brace Jovanovich, Inc., 1972), 284. For a more detailed analysis of Du Bois's activities during these years, consult Broderick, *W. E. B. Du Bois;* and Rudwick, *W. E. B. Du Bois.* For a discussion which focuses on Du Bois's economic thought during the depression, see Wolters, *Negroes and the Great Depression,* 230–65; and for one which interprets his conception of race, see Fullinwider, *Mind and Mood of Black America,* 47–71.

55. See for example a letter to the editor of the *Nation*, "Testimony in Defense," July 3, 1935, defending the white critic Benjamin Stolberg's attack on Du Bois's black chauvinism, signed by Sterling A. Brown, Ralph J. Bunche, Emmett E. Dorsey, and E. Franklin Frazier.

56. W. E. B. Du Bois, "The Negro Citizen," *Crisis*, XXXVI (May, 1929), 155. See also Du Bois's chapter, "The Negro Citizen," in Charles S. Johnson (ed.), *The Negro in American Civilization: A Study of Negro Life and Race Relations in the Light of Social Research* (New York: Henry Holt and Co., 1930), 461–70.

57. W. E. B. Du Bois, "U. S. Will Come to Communism, Du Bois Tells Conference," Baltimore *Afro-American*, May 20, 1933. See also W. E. B. Du Bois, *Dusk of Dawn* (New York: Harcourt, Brace and Co., 1940), 289, 295–96; and his "Education and Work," *Journal of Negro Education*, I (April, 1932), 68.

War.[58] But in the next few years, as he reassessed his career of militant protest, he decided that race prejudice was certainly as strong, if not stronger than it had been in 1910.[59] By 1934, he was urging the race to create a separate "economic nation within a nation." Du Bois would devote the bulk of his efforts during the rest of the decade to the promulgation of his racially oriented economic program.

He had long considered himself a Socialist of sorts, and early in the century had joined New York Local No. 1 of the Socialist party. But it was not until he was "stirred" by what he saw on a trip to the Soviet Union in 1928 that he became a believer. There, like many other famous American visitors, he saw socialism at work. He was most impressed with the Soviet Union's systematic attack upon the problem of poverty. Discarding the profit system, the government was organizing the natural, industrial, and human resources of the whole nation for the purpose of eliminating indigence.[60] Du Bois came away from the trip with the notion that American Negroes might be able to employ a similar system in an assault upon their economic problems.

Although Du Bois always applauded Soviet social experiments, he was very critical of the Communist party program in the United States. While admitting that if he was living in Russia, he would be "an enthusiastic Communist,"[61] he condemned the "young jackasses who are leading Communism in America today."[62] His two major criticisms of American communism were its advocacy of violent revolution and its inflexible definition of the class structure of society.

58. "Shall the Negro Be Encouraged to Seek Cultural Equality?" a debate between Du Bois and Lothrop Stoddard held in Chicago on March 17, 1929 (printed copy in the Arthur Schomburg Collection, New York Public Library), 8, 24; "Postscript," *Crisis*, XXXVI (September, 1929), 314.

59. Du Bois, *Dusk of Dawn*, 283.

60. *Ibid.*, 235, 287–88. Broderick, *W. E. B. Du Bois*, 144–49.

61. Du Bois, "U. S. Will Come to Communism."

62 W. E. B. Du Bois, "Postscript: The Negro and Communism," *Crisis*, XXXVIII (September, 1931), 314.

Du Bois had always doubted the practical value of violence. He maintained that "no program of force and revolution suits nor is likely to suit present conditions in the United States and it would be utterly idiotic for Negroes to assume that it will." The final change might come suddenly, or the beginning of change might start with violence, but change itself came "slowly and in long and disappointing years." Bitter over the disruptive tactics of the Communists at the Scottsboro trial of nine Negro youths accused of raping two white prostitutes, Du Bois concluded that "American Negroes do not propose to be the shock troops of the Communist Revolution, driven out in front to death, cruelty and humiliation in order to win victories for white workers."[63]

Like Miller, Du Bois was amazed at the naïveté of both the Communists and the young radicals who believed that the "class solidarity of laborers in the United States will hold across the color line and that the union of black labor with white labor will consequently bring a solution of the race problem."[64] This might be true in the distant future, but at present white labor "keeps Negroes out of the trades, refuses them decent homes to live in and helps nullify their vote. . . . The persons who are killing blacks in Northern Alabama and demanding blood sacrifices are the white workers." Ironically, it was the capitalists who stood against mob law and for justice in the long run—"Industrial peace increases their profits."[65]

Yet Du Bois advocated socialism as the solution to the race's economic problems. Like the young radicals, he was now aware that all power in society was channeled through well-organized con-

63. Du Bois, "As the Crow Flies," New York Amsterdam News, March 23, 1940; his "Russian Oppression and Revolution Have Left a Trail of Crimson Blood Through the Centuries," Philadelphia Tribune, August 20, 1931; and his "The Negro and Communism," 314–15.

64. Du Bois, "As the Crow Flies," New York Amsterdam News, March 23, 1940.

65. Du Bois, "The Negro and Communism," 315. See also Du Bois, Dusk of Dawn, 301; and his "Marxism and the Negro Problem," Crisis, XL (May, 1933), 103, 118.

glomerations.[66] And Du Bois was as convinced as they that the capitalistic system was doomed. He was not sure just when its demise would occur, but the depression made him "certain" that it was imminent. And he was just as certain that with the downfall of capitalism "we are going to stop the organization of work for private profit and substitute therefore work for public welfare." However, unlike the young radicals, Du Bois's socialism was racial, rather than working class, in orientation. He saw American Negroes as "the group that had gone least forward on this program of the exploitation of the many for the benefit of the few." Thus, he reasoned, as the group least contaminated by private enterprise, Afro-America was in the best position to "give to the world an example" of intelligent, cooperative society. Indeed, he saw it as the mission of the Negro to do so.[67]

Du Bois characterized his program as "modified" Marxism. It was modified because Negroes were not exploited along class lines: they were exploited by both the white capitalists and the white proletariat. Thus, the Negro's "only defense is such internal organization as will protect him from both parties."[68] Du Bois wanted American Negroes to recognize the reality of segregation and create a separate black Socialist economy. His position was one of the factors which led to his break with the NAACP in 1934.[69]

Most observers thought he was advocating segregation as an end in itself. They mourned the complete "capitulation" of the "tired" old warrior.[70] The younger critics did not like Du Bois's brand of self-proclaimed Marxism. To them he was not advocating

66. See Du Bois, *Dusk of Dawn*, 288–89; and his "Education and Work," 63.
67. Du Bois, "The U. S. Will Come to Communism."
68. Du Bois, "Marxism and the Negro Problem," 104, 118.
69. See Fullinwider, *Mind and Mood of Black America*, 64–69; Wolters, *Negroes and the Great Depression*, 266–301; Bernard Eisenberg, "James Weldon Johnson and the National Association for the Advancement of Colored People, 1916–1934" (Ph.D. dissertation, Columbia University, 1968), 65–70.
70. See such editorials as "Is Du Bois Slipping?" Philadelphia *Tribune*, March 8, 1934; and "Debs and Du Bois," Chicago *Defender*, March 31, 1934.

socialism, but "black chauvinism." "Like the typical liberal in confusion," scoffed one young radical, "he turned inward."[71]

Du Bois's new "practical philosophy" was based on the assumption that "it is not ours to argue whether we will be segregated or
whether we ought to be a caste. We are segregated; we are a caste.
This is our given and at present unalterable fact." Although integration was the "ultimate goal of Humanity," it would not be
achieved for perhaps a thousand years.[72]

Du Bois was not, as his critics generally assumed, suggesting that
Negroes should stop all efforts to achieve integration. Although
logically the end of his program would be a segregated society, he
never advocated segregation as an end in itself. He merely noted
that Negroes should change their emphasis, face the situation as it
really existed, and make the most of it. "Therefore let us not beat
futile wings in impotent frenzy, but carefully plan and guide our
segregated life, organize in industry and politics to protect and
expand it." To his critics Du Bois sarcastically retorted in his last
editorial in the *Crisis*: "If you have passed your resolution, 'No
segregation, Never and Nowhere,' what are you going to do about
it? Let me tell you what you are going to do. You are going back
to continue to make your living in a Jim Crow school; you are going
to dwell in a segregated section of the city."[73]

Du Bois's black Socialist economy was to be initially based upon
the development of consumers' cooperatives. He reasoned that the
approximately $150 million that Afro-Americans spent each month
represented their greatest source of power. If, under the leadership

71. Streator, "In Search of Leadership," 17. See also E. Franklin Frazier, "The
Du Bois Program in the Present Crisis," *Race*, I (Winter, 1935–36), 11–13.
72. W. E. B. Du Bois, "The Negro College," *Crisis*, XL (August, 1933), 177;
and his "Postscript," *Crisis*, XLI (April, 1934), 115. See also W. E. B. Du Bois, "A
Philosophy of Race Segregation," *Quarterly Review of Higher Education Among
Negroes*, III (October, 1935), 190.
73. See W. E. B. Du Bois, "Postscript," *Crisis*, XLI (June, 1934), 183; his "The
Negro College," 177; and his "Postscript," *Crisis*, XLI (June, 1934), 182.

of a "dictatorship of intelligence,"[74] they could be forged into a union of consumers, then they would be capable of exerting considerable force in society. However, this was only the beginning. He hoped, from the power and resources thus derived from consumers' cooperatives, to develop for Negroes a semi-autonomous "economic nation within a nation, able to work through inner cooperation to found its own institutions, to educate its genius, and at the same time . . . to keep in helpful touch and cooperate with the mass of the nation."[75] Private profit would be eliminated in this new nation. All proceeds would go to build up black industries and institutions.

The success of the cooperatives depended upon race loyalty, or what Du Bois termed "consensus." All of the Negroes in a neighborhood must pool their resources and purchase commodities wholesale direct from the producers—preferably, black producers. Thus they would cut out middle-men's costs. From the capital thus saved they were presumably to build up race industry and race agriculture and support race "genius."[76] Where this was not immediately possible, Du Bois advised that Negroes should at least support black merchants even if it meant paying higher prices for inferior quality. He did not include black businessmen among the exploiters of the black workers and thus did not believe that the black proletariat should revolt against the black bourgeiosie but should support it. Such race loyalty entailed much sacrifice, and Du Bois finally admitted that the sacrifice might be "for an ideal

74. W. E. B. Du Bois, "Forum of Fact and Opinion," Pittsburgh *Courier*, May 1, 1937. Du Bois's "creed for American Negroes today" also called upon the masses to follow the "Talented Tenth." See his "Forum of Fact and Opinion," Pittsburgh *Courier*, June 20, 1936.

75. W. E. B. Du Bois, "A Nation Within the Nation," *Current History*, XLII (June, 1935), 269.

76. For discussions of consumers' cooperation, see W. E. B. Du Bois, "A Negro Nation Within the Nation"; his "The Position of the Negro in the American Social Order: Where Do We Go From Here?" *Journal of Negro Education*, VIII (July, 1939), 551–70; and his *Dusk of Dawn*, 208–20.

which the present generation will hardly see fulfilled."[77] One gets the impression from reading Du Bois's proposals that the creation of a spirit of race solidarity was more important to him than the realization of any of his specific economic programs.[78]

Such suggestions led younger critics to believe that Du Bois was encouraging the development of a black bourgeoisie within the capitalistic system.[79] They were skeptical of the depth of Du Bois's commitment to the welfare of the black masses. "Imagine," commented a young Howard professor, the "fantastic idea" of organizing "the consumptive power of dispossessed tenant farmers and relief clients!"[80]

Du Bois's "black chauvinism" was not limited to the United States. He had long been a leading advocate of pan-Africanism. He saw between the African and the Afro-American a common heritage of slavery, discrimination, and insult. However, unlike Woodson, Du Bois did not confine himself to Negro nationalism. He saw this same heritage of exploitation in the histories of all the "darker races" of the world, and he did not believe that the problems of the Negro American could be solved "until the color problems of the world are well on the way toward settlement." His attitude was typified in his advice to young Afro-Americans, that their interests draw them nearer to the dark people outside of America than to their white fellow citizens.[81]

Du Bois's intense loyalty to the darker peoples sometimes clouded his objectivity. Perhaps the most salient example of this

77. Du Bois, "The U. S. Will Come to Communism"; his "Marxism and the Negro Problem," 104; and his "Position of the Negro in the American Social Order," 566.

78. Wolters, *Negroes and the Great Depression*, 258.

79. See E. Franklin Frazier, "The Du Bois Program in the Present Crisis," 11–13.

80. Emmett Dorsey, "The Negro and Social Planning," *Journal of Negro Education*, 5 (January, 1936), 108.

81. Du Bois, *Dusk of Dawn*, 117; his "Forum of Fact and Opinion," Pittsburgh *Courier*, April 25, 1936; and his "Pan-Africa and New Racial Philosophy," *Crisis*, XL (November, 1933), 247.

was his consistent defense of Japanese aggression in Manchuria during the 1930s. He hated to see two colored peoples—the Japanese and the Chinese—fighting, but he argued that the Japanese were clearly fighting to prevent European control of Asia and to bring about a union of the "yellow and brown race" so that it might take its "rightful leadership of mankind." Du Bois blamed the war on "all those white nations" that had enslaved China. In effect, Japan was liberating China despite China's wishes: "When China refused to organize herself, but made herself a part of imperial industry and English and French industrial expansion, Japan seized the opportunity, during the paralysis of European power, and undertook the duty herself."[82]

When he visited Manchuria in 1937, Du Bois did not report any of the atrocities which other correspondents observed. Most significant for him was the fact that he "could see nothing that savored of caste." It was inconceivable to Du Bois that the Japanese could be exploiting their own "cousins" for the selfish purposes of national interest. They were merely attempting to convince the Chinese of the efficacy of an allegiance which would "save the world for the darker races." As of August, 1941, he was still maintaining: "I want to see Japan the leader of Asia, with Asia's cooperation and consent."[83]

Du Bois was less interested in the European war. In April of 1941, he commented that "if Hitler triumphs the world is lost; if England triumphs the world is not found." The most promising aspect of a European war for Du Bois was the possibility that it would weaken the colonial powers and thus give the darker races

82. See, for example, Du Bois's comments immediately after the first invasion: "The Program of Peace in Manchuria," *Louisiana Weekly*, November 20, 1931. On racial aspect of war, see Du Bois, "Postscript," *Crisis*, XL (January, 1933), 20; and his "Forum of Fact and Opinion," Pittsburgh *Courier*, September 25, 1937.

83. Du Bois, "Forum of Fact and Opinion," Pittsburgh *Courier*, January 30, 1937; his "As the Crow Flies"; New York *Amsterdam News*, August 16, 1941; and his "Forum of Fact and Opinion," Pittsburgh *Courier*, October 23, 1937.

a chance to rise up.[84] As he had throughout the domestic crisis of depression, Du Bois continued to emphasize race solidarity even as he contemplated the impending disaster of world war.

While the young radicals considered Du Bois the arch-"black chauvinist," they referred to James Weldon Johnson as an "Uncle Tom." Johnson, the eminent poet, critic, and former executive secretary of the NAACP, was perhaps the best-known American Negro of his generation. For the young radicals, Johnson epitomized the obsolescent NAACP liberalism which they had bitterly denounced at the Amenia conference.

Johnson confided in his autobiography that he had often been treated roughly by the young intellectuals, "because I did not hold that all of the ills and disadvantages suffered by the Negro could be wholly accounted for by the theory of economic determinism."[85] He saw their monistic philosophy as "fashionable" and simplistic: "The factors involved are not only economic; they are also emotional, ethical, esthetical." It was, he asserted, absurd to reason that if the bulk of American Negroes did achieve economic security, race problems would dissolve into thin air: "It would be just as reasonable to believe that the millions of white Americans who are on the dole and utterly without economic security will for that reason become a class, segregated, jim crowed, disfranchised, lynched and denied a chance at such employment as there might be."[86] Late in 1934, Johnson attempted to formulate some solution to "the problem." *Negro Americans, What Now?* was ostensibly a reply to the segregationist teachings of Du Bois. But Johnson's actual differences with Du Bois were not as deep as were his differ-

84. Du Bois, "As the Crow Flies," New York *Amsterdam News*, April 19, 1941, and May 25, 1940, and June 1, 1940.
85. James Weldon Johnson, *Along This Way: The Autobiography of James Weldon Johnson* (New York: The Viking Press, 1933), 412.
86. James Weldon Johnson, "Communism and the Negro," New York *Herald Tribune Books*, July 21, 1935.

ences with the young radicals. He initially posited a number of possible solutions to the race's problems in the United States. First he ruled out mass exodus as impossible. Physical force was feasible for black Africans because of their numerical superiority, but it would mean extermination for Afro-Americans. Johnson next rejected communism in the United States because even if the revolution succeeded, Communists would still be recruited from the ranks of bigoted white Americans. Besides, he distrusted all "childlike" faith in the "miraculous efficacy on our racial situation of any economic or social theory of government."[87] Negro Americans faced a complex problem and no panacea would work.

By a process of elimination, Johnson arrived at what he concluded were the two most significant possibilities: continued efforts toward integration, or, on the other hand, "an acknowledgement of our isolation and the determination to accept and make the best of it." Johnson repudiated Du Bois's program because he thought the American Negro had insufficient resources to construct an economy of his own. More importantly, "the outcome of voluntary isolation would be a permanent secondary status, so acknowledged by the race." However, Johnson was not at an opposite pole from Du Bois. Although he would have been loath to admit it, he echoed Du Bois when he suggested that "we should gather all the strength and experience we can from imposed segregation." He advised Negroes to make their business enterprises and other "strictly group undertakings" as successful as possible.[88] He did not condemn as "chauvinistic" attempts to strengthen the race from within.

In fact, in his autobiography, he theorized that if integration became absolutely impossible, "there will be only one way of salvation for the race that I can see, and that will be through the making of its isolation into a religion and the cultivation of a hard, keen,

87. James Weldon Johnson, *Negro Americans, What Now?* (New York: The Viking Press, 1934), 5–6, 6–7, 9. For a discussion of Johnson's disagreements with Du Bois, see Eisenberg, "James Weldon Johnson," 71–75.
88. Johnson, *Negro Americans, What Now?* 12, 15, 17.

relentless hatred for everything white." Just as Du Bois, he believed that under those circumstances, this was the only means by which the Afro-American could maintain any self-respect.[89]

The principal difference between the two men was that Johnson did not believe that the time for this approach had yet arrived. Johnson's pessimism was not as deep as Du Bois's. Thus, group enterprises must at present be built up as a means "of *entering into, not staying out of* the body politic." This left the continuing effort to achieve Negro integration into the dominant society as the only acceptable solution. Looking back on his NAACP experience, Johnson suggested two basic "parallel" methods of approaching this: "our own development and the bringing about of a change in the national attitude toward us."[90]

Johnson conceded that at present "the fundamental question in our whole situation, the question of a fair and equal chance to earn our bread by our toil, is the most perplexing and unyielding with which we have to contend." He also agreed with the basic idea of giving "workers education" to black workers. However, unlike the young radicals who wanted to see industrial unions established, Johnson, who had long been critical of the labor movement, wanted Negroes to continue to "hammer away" at the old trade unions as they had been doing for the past twenty-five years.[91] He thought that the slogan, "Black and white workers unite!" was admirable, but he chided, "Nobody, as far as I am able to learn, has yet come forward with a feasible method for bringing about this unity."[92] Like Du Bois and the other race men, Johnson had lived through all of the disappointments of the first third of the century, and he saw little cause for the young radicals' unbounded optimism concerning the destruction of caste.

Unlike his younger critics, Johnson thought it was feasible that

---

89. Johnson, *Along This Way*, 412.
90. Johnson, *Negro Americans, What Now?* 17, 10.
91. *Ibid.*, 68–69; Eisenberg, "James Weldon Johnson," 131–33.
92. Johnson, *Negro Americans, What Now?* 72.

"we ourselves should raise our economic status by establishing businesses that would furnish us with the necessary capital and provide employment for our own people." This proposition "goes to the root of our trouble," he said. However, though Johnson wanted to see Negroes learning the techniques of big business and establishing small enterprises of their own, he was forced to admit that under the severe circumstances of the depression, "our greatest hope lies, probably, in our ability to adopt and make use of co-operative and collective methods."[93] But this was only a temporary method of meeting an emergency. Johnson's economic program was based on the status quo.

In the political realm, Johnson called for continued agitation for political rights and the intelligent use of the ballot wherever it had been obtained. He emphasized the importance of local elections because they were the ones in which Negro votes would be most felt. Unlike the Amenia radicals, who hoped for the rise of a separate labor party, Johnson advised Negroes to get into the parties already established or vote as independents.[94] The tacit assumption of Johnson's political program was that Negroes should vote according to their racial interests—the same advice liberal NAACP officials had been offering for years.

The second of Johnson's "parallel" methods—the "change in the national attitude"—was considered in the context of education. Johnson merely repeated the timeworn idea that white Americans should be taught "the truth about us." He emphasized that this education should set forth both the accomplishments of the race and the injustices which it had suffered. Of the two, the second was by far the more important. In his autobiography, Johnson concluded that "in large measure the race question involves the saving of black America's body and white America's soul." He hoped to bring about a change in the "hearts" of white men: "The only kind of revolution that would have an immediately significant effect on

93. *Ibid.*, 75, 79–80.   94. *Ibid.*, 59–60.

the American Negro's status would be a moral revolution—an upward push given to the level of ethical ideas and practices."[95] If white Americans could be "educated" concerning the injustices which they were perpetuating, then they might relent in their bigoted behavior: "Until white America heeds, we shall never let its conscience sleep."[96] Thus, like the "mossback" Kelly Miller, Johnson spoke ultimately in terms of morality instead of power.

Finally, Johnson suggested that all race organizations concerned with political, economic, or educational aspects of the race problem, should come under the general guidance of a "central machine." He suggested that the NAACP, the most successful organization already in existence, should assume the role of a Greater Association for the Advancement of Colored People.[97] Thus, Johnson anticipated the National Negro Congress idea of the young radicals, the only difference being that they would look to labor as the spearhead of such an organization, while Johnson looked back to the much-criticized liberal organization.

The young sociologist, E. Franklin Frazier, did indeed treat Johnson roughly in his reviews of *Negro Americans, What Now?*. Because Johnson's program was essentially a restatement of the policies of the NAACP, which were predicated on the status quo, Frazier dubbed him an "intellectual 'Uncle Tom.'" He charged that Johnson, like most of the older race leaders, supported the status quo because he was in reality speaking for the interests of his own small black middle class and not the impoverished black masses of the nation. Johnson's "opportunistic and 'common sense'" approach contained the "stock-in-trade arguments of numerous Negro 'leaders' who are unwilling to risk their own security."[98]

But most often the young radicals challenged the provinciality

95. *Ibid.*, 52–54; Johnson, *Along This Way*, 318, 411.
96. Johnson, *Negro Americans, What Now?* 101.
97. *Ibid.*, 36–40.
98. E. Franklin Frazier, "Quo Vadis?" *Journal of Negro Education*, IV (January, 1935), 129–31. See also, "What Now?" *The Nation*, XII (June, 1935), 692.

of the older men. They could not go beyond race; it had shaped—constricted—their whole lives. Time and again they had been disillusioned: from the disappointments of the Populist movement in the 1890s to the treachery of a president in the First World War. This historical experience had convinced them that caste was the primary problem facing the black man in the United States. It was a problem which each of them, in varying degree, despairingly believed would be a long time in solving. The naïve optimism of the younger radicals, they believed, was the result of inexperience.

Through all of the disappointing experiences of the first third of the twentieth century they had emerged as race spokesmen. This was their primary function in life. They were race spokesmen before they were academicians or historians or journalists. The race and its welfare received their almost undivided attention. They seldom commented on issues or events which did not in some way relate to racial matters.

Thus the charge of "provinciality" against them was at least partially justified. During the 1930s, when it became intellectually fashionable to conceive of almost all problems in terms of economic determinism, and when the crisis was so fundamental that it threatened all of society, they still clung loyally to their racial orientations. It was this, more than anything else, which appeared to separate them from the impatient radicals.

II

The Moratorium on Race

Writing early in the depression decade, the young newspaper columnist and literary critic, Arthur P. Davis, observed somewhat mockingly: "There is nothing to be ashamed of in the fact that one is colored, but heaven knows I can see nothing to be so proud of. A man who can make such a statement—in America—must be either a consummate fool or a colossal liar. . . . Some of my contemporary friends who make this statement I have yet to place." Davis was perplexed because "the issue of 'race' is too much with us." He noted the recent popularity of the moratorium idea and asked his readers: "Why not have a ten year moratorium on all discussions and writings on the race problem? This would give the present younger generation a chance to grow up without having their minds too warped." Davis thought that the racial provinciality of the race men was based upon their vested interest in it. And for that reason he finally concluded that his moratorium idea would probably fail: "But on second thought I find that this idea wouldn't work because if the moratorium were effective every so-called 'Big Negro' in the country would starve to death. This would probably be a good thing."[1]

Almost as if they were heeding Davis' call, the young radicals at the Amenia conference attacked this provinciality as well as the

1. Arthur P. Davis, "The Eternal Problem," Norfolk *Journal and Guide*, April 30, 1932.

methods and liberal ideology of the older leadership. In their published writings during the succeeding years they remained critical, but added their own positive solutions to the race's problems, solutions based essentially on the tenets of the Amenia manifesto.

The young radicals considered in this chapter had earned advanced degrees in the new scientifically oriented social sciences from the leading "white" universities of the North. They came away from this training with very different ideas from those to which many of the older race men had been exposed while in college.

Throughout the 1920s increasing numbers of anthropologists and psychologists, led by Franz Boas, began to successfully challenge widely held beliefs about innate cultural, temperamental, and mental differences between the races. Boas demonstrated that cultural, and perhaps even some physical, differences were determined by environment, not by heredity.[2] Psychologists also were increasingly won over to the idea that it was impossible to discern any valid evidences of differences in mental ability according to race. Most of those which had been discovered by earlier psychologists were induced again by environmental variations.[3] By the 1930s social scientists dealing with the subject of race could not even agree upon what race was.[4] Most of them, however, did agree that so-called "racial differences" could be altered or even eliminated by changing the environment. By the 1930s a belief in racial inferiority or superiority was no longer intellectually respectable in the American academic community.[5]

2. See Peter I. Rose, *The Subject Is Race: Traditional Ideologies and the Teaching of Race Relations* (New York: Oxford University Press, 1968), 39–40; Thomas F. Gossett, *Race: The History of an Idea in America* (New York: Schocken Books, 1965), 418–30.

3. Gossett, *Race*, 424–26.

4. Rose, *The Subject Is Race*, 68–69.

5. Gossett, *Race*, 424. Gunnar Myrdal noted this environmentalist emphasis in *An American Dilemma: The Negro Problem and Modern Democracy* (New York:

The young radical social scientists emerged from this academic environment with the idea that race was, more than anything else, a useful myth which had been perpetuated by powerful whites and manipulated by the black leadership class for its own selfish interests. Although in their private correspondence and memoranda they often saw the value of intraracial unity, in their published works they practically ignored the idea, and even sometimes treated it with contempt. Perhaps they did so in order to counter the chauvinistic preachings of men like Du Bois.

Also, these young men came to intellectual maturity during a time of acute economic crisis—a time when it was fashionable for intellectuals from all backgrounds to proclaim along with Edwin Seaver that "our liberalism has been put to the test and has been found wanting."[6] The young radicals scorned liberals, both black and white. They were dissatisfied with the accomplishments of liberal race organizations like the NAACP. Such organizations, they asserted, had confined their efforts principally to the realm of civil rights. This was beneficial to the middle and upper classes, but it ignored the black masses, whose problems, the young radicals believed, emanated from the exploitation of labor by private capital. In private the radicals criticized white liberals active in such organizations for being too cautious and for confronting basic social and economic problems with palliatives rather than fundamental solutions. Black and white liberals within these organizations were too firmly committed to the status quo to entertain any notions of drastic change.[7] The old interracial coalition of liberals had failed;

Harper & Row, Publishers, 1944), 1036. S. P. Fullinwider, *The Mind and Mood of Black America: Twentieth-Century Thought* (Homewood, Ill.: Dorsey Press, 1969), develops the idea that the "sociological imagination" began to predominate during the 1930s. See pp. 92–122, 172–73

6. In Samuel Schmalhausen (ed.), *Behold America!* (New York: Farrar and Rinehart, Inc., 1931), 586.

7. See Ralph Bunche, "The Programs, Ideologies, Tactics and Achievements of Negro Betterment and Interracial Organizations," memorandum for the Carnegie-

it was time, the young radicals contended, for a new coalition based upon the solidarity of black and white labor.

The young radicals were also critical of New Deal liberalism. Liberals in and out of the New Deal were generally little concerned with the difficulties of black people. They developed no systematic conception of the unique nature of black problems and hence no coherent plan for dealing with them.[8] Generally speaking, if they considered the plight of blacks at all, they viewed them not as victims of racial proscription but as lower-class victims of economic forces. The problems of Negro tenant farmers in the South were essentially the same as those of the white tenant farmers. The racial problem was at bottom, they thought, an economic class problem which would be solved when those facing all poverty-stricken Americans were solved. Many of the liberals also thought that the severe economic crisis would actually drive black and white workers together as they became increasingly aware of their common economic problems.[9]

Although the young radicals tended to agree with the idea that the fundamental problem facing Afro-Americans was economic exploitation and that the ultimate solution would be black-white worker solidarity, they were severely critical of the New Deal's

---

Myrdal Study (MS in the Schomburg Collection of the New York Public Library), 147–48; Raymond Wolters, *Negroes and the Great Depression* (Westport, Conn.: Greenwood Publishing Corp., 1970), 318–21. Interestingly enough, this attack on white liberals was largely confined to such unpublished memoranda and to private correspondence.

8. See Wolters, *Negroes and the Great Depression*, x; Allen Kifer, "The Negro and the New Deal" (Ph.D. dissertation, University of Wisconsin, 1961), 272; John B. Kirby, "The Roosevelt Administration and Blacks: An Ambivalent Legacy," in Barton J. Bernstein and Allen J. Matusow (eds.), *Twentieth Century America: Recent Interpretations* (2nd ed. rev.; New York: Harcourt Brace Jovanovich, Inc., 1972), 269, 286; and Peter J. Kellogg, "Northern Liberals and Black America: A History of White Attitudes, 1936–1952," (Ph.D. dissertation, Northwestern University, 1971), vi–vii, 20–22. Kellogg's study focuses on the opinions expressed in two major liberal journals, the *New Republic* and *The Nation*.

9. Kirby, "The Roosevelt Administration and Blacks," 270–72; Kellogg, "Northern Liberals and Black America," 3–13, 20–22.

effect, or lack of effect, on black Americans.[10] Additionally, the New Deal's economic remedies were designed to preserve a free enterprise system which the radicals wished to see destroyed.

Because the young radicals challenged American capitalism, elder critics such as Kelly Miller erroneously placed them in the same category as "reds." Although, particularly during the Party's "United Front" phase (1935–1939), the young radicals often sympathized with such Communist proposals as black-white labor solidarity and destruction of free-enterprise capitalism, they were never as far left as the "reds." They remained independent of the Party and were frequently critical of its policies. The young radicals never condoned the idea of violent revolution. They vehemently disapproved of the Party's insistence, during the early years of the decade (1928–1934), that blacks constituted a separate nation within the United States and should thus demand "self-determination." Although Party theoreticians insisted that this question was predicated upon national and not racial considerations, the young radicals thought it suspiciously akin to a racially chauvinistic approach.[11] And later in the decade when the Party was attempting to create a "united front" with liberal race leaders, the young radicals continued to be critical of those leaders. These young radicals never surrendered their independence of thought to the dictates of any politicians. Almost without exception, those writers who did join the Party and submit to its discipline forfeited their individual

10. See some of the critiques of the New Deal which were delivered at the 1935 Howard Economic Conference, especially E. Franklin Frazier, "The Effects of the New Deal Farm Programs Upon the Negro," and Ralph Bunche, "A Critique of New Deal Social Planning," both published in the *Journal of Negro Education*, V (January, 1936).

11. See Wilson Record, *The Negro and the Communist Party* (Chapel Hill: University of North Carolina Press, 1951), 55–56, 60–61, 120–34. For an analysis by a black Party theoretician which attempts to distinguish between race and nationality as a basis for "self-determination in the black-belt," see Harry Haywood, "The Theoretical Defenders of White Chauvinism in the Labor Movement," *Communist*, X (June, 1931), 505–506.

identities. Their writings, unlike those of the young radicals, never deviated from whatever the current Party line happened to be.[12]

The optimism of the young radicals concerning the efficacy of black and white labor solidarity was perhaps induced by the relatively successful efforts of John L. Lewis' United Mine Workers and the International Ladies Garment Workers Union to organize all workers in their respective industries regardless of race. Many black organizers were employed both in the North and the South in the great organizing campaigns which commenced in the summer of 1933.[13] The young radicals' faith in working-class unity would continue to be reinforced after 1935 when the newly organized CIO promoted organizing drives in the steel and automobile industries which successfully brought many thousands of black workers into the unions on an egalitarian basis.[14] Thus, although the old AFL continued its discriminatory practices against black workers—a condition which continued to motivate a deep distrust

12. See Record, *The Negro and the Communist Party*, 107–108, 179–80; Harold Cruse, *The Crisis of the Negro Intellectual* (New York: William Morrow & Company, Inc., 1967), 146–48. Though I do not agree with all of Cruse's conclusions, I am forced to agree with both Cruse and Record that the influence of the Party on black writers was stifling and that it induced a stance, in Cruse's words, of "imitative posturing." After carefully perusing the writings of men such as Cyril Briggs, Otto Hall, William Patterson, Langston Hughes, Eugene Gordon, and Ben Davis, Jr., in various Party publications such as the Harlem *Liberator*, the *Daily Worker*, the *New Masses* and the *Communist*, I could not improve on the observations of Record and Cruse. The articles of the pre-united front era are given over largely to mud-slinging at figures such as Du Bois, Miller, and Johnson, while the intellectual content throughout the decade was often on the level of sloganeering. Probably the most glaring examples of the Party's stultifying influence on talented black writers can be found among the poets and novelists, and this influence will be examined in Chapters V, VI, and VII.

13. Wolters, *Negroes and the Great Depression*, 305–307. See also Herbert Northrup, *Organized Labor and the Negro* (New York: Harper & Brothers, 1944), 154–71; and Horace R. Cayton and George S. Mitchell, *Black Workers and the New Unions* (Chapel Hill: University of North Carolina Press, 1939), 314–68.

14. James S. Olson, "Organized Black Leadership and Industrial Unionism: The Racial Response, 1936–1945," *Labor History*, 10 (Summer, 1969), 477; Sumner M. Rosen, "The CIO Era, 1935–1955," in Julius Jacobson (ed.), *The Negro and the American Labor Movement* (Garden City, N.Y.: Doubleday & Co., Inc., 1968), 194–95; and Cayton and Mitchell, *Black Workers and the New Unions*, 212.

of organized labor among many, if not most, blacks [15]—the young radicals had some valid reasons for their faith in black and white working-class unity.

The headquarters for the most articulate group of the young radicals was Howard University. During the 1930s Abram Harris became chairman of the department of economics, E. Franklin Frazier assumed leadership of the department of sociology, and Ralph Bunche became head of the political science department.

Abram Harris was a Columbia-trained economist. In collaboration with the white scholar Sterling Spero, he published the classic study, *The Black Worker* (1931), which traced the history and present status of Negro labor in the United States. Harris, unlike so many of the older generation, was severely critical of the teachings of Booker T. Washington. He deplored Washington's advocacy of loyalty to employers and his failure to enlighten Negroes about the "problems peculiar to the wage earner in modern industry." At the turn of the century, the economic philosophy in which Washington placed his faith "was becoming more fictitious than ever." The prevailing notion of the eighteenth and nineteenth centuries, that a man with limited capital could raise himself into wealth and power through hard work and thrift, was being discredited by the spread of immense combinations capitalized in the hundreds of millions of dollars.[16] Instead of realistically teaching Negroes that they could gain the strength they needed to compete with organized industry by affiliating with labor unions, Washington preached a romantic myth. Most regrettably, this myth was

15. Marc Karson and Ronald Radosh, "The American Federation of Labor and the Negro Worker, 1894–1949," in Jacobson (ed.), *The Negro and the American Labor Movement*, 162–87; Olson, "Organized Black Leadership and Industrial Unionism," 474–75; and Cayton and Mitchell, *Black Workers and the New Unions*, 371.
16. Abram Harris and Sterling Spero, *The Black Worker: The Negro and the Labor Movement* (New York: Columbia University Press, 1931), 50–51. All quotes from the book are taken from chapters which were written by Harris.

still hindering the progress of Negro labor, because the middle-class Negro leadership clung to it and continued to be "pro-employer in sympathy and outlook."[17] Harris noted that in nearly every important controversy between organized labor and capital in which the Negro had been involved, this leadership had sided with capital.

Harris hoped to see the establishment of industrial unionism because he thought that such unions, having jurisdiction over an entire industry, would threaten their own existence by neglecting any large section of workers in that industry. He further noted that "because the ideology of industrial unionism is usually socialist or radical, the industrial union signifies aggressive and comprehensive working-class alignment, and is, therefore, more solicitous than the conservative trade union about the welfare of underprivileged minorities like the Negro." He stressed that Negroes should try to avoid setting up separate unions of their own, even if it was expedient. Such self-imposed segregation would hinder the development of a class consciousness.[18]

While Harris praised the efforts of the Communists to instill class consciousness among the Negro masses, he thought them naïve in anticipating a worker's revolution in the United States. They were too eager to see in any sign of unrest the beginning of a general revolt. "The communists are forced to run from pillar to post, with an eye for any dissatisfaction that can be seized upon for its revolutionary possibilities. Thus they see revolution where there is only conservatism." If change was to come, it would not be through violence. Even more disconcerting to Harris was the Communists' "formulation of a fatuous romance like their Negro Socialist Soviet Republic of the United States."[19] It was too much

17. *Ibid.*, 373.   18. *Ibid.*, 326, 74.
19. *Ibid.*, 429, 425. See also Abram Harris, *The Negro As Capitalist: A Study of Banking and Business Among American Negroes* (Philadelphia: The American Academy of Political and Social Science, 1936), 184.

akin to the "black chauvinism" which Harris and his young colleagues detested.

Harris took a closer look at race chauvinism in his other major economic study of the decade, *The Negro as Capitalist* (1936). This was published after Du Bois had set forth his new program for a Negro economic nation within the nation. Harris took specific aim at the inadequacies of the Du Bois scheme. He noted that the Negro's hope of creating an independent economy dated back to pre-Civil War days, but recently the idea had taken two forms: the individualistic economics of Washington which would develop a black economy upon a strictly competitive and private-profit basis and Du Bois's plan for a separate cooperative economy based upon consumer's cooperatives. Despite Du Bois's socialistic protestations, Harris concluded that it was impossible to draw any significant distinction between the two. "They shade imperceptibly into each other. Their common ideology is middle class."[20]

Harris astutely observed that none of the advocates of a separate black economy had satisfactorily explained how such a system could develop and function in the face of persistent industrial integration, business combinations, and the centralization of capital control. He thought that Du Bois's call for "self-sacrifice and enterprise" in light of these circumstances was simplistic. Harris was not as optimistic about the inevitability of capitalism's demise as was Du Bois. Thus, he concluded that "as long as capitalism remains it is reasonably certain that the main arteries of commerce, industry, credit and finance will be controlled by white capitalists" and that the "great mass of black and white men will continue dependent upon these capitalists for their livelihood."[21] Economically speaking, Harris' study demonstrated that the independent black economy was a fantasy.

20. Harris, *The Negro As Capitalist*, ix, 180.
21. *Ibid.*, ix.

In addition to attacking the economic weaknesses of Du Bois's chauvinistic program, Harris also launched into an attack upon black middle-class chauvinism in general. He characterized the middle class as a parasitical group which was fostering such movements as the "Don't Buy Where You Can't Work" campaign for its own selfish interests. Besides giving business to black enterprises, the logical end of this program would be the displacement of white workers by black workers which would only "serve further to widen the breach between white and black labor." The jobs which the campaigners were demanding were white collar positions for the middle class. "In the final analysis," concluded Harris, "it would be the hundreds of thousands of black workers in white industry who would have to bear the cost of the movement's success in obtaining a few thousand jobs for Negro clerks, salesmen, and managers."[22]

Harris also noted that middle-class black chauvinism was "becoming as vicious in its social aspects as it is reactionary in the economic." He attributed the rapid rise of anti-Semitism in Harlem during the 1930s to the black businessmen of the community, who blamed their own failures upon the successful encroachments of Jewish merchants. The black merchants started a "Buy Black" campaign, not out of any real feeling of race loyalty, but merely to line their own pockets: "It is silly to see anything especially Jewish in the exploitation. If there is exploitation of the black masses in Harlem, the Negro business man participates in it as well as the Jew, while both . . . are governed by higher forces that are beyond their control."[23] For Harris, a capitalist was still a capitalist, whatever his ethnic background.

Despite Harris' attempts to be scientifically objective, the black businessman emerged from his study as a villain. The black businessman was not the unselfish, dedicated race-uplifter that Woodson had hoped for—he was not so loyal to the race that he would be willing to make the necessary sacrifices. On the contrary, "What

22. *Ibid.*, 180–81.   23. *Ibid.*, 183.

the Negro business man wants most of all is freedom to monopolize and exploit the market they [the black masses] provide. They cannot see that they have no greater exploiter than the black capitalist who lives upon low-waged if not sweated labor, although he and his family may, and often do, live in conspicuous luxury."[24] Black business or businessmen could offer no salvation to the masses of the race.

Like most of the radicals, Harris functioned principally as a critic. But he did have a program of his own. In 1934 he was asked by the NAACP to revamp its policies in the light of contemporary conditions. Heading an investigative committee which included such young radicals as Sterling Brown, Ralph Bunche, and E. Franklin Frazier, and older liberals like James Weldon Johnson, Harris proposed a new scheme the published portion of which was patterned closely after the Amenia manifesto.[25]

Harris first noted that the NAACP had been operating under the guidance of obsolete principles of eighteenth-century liberalism. In an age of rampant capitalism which left the masses of people powerless against the depredations of organized wealth, the association still clung to a laissez faire political economy. He argued that civil rights would do the Negro little good until after he had achieved a semblance of economic power. The association must organize the laboring masses. Harris assumed that the problems and interests of white and black labor were essentially the same. He advised the association that "instead of continuing to oppose racial discrimination on the job and in pay and in various manifestations of anti-Negro feeling among the workers, we should attempt to get Negroes to view their special grievances as a natural part of the larger issues of American labor as a whole."[26] Harris was aware

24. *Ibid.*, 184.
25. See Fullinwider, *Mind and Mood of Black America*, 183. For an interesting and much more detailed discussion of the Harris report which employs internal evidence, see Wolters, *Negroes and the Great Depression*, 302–52.
26. Harris, as quoted in Emmett Dorsey, "The Negro and Social Planning," *Jour-*

of black America's deep distrust of organized labor, and he emphasized the point that one of the most important blocks in the path of labor solidarity was the black worker's attitude. He also thought that the association should attempt to teach white workers that as long as they discriminated against black workers, there would be a continuing pool of cheap labor at the disposal of the capitalists. Until the workers, black and white, realized the absolute necessity of labor solidarity, they would continue to be economically—and, therefore, politically and socially—powerless.

In order to produce solidarity, Harris proposed that the association establish workers' and farmers' councils for the purpose of "workers' education." The councils were to demonstrate the mutual economic interests of white and black workers, inculcate an industrial rather than trade union consciousness, and lay a foundation for united political action. In the future, this political unity might lead to the establishment of a separate political party. In the present, however, it consisted of "intelligent" use of the ballot and the application of immediate pressure for such social legislation as old age pensions, child and female labor protection, and the elimination of lynching and legalized Jim Crow. He emphasized that these councils were "not to be established in a separatist or racial spirit"; white workers would be encouraged to join. He also cautioned that the councils should not be mere debating societies, but should take an active part in strikes, lockouts, and labor demonstrations.[27] Significantly, Harris' program was designed to work within the general bounds of the status quo. The NAACP took Harris' program under consideration, then dropped it. It continued, however, to serve many of the younger intellectuals as a feasible model of what should be done.[28]

---

nal of Negro Education, V (January, 1936), 108–109. The program was reprinted at the end of Dorsey's article.

27. Ibid., 109.

28. See for example, ibid., 105–109; and Ralph Bunche, "Triumph? or Fiasco?" Race, 1 (Winter, 1935–36), 93–96.

While Harris had noted the romanticism of race men like Du Bois, his colleague at Howard, E. Franklin Frazier, expanded the concept of romanticism into the central motif of his sarcastic critique, "The Du Bois Program in the Present Crisis." This article was perhaps the bitterest attack of the decade upon the older race men in general and Du Bois in particular. Like most of Du Bois's critics, Frazier distrusted the legitimacy of the aging leader's conversion. For despite Du Bois's concentration on the economic improvement of the black masses, Frazier was certain that he remained the haughty, "genteel" aristocrat who had no real conception or "sympathetic understanding" of the plight of the black proletariat. His image of the black masses was a "dazzlingly romantic picture." Like most of the older leadership, he was really interested in the welfare of the privileged black middle class. "The voice of Du Bois," wrote Frazier, "is genuine only when he speaks as a representative of the Talented Tenth."[29]

Thus, Frazier thought it was absurd when Du Bois called for a Negro nation within a nation. Although he might prattle romantically about the ideal black society, "nothing would be more unendurable for him than to live within a Black Ghetto or within a black nation—unless perhaps he were king, and then he probably would attempt to unite the whites and blacks through marriage of the royal families." More seriously, Frazier was worried that "if a Fascist movement should develop in America, Du Bois would play into the hands of its leaders through his program for the development of Negro racialism."[30]

As for Du Bois's socialistic pronouncements, Frazier thought that they were also hopelessly romantic. For Du Bois socialism was "a far-off, divine event toward which all creation moves."[31] It was incomprehensible to Frazier how Du Bois could preach his peculiar

---

29. E. Franklin Frazier, "The Du Bois Program in the Present Crisis," *Race*, I (Winter, 1935–36), 11–12.
30. *Ibid.*, 12–13.   31. *Ibid.*, 12.

brand of socialism to Negroes while ignoring whatever might happen to the rest of society. Even within the black community, Frazier thought that Du Bois's system of consumer's cooperatives was impracticable. Like Harris, he noted that such a system presupposed a certain amount of capital on the part of the consumers. He suggested that if the destitute black masses adopted such a plan, they could use "Share Your Poverty" as a slogan.[32]

Frazier was outraged because Du Bois was trying to wean the black masses away from the white workers and economic radicals. His immediate program of establishing separate cooperatives within the American capitalistic system would "set up false hopes for the Negro and keep him from getting a realistic conception of capitalist economy and the hopelessness of his position in such a system." In fact, Frazier condemned all of the old leadership for ignoring the fact that the status of the race in America had been determined "by those economic forces which have shaped the country at large."[33] Unlike the race men, Frazier thought that black America's problems were essentially a part of the larger problems of the dominant society.

The major problem confronting society during the 1930s was economic, and Frazier tended to see most problems in that context. By the middle of the decade he was quite certain that "the development of the Negro's status in the United States . . . has been bound up, in the final analysis, with the role which the Negro has played in the economic system."[34] The older generation had been too preoccupied with race prejudice. "While everyone is aware of the fact that such social factors as racial prejudice have accelerated certain features of the system," wrote Frazier, "the relentless operation of dominant economic forces have brought about the degradation of

---

32. *Ibid.*, 13.   33. *Ibid.*
34. E. Franklin Frazier, "The Status of the Negro in the American Social Order," *Journal of Negro Education*, V (July, 1935), 307.

white and black alike."[35] The Negro's problems were more the result of being poor than of being black.

Moreover, Frazier did not share the race men's pessimism. Even
in the South, he noted, "There are signs that the question of the
status of the Negro is losing its purely racial character and is becoming tied up with the struggle of white and black workers
against the white landlords and capitalists."[36] He noted approv-
ingly the fact that black farmers were rejecting the old individualistic ethos of Washington and joining such bodies as the Southern
Tenant Farmers Union.[37]

In contrast to Kelly Miller, Frazier was optimistic about the Negro's future in the city. The urbanization of the Negro represented
his "second emancipation." The urban Negro was rapidly identify-
ing himself with the industrial proletariat. With his increasing
labor consciousness came an understanding of the rudiments of
the use of power and an awareness that " 'good will' on the part of
sentimental whites will not help him."[38]

Frazier was quite certain that cooperation with the white workers in the struggle for power with the owning classes offered the
Negro "the only hope of his complete emancipation." Frazier, like
Harris, thought that the decision for cooperation rested largely on
the black man's shoulders. "The increasing conflict between the
workers and the employers," he wrote, "is forcing the Negro to
make common cause with white workers."[39] In light of the violent
race prejudice among white workers, older race men thought that

35. E. Franklin Frazier, "Seventy Years too Late," *Journal of Negro Education,*
V (April, 1936), 273.

36. Frazier, "Status of the Negro," 300.

37. Frazier, "Seventy Years too Late," 274.

38. E. Franklin Frazier, "Negroes in the United States: 1920–32," *Journal of
Negro Education,* V (January, 1936), 137. See also Frazier, "Status of the Negro,"
305, 307.

39. Frazier, "Status of the Negro," 305, 307. See also "Southern Resources,"
Journal of Negro Education, VI (January, 1937), 82.

idea—that black workers could decide to make a "common cause"
—was utterly absurd.

Frazier's emphasis in his polemical tracts on the need for interracial solidarity was not just the reflection of a radical ideology, it
was also based on his research as a sociologist. In all of his sociological studies of the Negro family during the 1930s, Frazier operated on the assumption that complete assimilation of the values,
culture, and institutions of the dominant white society was the only
means by which Negroes could gain complete equality.[40]

Frazier had studied under Robert Park at the University of Chicago during the 1920s. It was Park, more than any other sociologist,
who had redirected the study of race relations away from an emphasis on race and racial differences and toward an emphasis on
the ideas of caste, class, and status. Following Park's lead, increasing numbers of sociologists were won over to the idea that racial
antagonism was to a large extent the product of an exaggerated
social distance between the races. Park also maintained that relations between the races were not static, but dynamic. He theorized
a pattern in the evolution of race relations. Whenever two different
races came into contact, conflict and competition would be inevitable. Then a period of stability would follow in which one race
dominated and the other was forced to accommodate. Eventually,
the race which was forced into the accommodating position would
pass through the process of assimilation. Park was most interested
in the accelerating affect which the city was having on this dynamic process. In the cities he believed that caste was breaking

40. Frazier's books included *The Negro Family in Chicago* (Chicago: University
of Chicago Press, 1932); *The Free Negro Family* (Nashville, Tenn.: Fisk University
Press, 1932); *The Negro Family in the United States* (Chicago: University of Chicago Press, 1939); and *Negro Youth at the Crossways* (Washington, D.C.: American
Council on Education, 1940). The first two books were essentially preparatory
studies for *The Negro Family in the United States*, and the fourth was based on
similar materials. For another analysis of Frazier's sociological ideas, see Fullinwider,
Mind and Mood of Black America, 100–106.

down and that the social distance between the races on various class levels was disappearing. There was what the Swedish sociologist, Gunnar Myrdal, called an "optimistic bias" built into Park's theorizing.[41] E. Franklin Frazier shared this bias. He believed that assimilation would be the ultimate fate of the black man in the United States.

In his study of the family, Frazier was concerned with finding how the Negro, "stripped of the relatively simple preliterate culture in which he was nurtured, has created a folk culture and has gradually taken over the more sophisticated American culture." In contrast to men like Du Bois and Woodson, whose belief in cultural carryover supported their chauvinism, Frazier followed the lead of Franz Boas. He denied the existence of any cultural carryover from Africa. The Afro-American slave underwent a process of "dehumanizing" which cut off all memory of his African heritage and transformed him into an "animate tool."[42]

In contrast to the norm of society, Frazier pictured the typical Negro family in slavery as being unstable and matriarchal. The "peculiar institution" encouraged sexual promiscuity and familial irresponsibility, especially on the part of males. Very few Negroes, thought Frazier, had any opportunity to be real humans: "The emergence of the slave as a human being was facilitated by his assimilation into the household of the master race. There he took over

41. For an analysis of Robert Park's theories on race relations, see E. Franklin Frazier, "Sociological Theory and Race Relations," *American Sociological Review*, XII (June, 1947), 269–71; John H. Bracey, Jr., August Meier, and Elliott Rudwick (eds.), *The Black Sociologists: The First Half Century* (Belmont, Calif.: Wadsworth Publishing Company, 1971), 5–7; and Fullinwider, *Mind and Mood of Black America*, 100–104, which effectively demonstrates Park's influence on Frazier's thinking. Gunnar Myrdal criticized the "optimistic bias" of men like Park and pointed out how in its fatalistic determinism it often led to a "do-nothing" bias. See *An American Dilemma*, 1038–1057. A more recent critical analysis of the biases of social scientists during the 1930s and 1940s, including those of Myrdal, can be found in Lewis Killian and Charles Grigg, *Racial Crisis in America: Leadership in Conflict* (Englewood Cliffs, N.J.: Prentice-Hall, Inc., 1964), 15–19.
42. Frazier, *The Negro Family in the United States*, 479, 43, 479.

more or less the ideas and attitudes and morals and manners of his masters."[43] Frazier's measure of "humanity" was the white master class. The only Negroes able to become more "human" were the mulatto servant class.

The great bulk of Negroes, both before and after emancipation, remained tied to the soil and isolated from white society. These were the people who, living "in relative isolation . . . developed a folk culture with its peculiar social organization and social evaluations." Typical of this folk culture again was the matriarchal family and the acceptance of "widespread illegitimacy." For Frazier this was deviant behavior. However, there were those few "ambitious and energetic" freedmen who managed to "get some education and buy homes." These Negroes, to some extent, escaped from the folk culture and started "small nuclei of stable families with conventional standards of sexual morality." For Frazier they represented "the highest development of Negro family life up to the opening of the present century."[44]

The most significant influence upon the Negro family after emancipation was the rapid urbanization of the twentieth century —a process that was still much in motion while Frazier was writing. He noted that the initial impact of the city had almost completed the disintegration of the Negro family as it had existed in the rural South. The city became the home of "Roving Men and Homeless Women." The freedom of the city at first pushed Negroes even further away from the "conventional standards" into the "final stages of demoralization." But Frazier concluded, optimistically, that if there was a "City of Destruction," there was also a "City of Rebirth."[45] In the city, the old deviant folk culture was cast off and the culture of the dominant society more easily assimilated.

For example, as the Negro became an industrial worker in the

43. *Ibid.*, 41.   44. *Ibid.*, 483–84.
45. *Ibid.*, 288. These are the titles to Parts IV and V of the book.

city and received adequate compensation, the father tended to become the chief breadwinner and thereby assumed a responsible—conventional—position in the family. Economic opportunity was in the city, not on the farm, and Frazier believed that if the Negro could earn a conventional wage, he could lead a conventional family life. After all, "the condition of the black worker is determined by the same forces in our economic system which affect the life of the white worker." In addition to economic opportunity, the city offered proximity to whites, and in the flux of the city, caste barriers were less rigid. Thus the process of assimilation, acculturation, and even amalgamation was happily accelerated.[46]

Frazier wanted to achieve the race's salvation through its eventual disappearance, culturally and biologically. His own lack of "sympathetic understanding" of the black masses whom he championed can be seen in those accomplishments which he most valued. For example, he did not value the philosophy and life-style behind the blues; instead, he saw that the very fact that "the Negro has succeeded in adopting habits of living that have enabled him to survive in a civilization based upon laissez faire and competition, itself bespeaks a degree of success in taking on the folkways and mores of the white race."[47] It is not surprising that Frazier was never mistaken for a racial chauvinist. What is surprising is that as a sociologist he saw some value in the individualistic ethos which he condemned as a radical polemicist.

If Frazier wanted to see the end of the race in the future, Ralph Bunche often ignored its existence in the present.[48] Bunche firmly believed that the racial nature of the "Negro problem" in the United States had been seriously exaggerated. "The customary racial approach to this vital problem tends to put the cart before the

46. *Ibid.*, 475, 486–87, 474, 488.   47. *Ibid.*, 487.
48. See especially Ralph Bunche, *A World View of Race* (Washington, D.C.: The Associates in Negro Folk Education, 1936), 84–85.

horse and blinds itself to factors which are far more significant than those of mere race."[49] Bunche thought that this was a result of a widespread misconception concerning the "true position" of the Negro in society: "The Negro is said to be a 'racial minority' group, but this is true only in a narrow and arbitrary sense. Economically, the Negro primarily is identified with the peasant and proletarian classes of the country, which are certainly not in the minority." And even culturally, "the Negro reflects the prominent characteristics of the section of the country and the class with which he is identified."[50]

Bunche thought that the concept of race probably possessed little, if any, scientific validity. But as an ambiguously defined concept, it had been a useful device for the cultivation of group prejudices. "Racialism is a myth, albeit a dangerous one, for it is a perfect stalking-horse for selfish group politics and camouflage for brutal economic exploitation." The most important manipulators of this myth were the "ruling classes," who employed it to keep the black and white masses apart,[51] and the older race leaders, who used it to maintain their own positions of power.

While not as sarcastic as Frazier, Bunche was the most persistent critic of the methods and ideologies of the older race men who had, he believed, perpetuated the race myth. Negro leadership had "traditionally put its stress on the element of race; it has attributed the plight of the Negro to a peculiar racial condition." He regretted that "leaders and organizations alike have but one end in view— the elimination of 'discrimination against the race.'" They ignored the fact that as long as the black and white masses did not understand their common economic interests, "neither prayer, nor logic,

49. Ralph Bunche, "Education in Black and White," *Journal of Negro Education*, V (July, 1936), 353. See also Bunche, *A World View of Race*, 81, 91.

50. Bunche, "Education in Black and White," 353–54.

51. Bunche, *A World View of Race*, 25; Ralph Bunche, "A Critical Analysis of the Tactics and Programs of Minority Groups," *Journal of Negro Education*, IV (July, 1935), 309. See also *A World View of Race*, 67.

nor emotional or legal appeal can make much headway against"
race prejudice.[52] Bunche characterized them as "floundering about"
in their "ghettoes of thought" guiding Negroes "up the dark, blind
alley of black chauvinism."[53] Du Bois sarcastically retorted that
Bunche apparently hoped to establish a new slogan for American
Negroes: "All save Race is our soul's salvation."[54]

Du Bois's pan-Africanism was a prime example of the black
chauvinism which Bunche opposed. Romantic black chauvinists
assumed that "both the white and black peoples of the earth have
a common fundamental interest in the color of their skin." They
completely ignored class, religious, cultural, linguistic, national,
and other differences among both white and black peoples. Men
like Du Bois could not see that for either a white or a black man
"it is scarcely more pleasant to be exploited and oppressed by privileged members of one's own race than by members of some other
race."[55] Like Harris and Frazier, Bunche was skeptical of the economic programs endorsed by the race leaders. He did not believe
that the Negro had the resources to succeed in private enterprise,
and he was disgusted with those leaders who continued, in the
crisis of the depression, to feed black Americans "on the traditional
American illusion that even the man or group on the very lowest
rung of the economic ladder can, by industry, thrift, efficiency, and
perseverance, attain the top rung."[56] The American capitalistic
system no longer permitted it.

He also doubted the ability of consumer cooperatives to compete

52. Bunche, "A Critical Analysis of the Tactics and Programs of Minority
Groups," 310–11. See also his A World View of Race, 83–84; and his "The Programs
of Organizations Devoted to the Improvement of the Status of the American Negro,"
Journal of Negro Education, VIII (July, 1939), 540.
53. Bunche, "The Programs of Organizations," 540; and his A World View of
Race, 84.
54. W. E. B. Du Bois, "The Position of the Negro in the American Social Order:
Where Do We Go From Here?" Journal of Negro Education, VIII (July, 1939), 561.
55. Bunche, A World View of Race, 95.
56. Bunche, "The Programs of Organizations," 542; and his "A Critical Analysis," 314.

successfully against huge industrial and commercial conglomerations. He was even more critical of the boycott movements, such as the "Don't Buy Where You Can't Work" campaign. Such action could create no new jobs, but could only gain jobs for Negroes by the displacement of whites: "At best, it could create only a vicious cycle of job displacement." At worst, it widened "still further the already deplorable gap between the white and black working-classes of the nation, by boldly placing the competition for jobs on a strictly racial basis." Bunche reminded the boycotters that "the Negro is not out of a job simply because he is a Negro, but, rather because the economic system finds itself incapable of affording an adequate number of jobs for all."[57]

The older leaders' efforts, however, had not been concerned chiefly with economics, but with civil rights. Like Harris, Bunche felt that groups such as the NAACP were still operating on the basis of outmoded democratic liberalism. They placed their faith in the ballot and in the courts. "The inherent fallacy of this belief," commented Bunche, "rests in the failure to appreciate the fact that the instruments of the state are merely reflections of the political and economic ideology of the dominant group, that the political arm of the state cannot be divorced from its prevailing economic structure, whose servant it must inevitably be."[58]

Bunche asked if the Negro would be any better off if he were able to throw off his racial identity, suddenly turn white and assume all of the rights which the white man theoretically possesses. Bitterly, he concluded: "Paper rights and political privileges have not protected millions of the white population from abject wage slavery, if indeed they can find the chance to sell themselves into it; they have carried the ballot to the bread lines."[59] Significantly, the "millions of the white population" to which he was referring

57. Bunche, "A Critical Analysis," 313–14. See also his "The Programs of Organizations," 544.

58. Bunche, "The Critical Analysis," 314–15.

59. Bunche, A World View of Race, 85–86.

were "the inhabitants of Tobacco Road . . . the wage slaves of the factory, mill and mining towns." Even the well-trained young social scientist could indulge himself in romanticism.

Bunche also thought that the efforts of organizations, such as the Urban League and the NAACP, to achieve interracial conciliation were "dubiously valuable." Their efforts to achieve "good will" were genteel. "They can be militant, but only politely so; they can attack, but not too harshly; they must entreat, bargain, compromise and capitulate in order to win petty gains."[60] Their dependence upon liberal white philanthropic good will left them powerless.

Bunche was also impatient with those who placed their faith in the Constitution as a guardian of American liberties. He explained that the Constitution was a very flexible instrument and that, like the government, "it cannot be anything more than the controlling elements in American society wish it to be."[61]

Finally, Bunche ruled out attempts to gain justice in the courts. He alleged that laws and decisions contrary to the will of those in power could not be enforced. More important was the fact that even the Supreme Court could "effect no revolutionary changes in the economic order, and yet the status of the Negro, as that of other groups in the society, is fundamentally fixed by the functioning and the demands of that order."[62]

Bunche joined Harris and Frazier in advising that "the only hope for the improvement in the condition of the masses of any American minority group is the hope that can be held out for the betterment of the masses of the dominant group. Their basic interests are identical."[63] Any realistic program would have to be based on the power derived from white and black labor solidarity. The need for power was the element which most of the older leaders had ignored. Bunche sought a means by which the black masses could be

60. Bunche, "A Critical Analysis," 316. See also his "The Programs of Organizations," 546–47.

61. Bunche, "A Critical Analysis," 315.

62. Ibid., 316–17.   63. Ibid., 320.

instructed in the use of power through an "ideology of organized labor." By the time of the Howard Economic Conference in 1935, he thought that this might be achieved through a national Negro congress.

Kelly Miller indicted the Howard Economic Conference as "red" and Ralph Bunche, one of its radical organizers, as a heretic.[64] For although he had served as a member of the famous "Black Brain Trust," Bunche irreverently attacked the middle-class pragmatism of the New Deal: "The New Deal follows the classical pattern of middle-class planning by compromise with Big Business,— a policy fatal to the interests of labor."[65] Naturally, he and the young radicals and Communists thought that black and white labor should unite to combat such a situation. They agreed among themselves that a national Negro congress might, among other things, be able to encourage this. At the suggestion of Bunche and John P. Davis, secretary of the Joint Committee on National Recovery, "a select group of leaders" was invited to discuss plans for such a gathering at Bunche's residence immediately after the adjournment of the conference.[66]

These conferees agreed that they did not want to establish yet another organization. Their purpose was to bring together the existing labor, religious, civic, racial, and interracial organizations into some semblance of unity. They thought that if such organizations could work together, instead of at cross purposes, then they could more efficiently educate Negroes, mold public opinion, and apply pressure for the rights of Negro citizens.[67]

64. Kelly Miller, "Kelly Miller Says—," Chicago *Defender*, June 8, 1935; and "Kelly Miller Says H. U. Prexy Presided Over One Session of Red Conference," Baltimore *Afro-American*, June 1, 1935.

65. Bunche, "A Critique of New Deal Social Planning As It Affects Negroes," 62.

66. Bunche, "The Programs, Ideologies, Tactics and Achievements," II, 319.

67. *Ibid.*, 319–20. For further analyses of the National Negro Congress, see Wolters, *Negroes and the Great Depression*, 353–82; Cruse, *The Crisis of the Negro Intellectual*, 171–80; Fullinwider, *Mind and Mood of Black America*, 185–86; Record, *The Negro and the Communist Party*, 153–62; and especially Lawrence S. Wittner, "The National Negro Congress: A Reassessment," *American Quarterly*, XXII (Win-

The National Negro Congress convened in Chicago, on February 14–16, 1936, with an attendance of over 800 delegates representing 585 organizations. Kelly Miller, James Weldon Johnson, Du Bois, Robert Russa Moton, and other old-guard leaders were conspicuously absent. One leftist observer interpreted this as evidence that the congress was seeking a new race leadership and gleefully reported that "certainly we must say that for once at least 'God's dark chillun' were 'red' in spirit if nothing more."[68]

Kelly Miller agreed, but for different reasons. The congress was led in the main by the younger intelligentsia, "impelled by the same inchoate and undefined spirit of unrest and dissatisfaction which caused the recent Harlem riot." Once again, he was disgusted because religion, philanthropy, and patriotism, "the three pillars upon which the life and hope of the race have been built, were either ruthlessly flouted or tepidly tolerated out of a sense of salutary prudence."[69] His charge, that the congress was a mere Communist front organization, was prophetic, as the young radicals would later discover.

However, the congress was not yet dominated by the Communists. The delegates passed resolutions that would satisfy both ardent Communists and black businessmen and chose the much respected A. Philip Randolph as president.

It was this very lack of consistency which disappointed Bunche. As he reviewed the proceedings, he noted that though the ideology of organized labor had been dominant, there had been too many other, contradictory ideologies—especially the support for bigger

---

ter, 1970), 883–901. Wittner argues rather persuasively that the failure of the original nonsectarian and racial aims of the Congress was due to more than just the influence of the Communist party; the CIO and the increasing lack of racial homogeneity were also important. Wittner perhaps does not give enough attention to the power of the Communists within many of the CIO affiliates.

68. Louis Emanuel Martin, "The National Negro Congress," *Challenge,* I (June, 1936), 31–32.

69. "Kelly Miller Calls Negro Congress A 'Leftward Drift,'" Pittsburgh *Courier,* February 14, 1936.

and better black business—supported by the congress. The breadth of the coalition, which the organizers hoped would produce strength, was its basic weakness. Bunche hoped that the next congress, to meet in 1937, would be composed only of representatives of organizations actively engaged in the labor struggle. But the 1937 congress, which met at Philadelphia, was made up of the same elements and passed essentially the same resolutions as the year before. Again Bunche was disappointed.[70]

Although Bunche was dissatisfied with the congress' ideological ambiguity, the organization did become quite an effective force for a few years during the late 1930s. During the first two years of its existence its most important work was done on the local level within the black community. The organization had local branches in approximately seventy cities and in many of them it led successful campaigns for improved employment opportunities, better housing conditions, and more adequate relief work within the black community.[71] After 1938 the grass-roots character of the organization declined and the national office increasingly dominated activities. Although it was originally a nonsectarian and essentially racial organization, Secretary John P. Davis, who sometime during these years became a Communist, moved it more and more into Party politics and a coalition with big labor.[72] Following the Party's "united front" line, Davis, who at one time had been one of the New Deal's most caustic critics, threw the support of the congress squarely behind Roosevelt and all liberal New Dealers. Also during this period the congress played an important part in helping the CIO's Steel Workers Organizing Committee to organize black

70. Bunche, "Triumph? Or Fiasco?" 93–96. See the two pamphlets: *1936—National Negro Congress Resolutions*, and *1937—National Negro Congress Official Proceedings*, both in the National Negro Congress vertical file, Schomburg Collection, New York Public Library. Bunche, "The Programs of Organizations," 547.

71. Wittner, "The National Negro Congress: A Reassessment," 887–90.

72. *Ibid.*, 886, 890–95. For an analysis of John P. Davis' perilous voyage from the Republican party to the Communist party during the 1930s, see Wolters, *Negroes and the Great Depression*, 373–75.

workers in the steel industry. This was one of the goals which the young radicals had hoped to see accomplished. However, unbeknownst to them, the congress, which had been strapped for funds throughout much of its existence, was beginning to receive substantial financial support from the CIO and many of its affiliated unions.[73] Many of these affiliates were dominated by the Communist party. The extent of CIO and, more importantly, Communist control of the congress became readily apparent during its third and final meeting in 1940.

After this meeting Bunche was bitter because the congress had become little more than a Communist front organization. John P. Davis and other Communist leaders had turned the congress into a forum for Soviet foreign policy. Thus the young radicals' one concrete attempt to organize and educate the masses had been, in Bunche's opinion, "perverted" by the Communists.[74]

While Bunche, like most of the non-Communist radicals, never advocated the Communist cause, he had been at first sympathetic with the Party's efforts to educate the masses in the lessons of class consciousness.[75] But in the latter half of the decade, as the Party shifted its emphasis away from domestic problems to inconsistent pronouncements on international affairs, Bunche became disillusioned. "The Negro interest for the Communists is tied to the uncertain and constantly shifting foreign policy of the Soviet Union,"[76] he wrote in 1940.

Ironically, Soviet foreign policy in 1940 temporarily coincided with the advice of much of the older leadership: American Negroes should ignore the war in Europe and concentrate on democracy at

73. Wittner, "The National Negro Congress: A Reassessment," 890–96; Wolters, *Negroes and the Great Depression*, 367–68. For an analysis of the effectiveness of the congress' activities in creating a favorable opinion toward organized labor in the black community, see Cayton and Mitchell, *Black Workers and the New Unions*, 202–206.

74. Bunche, "The Programs, Ideologies, Tactics and Achievements," 357–69.

75. Bunche, "A Critical Analysis," 312; and his *A World View of Race*, 36.

76. Ralph Bunche, "The Role of the University in the Political Orientation of Negro Youth," *Journal of Negro Education*, IX (October, 1940), 577.

home. Bunche vehemently disagreed with this: "The Negro faces grave danger from the repercussions of a Nazi victory in Europe."[77] He castigated the older leadership for relinquishing discussion of issues more fundamental even than race—such as world war—to the dominant white leadership. In doing so, they were imposing segregation upon themselves.[78]

As the war crisis drew nearer, Bunche joined the consensus of opinion among most black intellectuals, maintaining that the Negro should not cease to agitate for his rights,[79] but still he argued that the Negro should not threaten to remain aloof from the war effort in order to extort concessions from the dominant society. Unashamedly, Bunche proclaimed: "American democracy is bad enough. But in the mad world of today I love it, and I will fight to preserve it."[80] As always with Bunche, the needs of the race took a back seat to those of the larger society.

It was precisely this de-emphasis of race which most significantly distinguished the young radicals from their elders. The older generation could never get beyond the fact of race. The young men thought that they could; in fact, they often operated on the assumption that they already had done so. They were social scientists, recently instructed in the latest social theories which contended that race was indefinable. They were also young intellectuals, receptive to the intellectual currents of the time. During the depression, it became "fashionable," as Johnson pointed out, to look at all problems in an economic frame of reference. The economic interpretation seemed to fill the void which was left by the elimination of the race motive.

77. *Ibid.*
78. Bunche, "The Programs of Organizations," 549–50.
79. Ralph Bunche, "The Negro in the Political Life of the United States," *Journal of Negro Education*, X (July, 1941), 583. See Richard M. Dalfiume, *Desegregation of the U. S. Armed Forces: Fighting on Two Fronts, 1939–1953* (Columbia: University of Missouri Press, 1969), 111–12, for a discussion of the fighting on "two fronts" idea.
80. Bunche, "The Role of the University," 579.

Thus, they chastized their elders for emphasizing civil rights, which would principally benefit the black bourgeoisie, and for ignoring the basic problem of the black masses which was economic. They ridiculed the older leaders for a lack of "sympathetic understanding" of the black masses, and for failing to communicate with them. And yet, the young radicals only published books, or sophisticated articles for academic journals, while many of the older leaders wrote columns for the Afro-American press. Most of the young radicals, in their university environments, were as isolated from the black masses as were the "marginal men" they condemned. No matter how much they may have wished to avoid the fact, they were of the same class.

Nor, in the end, could they avoid the problem of race. As Du Bois so aptly pointed out, they were teaching in black universities, publishing articles concerning the problems of the race, and in race journals for the most part, and were submitting plans which were designed to alleviate the problems of black people. As events of the war years would prove, race was indeed a major problem facing modern society.

III

Variations on a
Racial Theme

There were many prominent black intellectuals who either did not take sides in the debate between the Amenia radicals and the older race men, or who took part but did not consistently adhere to the thinking of either side. The older race men and the young academic radicals represented only two opposite poles of thought during the depression years. The thinking of many, perhaps even most, black writers was deeply influenced by both but followed neither exclusively. These men, each in his own way, were equally concerned with the problems of both race and class. Roy Wilkins, for example, although a young man, was one of those NAACP officials who had been criticized at Amenia. Although in private he was also critical of the association's inability to attack the race's special problems within the context of the larger issues facing the nation, he generally supported the association's policies in his published comments. Though he remained a race man to the core he also eventually became a strong supporter of the idea of white and black labor solidarity. Horace Mann Bond, a young southern educator, held the same antichauvinist views as the radicals, but he frequently looked back to Booker T. Washington for guidance in social and economic affairs. Wilkins, Bond, and others such as Horace Cayton and Ira DeA. Reid, who held views somewhere between those of the older race men and the young radicals, were just beginning their careers in the 1930s. They did not yet possess the influence of men like A. Philip Randolph, Charles S. Johnson, George S. Schuyler, and William Pickens whose views will be considered in this chapter.

The thought of these four men cannot be categorized as either traditionally racial or newly radical, for they incorporated elements of both into their own thinking. Like the race men, they were concerned with black men's problems as a racial minority; like the radicals, they also saw the race's problems in a class context. Each of these men offered his own alternative to the approaches of the older race leaders and the young radicals, sometimes leaning toward one and then toward the other.

The labor organizer, A. Philip Randolph, combined the roles of economic radical and race spokesman. As an economic radical he set forth many of the ideas that were taken up by the young radicals. As a race spokesman he called upon Negroes to depend upon themselves in their struggle for equality—a theme constantly repeated by the older race leaders during the 1930s. While Randolph, like the young radicals, concentrated most of his efforts upon finding solutions to the race's economic problems, he could not view the race's situation solely within an economic frame of reference. "Black America," he observed, "is a victim of both class and race prejudice and oppression."[1] Unlike his young radical admirers, he had had considerable experience with the reality of race prejudice among the white working class.

During the 1930s Randolph became one of the best-known Negroes in the United States. He first achieved prominence as the organizer and president of the all-black Brotherhood of Sleeping Car Porters. After more than a decade of fierce struggle, Randolph capped his successes as a labor leader in 1937 by winning from the

1. "Randolph's Speech," *1936—National Negro Congress Resolutions*, in the National Negro Congress vertical file, Schomburg Collection, New York Public Library, 2.

Pullman Company recognition for his union and a very favorable contract for the porters. He was the first Negro to achieve any real power within the conservative AFL. Throughout the 1940s and 1950s Randolph would persist in an almost single-handed struggle to pressure the AFL into eliminating discriminatory practices within its affiliates.[2] His accomplishments in organized labor earned him such widespread respect within the Negro community—especially among the young radicals—that he easily won election as president of the National Negro Congress in 1936 and 1937.

Randolph achieved his greatest fame, however, as chairman of the March on Washington Movement. In June of 1941, his threat of a march on the nation's capital helped to persuade President Roosevelt to issue the famous Executive Order 8802 which, on paper at least, guaranteed equal employment opportunities for blacks in all defense industries. The March on Washington Movement was based upon a philosophy of black power which Randolph had propounded throughout the decade. Both as a labor and a race leader, he taught that organization is the basis of real power.

While Randolph admitted that the race had its own peculiar problems, he associated its fundamental economic problems with those of labor in general. After all, the great majority of Negroes were workers. With the coming of the depression, the Negro's chief problems, as with all workers, were unemployment, long hours, and low wages.[3]

2. See Marc Karson and Ronald Radosh, "The American Federation of Labor and the Negro Worker, 1894–1949," in Julius Jacobson (ed.), The Negro and the American Labor Movement (Garden City, N.Y.: Doubleday & Co., Inc., 1968), 163–87; Lawrence S. Wittner, "The National Negro Congress: A Reassessment," American Quarterly, 22 (Winter, 1970), 895. For biographical sketches of Randolph, see Jervis Anderson, "Profile: A. Philip Randolph," New Yorker, December 2, 9, 16, 1972; Edwin R. Embree, 13 Against the Odds (New York: The Viking Press, 1944), 211–30; and James J. Flynn, Negroes of Achievement in Modern America (New York: Dodd, Mead & Company, 1970), 235–48.

3. A. Philip Randolph, "The Economic Crisis of the Negro," Opportunity, IX (May, 1931), 145–49. See also his "What the Universal Economic Depression Has Meant to Members of the Race," Chicago Defender, January 14, 1933; and his

He vehemently opposed those who asserted that successful black business would offer a substantial increase in jobs for Negroes. Like Abram Harris and the young radicals, he thought that capitalists came in all colors, even black, and that their interests were essentially opposed to those of the workers.[4] Besides, even if the black capitalists could subsume their interests to those of the workers, their chances for success in the modern industrial order were nil because of the "increasing concentration and centralization of financial and industrial power into fewer and fewer hands."[5] Randolph thought that permanent full employment would come only with "the collective ownership, control and operation of the social productive and distributive instrumentalities in our industrial society."[6] In the meantime, he advised that "only through the exercise of power attainable through the organization of wage earners is it possible increasingly to exact higher wages and shorter hours."[7]

In addition to its economic gains, Randolph thought that organized labor could exert considerable political influence as well. Very early in the decade he called for social legislation which would be enacted later in the New Deal. He thought that politically active labor could pressure the government to institute programs for old age and unemployment insurance, to establish a program of public works, to enact legislation protecting child and female labor, to give recognition to the Soviet Union and to provide the states with a "hunger loan."[8] Significantly, many of these measures were later called for by the radicals at Amenia.

Randolph also promoted worker education. Like Abram Harris,

"Randolph Analyzes World Economic Situation as It Effects Race," Chicago *Defender*, January 21, 1933.

4. See A. Philip Randolph, "Propaganda Against Jews," *The Black Worker: Official Organ of the Brotherhood of Sleeping Car Porters and Mouthpiece of the Negro Workers of America*, August, 1938.

5. Randolph, "The Economic Crisis of the Negro," 149.

6. *Ibid.*   7. *Ibid.*, 148.

8. "Randolph Analyzes World Economic Situation as it Effects Race." See also Randolph, "The Economic Crisis of the Negro," 148.

he thought that this would be especially necessary for black workers. It would give them a proper understanding of the uses of power and of the new economic system which would take the place of private capitalism. He called upon the " 'best minds' of the race" to form a supreme economic council which would direct this educational process.[9] As early as 1931, he was anticipating the National Negro Congress.

While Randolph hoped that worker education would instill a genuine class consciousness among the black workers, he still thought "our salvation lies within." Unlike the young radicals, Randolph had no illusions about the depth of racial prejudice among the white workers. Experience had taught him that Negroes could not merely appeal to the conscience of the white workers to gain admittance into the labor unions: they would have to force their way in. The black workers as a group would have to organize themselves to amass enough power to gain the respect or fear of the white workers. He criticized the black masses for their apathy and for their dependence upon outside help. Significantly, during the early, difficult years of organizing the Brotherhood of Sleeping Car Porters, Randolph had declined financial help from white organizations, arguing that black Americans should pay the price of their own struggle.[10] He noted that other ethnic minority groups had been confronted with the barriers of prejudice, "but they won respect, developed power, raised their standards of living and built up organizations because they possessed the character, spirit and will to do so." If other groups had succeeded, Randolph was certain that black Americans could as well.[11] He repeated this advice frequently throughout the decade and occasionally expressed it in

9. Randolph, "The Economic Crisis of the Negro," 149.
10. Anderson, "Profile: A Philip Randolph," Part II, 87–88.
11. Randolph, "The National Negro Labor Conference," *The Black Worker*, January 15, 1930. See also Horace R. Cayton and George S. Mitchell, *Black Workers and the New Unions* (Chapel Hill: University of North Carolina Press, 1939), 426–29, for a similar argument.

terms of "pride of race,"[12] sometimes sounding like many of the older race leaders.

Randolph always conceived of the National Negro Congress as essentially a race organization and during his tenure as its president he continued to encourage race solidarity. For a brief period, however, he attempted to coordinate these appeals with the idea of a "united front." He tentatively accepted the feasibility of a united front with the "white working brothers," the extreme radicals, and any other "progressive and liberal agencies of the nation whose interests are in common with Black America."[13] He stated emphatically that although there were many Communists in the National Negro Congress, the organization was by no means under the control of any single political party or ideology.[14] An active Socialist since before the First World War, Randolph had never sympathized with the violent ideology of the Communists. During the united front period of 1936–1937, however, he was able to at least coexist with them and even on occasion praise the "stalwart Stalin" for defending the "heritage of the proletarian revolution against world fascism."[15] For a time, at least, he believed that the united front was a reality.

As president of the congress, Randolph essentially adhered to the same program he had supported throughout the early years of the depression, with perhaps more emphasis upon the idea that "the problems of the Negro peoples are the problems of the workers." At the top of his list of remedies Randolph placed "the struggle of the workers against exploitation of the employers." Although his own Brotherhood of Sleeping Car Porters was a part of the AFL,

12. See A. Philip Randolph, "The Herndon Case," *The Black Worker*, June 15, 1935.

13. "Randolph Says Race Congress Not Communist," Pittsburgh *Courier*, February 28, 1936; A. Philip Randolph, "The Crisis of the Negro and the Constitution" (Presidential Address) 1937—*National Negro Congress Official Proceedings*, 11.

14. "Randolph's Speech," 5; Randolph, "The Crisis of the Negro and the Constitution," 7.

15. "The New Year," *The Black Worker*, January, 1937.

Randolph emphasized the importance of industrial unions like the CIO as the instrument of this struggle. "The industrial union is important in this stage of economic development," he maintained, "because modern business has changed in structure and assumed the form of giant trust and holding companies, with which the craft union can no longer effectively grapple."[16] But he did not rule out the value of the craft unions and he pleaded with the AFL and the CIO to end their feud because "neither one should be raised in importance above the concept of labor solidarity."[17]

A second important instrumentality which he thought the workers must employ in their struggle against "economic exploitation, war and fascism" was an independent working-class political party. Randolph hoped this would take the form of a farmer-labor coalition. He believed that a third party would offer an alternative to the capitalistic Republicans and New Deal Democrats. "They are the political committees of Wall Street and are constructed to serve the profit making agencies and therefore can no more protect or advance the interests of the workers than can a sewing machine grind corn. It is poor working class wisdom to fight big business for economic justice on the industrial field and vote for it on the political."[18] Young radicals such as Ralph Bunche avidly concurred with the labor program Randolph presented to the congress.[19]

Randolph thought that when the workers achieved this labor program, many of the Negro's problems would be solved simultaneously. But he cautioned that Negroes still had their unique problems: segregation, disfranchisement, and peonage. He felt that these strictly race problems would have to be solved by the race itself because it had the most at stake. As in the past, he reiterated: "The Negro peoples should not place their problems for

16. "Randolph's Speech," 2–3.
17. "The Crisis of the Negro and the Constitution," 10.
18. "Randolph's Speech," 3–4.
19. See Ralph Bunche, "Triumph? Or Fiasco?" *Race*, I (Summer, 1936), 95.

solution down at the feet of their white sympathetic allies, which has been the common fashion of the old school Negro leadership, for, in the final analysis, the salvation of the Negro, like the workers, must come from within."[20] If this had been uttered by a man like Du Bois, the young radicals would have vociferously attacked it as black chauvinism.

By the time of the last congress in 1940, Randolph was more than ever convinced that Negroes would have to save themselves. It had become increasingly apparent that the congress was no longer essentially a race organization. It had fallen under the control of the CIO and the Communist party. Randolph was especially perplexed by the Communist party influence. He realized that the Party had no genuine interest in the black man or in American labor. Furious, he told the assembled delegates at the 1940 congress: "The Communist Party is not primarily, or fundamentally concerned about the Negro or labor in America, but with the fulfilling and carrying out of the needs and demands for the consolidation of the foreign position of the Soviet Union in world politics."[21] He thought that American Negroes would not long follow any organization which accepted dictation from the Communist party. In fact, he bitterly concluded, "The American Negro will not long follow any organization which accepts dictation and control from any white organization."[22]

Power, thought Randolph, could only be effectively utilized in the best interests of the race if it was in the hands of the race: "Yes, salvation must come from within. Charity and philanthropy from the Left, or the Communists or Socialists, is just as unsound, illog-

20. "Randolph's Speech," 4–5. See also, Randolph, "The Crisis of the Negro and the Constitution," 11.

21. A. Philip Randolph, "The World Crisis and the Negro People Today" (Randolph's speech at the 1940 National Negro Congress, published as a pamphlet, n.p.; n.d., in Randolph vertical file, Schomburg Collection, New York Public Library). See also A. Philip Randolph, "Why I Would Not Stand for Re-election for President of the National Negro Congress," The Black Worker, May, 1940.

22. Randolph, "The World Crisis," 25.

ical and objectionable as the charity and philanthropy from the right, the capitalists. For with charity and philanthropy go control since the power over a man's subsistence is the power over his will."[23]

Like Ralph Bunche, Randolph felt that he had been betrayed by the far left. He walked out of the 1940 congress and left it to die a slow death as a Communist front organization. The united front turned out to be a fraud and a failure. But Randolph's next major undertaking, the March on Washington Movement, would prove more successful.

With the approach of war in 1940–1941, the depression ended for many Americans—at least for many white Americans. The rapidly expanding defense industries absorbed masses of workers but "last hired, first fired" still governed black labor relations. As early as September of 1940, various Negro groups around the country started calling for some kind of mass pressure to be exerted on the federal government to bring about an end to such discriminatory practices.[24] Like so many other black Americans, Randolph was bitter. "The whole National Defense setup," he charged, "reeks and stinks with race prejudice, hatred, and discrimination."[25] In January,1941, he issued a call to black Americans in which he proposed that they should march on the nation's capital ten thousand strong and demand equal opportunities in the armed forces and defense industries.[26]

Randolph's call was highly significant because it was directed to the masses of blacks. It was widely published in the Afro-

23. *Ibid.*, 15.
24. Richard M. Dalfiume, *Desegregation of the U.S. Armed Forces: Fighting on Two Fronts, 1939–1953* (Columbia: University of Missouri Press, 1969), 115–16.
25. " 'Defense Rotten'—Randolph; Let's March on Capital 10,000 Strong, Urges Leader of Porters," Pittsburgh *Courier*, January 25, 1941.
26. *Ibid.* For a detailed analysis of the March on Washington Movement, see Herbert Garfinkel, *When Negroes March: The March on Washington Movement in the Organizational Politics for FEPC* (Glencoe, Ill.: The Free Press, 1959). Also see Dalfiume, *Desegregation of the U.S. Armed Forces*, 115–23.

American press, not just in sophisticated race journals. It was the most concise and simple explanation of the use of power which any black intellectual published during the whole depression decade. Randolph did not just talk about the black masses, he talked to them.

He first observed that interracial cooperation and appeals to conscience were of dubious value; the virtue and rightness of a cause are not alone the condition and cause of its progress and acceptance. "Only power," he wrote "can effect the enforcement and adoption of a given policy, however meritorious it may be. . . . Power and pressure are the foundation of the march of social justice and reform." Looking back, no doubt, upon his experiences with the National Negro Congress and other similar assemblages of black intellectuals, Randolph next informed his readers that "power and pressure do not reside in the few, the intelligentsia, they lie in and flow from the masses. Power is the active principle of only the organized masses, the masses organized for a definite purpose." Based upon this theory, Randolph concluded that it was quite apparent that "Negro America must bring its power and pressure to bear upon the agencies and representatives of the Federal Government to exact their rights in National Defense employment and the armed forces of the country."[27]

Randolph spent the next few months organizing the March on Washington Committee. By May, Walter White, Frank Crosswaith, Rayford Logan, Lester Granger, and other leaders had joined him on the all-black committee. Randolph denied that the March on Washington Movement was chauvinistic despite the fact that no whites were permitted to participate. It was just that the problem was essentially the Negro's, and he thought that the black man would be likely to fight with more conviction for something which was in his own self-interest. "We call not upon our white friends to march with us. There are some things Negroes must do alone.

27. " 'Defense Rotten'—Randolph."

This is our fight and we must see it through."[28] He also denied charges that he was attempting to undermine national unity in a time of crisis. He pointed out that there could be no unity as long as one tenth of the people were denied their basic rights as American citizens."[29]

There was really no doubt as to where Randolph's loyalties were. Although he had long been a committed pacifist—he had been imprisoned for antiwar activities during World War I—Randolph had consistently supported American preparedness and aid to the allies both before and after his activities in the March on Washington Movement.[30] Unlike Du Bois and the journalist, George S. Schuyler, Randolph saw a great deal of difference between imperialistic Great Britain and racist Nazi Germany. "By every standard of decency and civilization," he told Negro Americans, "democratic England is as different from totalitarian Germany and Italy as New York is from Georgia . . . her imperialist history notwithstanding."[31] If the Nazis won the war, Negroes and other minority groups would be "liquidated or put into concentration camps."[32] After Pearl Harbor, Randolph called upon black America to "close ranks," but he added that the fight for democracy abroad must not hinder the continuing fight for democracy at home.[33]

As a race spokesman, Randolph might be considered a black nationalist. After all, he promulgated a feasible program of black

28. A. Philip Randolph, "Let the Negro Masses Speak," *The Black Worker*, March, 1941.

29. " 'Defense Rotten'—Randolph."

30. See A. Philip Randolph, "war," *The Black Worker*, September, 1939; his "National Defense," *The Black Worker*, June, 1940; and his "The Negro and the War," *The Black Worker*, November, 1941.

31. A. Philip Randolph, "England's Fight, Our Cause," Pittsburgh *Courier*, February 8, 1941.

32. " 'The Negro Has A Great Stake In This War'—Randolph: If the United States Loses, The Negro Is Through in the Western World," Pittsburgh *Courier*, December 20, 1941.

33. Randolph, "The Negro and the War."

power. But unlike most of the nationalists of his time, he conceptualized his theories of black power in hard, realistic terms. He did not, like Du Bois and so many others, attempt to construct a romantic mystique about the race. He thought, for example, that Japan was nothing more than a selfish imperialist nation seeking to exploit the unrest of colored people in the United States who had absolutely no interests in common with the Japanese.[34] Instead, Randolph merely saw a group of exploited black people who possessed potential power in their numbers, and he conceived a plan for channeling that power for their advancement. It will never be known whether the March on Washington would actually have brought 100,000 or even 10,000 black protestors to Washington, D.C., but the mood of black Americans was angry enough to make it seem like a real possibility. The unrest of black people in this country,[35] plus Randolph's threat to maneuver it into a massive protest movement, possessed enough force to win apparent concessions from a president. It is possible that Randolph did not force President Roosevelt into any substantive concessions which he was not already prepared to make,[36] and it is true that Randolph did not get all he was asking for (such as an end to segregation in the armed forces), and that Executive Order 8802 did not end discrimination in defense industries, but it did put the federal government officially on record in opposition to racial injustice. And the apparent pervasiveness of anger in the black community which responded to the appeal of the March on Washington Movement forced black leadership into a rare unity. By the summer of 1941, the movement enjoyed nearly unanimous support among black leaders, both moderate and militant. The coming of the war would motivate a near unanimity among blacks on the issue of demanding immediately

34. See Randolph, "The World Crisis," 13.
35. See Garfinkel, *When Negroes March*, 21–27; and Dalfiume, *Desegregation of the U.S. Armed Forces*, 108–12.
36. Dalfiume, *Desegregation of the U.S. Armed Forces*, 117–21.

the rights of citizens in a democracy which was allegedly fighting for the survival of democracy.[37]

Randolph was a doer. While most black intellectuals spent their time reflecting on and writing about race problems, he had actively done something to alleviate them. In contrast to Randolph, Charles S. Johnson assumed the conventional role of thinker. Johnson was, in fact, almost entirely the opposite of Randolph. Randolph was an economic radical; Johnson was a conservative. Randolph was a race man with some chauvinistic tendencies; Johnson made conscious efforts to avoid black nationalism. As a social scientist, Johnson went out of his way to try to be objective. On one occasion, for example, he even admitted the possibility of racial inferiority: "The assumption holds, at least tentatively, that the inefficiency of Negro pupils is at least as much a function of a poor educational system and an inferior background, as of an inferior, inherited mental constitution."[38] For a race man such a statement would have been utter heresy.

Although the young radicals sometimes classified him with the older leadership—he was only a year older than Frazier—because he failed to criticize the capitalistic system and adhered to the old methods of improving race relations, Johnson shared their desire to look at race problems with scientific objectivity. He was pleased to note during the depression years the increasing "substitution of realism for emotional outburst,"[39] and he advised Negro college youth to continue to "cultivate a stark objectivity about themselves and about their thinking about themselves." He thought that they should be taught to recognize and concede the race's weaknesses

37. Garfinkel, When Negroes March, 23–27, 54–55; and Dalfiume, Desegregation of the U.S. Armed Forces, 111–12, 126–28.
38. Charles S. Johnson, The Negro in American Civilization: A Study of Negro Life and Race Relations in Light of Social Research (New York: Henry Holt and Co., 1930), 287.
39. Charles S. Johnson and Willis D. Weatherford, Race Relations: Adjustment of Whites and Negroes in the United States (Boston: D. C. Heath and Co., 1934), 542.

because unless they were honest about these, they could not expect to be believed when they spoke of their virtues.[40]

Johnson, like E. Franklin Frazier, was trained in sociology under Robert Park at the University of Chicago. After spending a number of years as director of the Urban League's Department of Research and as editor of its journal, *Opportunity*, Johnson settled down as chairman of the department of social sciences at Fisk University in 1928. During the depression he published numerous influential scholarly books and articles on the condition of the American Negro.[41]

Johnson found little that was unique in Negro American culture. Like Frazier, he accepted Boas' theory about the absence of African cultural survivals among American Negroes.[42] Nor did he believe that the Negro in this country had evolved a subculture that was distinct in any of its essentials from the dominant culture. "The Negro group in America," he concluded, "having no unique culture of its own, lives on different planes of the American culture."[43] He granted that the standards of living among whites and blacks were different, but the difference was not cultural. "One," he emphasized, "is simply higher in the scale than the other." He noted that the code of morals by which Negroes live, "however imperfectly," was European; the system of marriage was monogamy; the standards of justice and law were American; vested property rights, the machine pattern of culture, were all European. He concluded that "any American Negro who tried to live otherwise than by these

40. Charles S. Johnson, "On the Need for Realism in Negro Education," *Journal of Negro Education*, V (July, 1936), 381.

41. For biographical accounts of Johnson, see Embree, *13 Against the Odds*, 47–70; John H. Bracey, Jr., August Meier, and Elliott Rudwick (eds.), *The Black Sociologists: The First Half Century* (Belmont, Calif.: Wadsworth Publishing Company, 1971), 7–11; and for a highly interpretive analysis, see S. P. Fullinwider, *The Mind and Mood of Black America: Twentieth Century Thought* (Homewood, Ill.: Dorsey Press, 1969), 107–15.

42. Johnson and Weatherford, *Race Relations*, 94.

43. Charles S. Johnson, "The Education of the Negro Child," *Opportunity*, XIV (February, 1936), 38.

codes and standards would quickly be crushed for his non-con-formity." Conformity, he thought, was the "test of survival."[44] Like Frazier, when he spoke of cultural "advance" or "development," it was always in terms of a closer conformity to the currently "approved American standards."[45]

Thus, even when he studied southern rural folk culture, Johnson saw little that was original. He thought it was merely an out-dated imitation of the early American frontier culture. "Their dialect," he related, "is in part a survival of the English of the colonists, their superstitions most often are borrowed from whites . . . their folk lore is scarcely distinguishable from that brought over from Europe by the early colonists, their religious emotionalism is similar to that commonly demonstrated in white Methodist camp meetings until very recently." He added that the patterns of social behavior to which Negroes were exposed, whether set by planters or poor whites, "cannot be said to have been ideal, from the point of view of current standards."[46] Johnson felt that it was not es-sentially a different style of life, but a "backward" version of the dominant style which differentiated blacks from whites.

Like so many other sociologists of the time Johnson attributed the Negro's "backward" life-style to "cultural lag." While the rest of American society had moved into the mechanized twentieth century, the Negro, for the most part, lived the peasant existence of the late eighteenth and early nineteenth centuries. He observed that this was because the Negro, particularly in the rural South, led an isolated existence. This isolation permitted the perpetuation of the old folk beliefs and customs and, "as a consequence, the Negro child inherits a set of folkways which, while perhaps quaint and,

44. Johnson and Weatherford, *Race Relations*, 547.
45. Charles S. Johnson, *A Preface to Racial Understanding* (New York: Friend-ship Press, 1936), 64. See also Johnson and Weatherford, *Race Relations*, 456–57.
46. Charles S. Johnson, *The Shadow of the Plantation* (Chicago: University of Chicago Press, 1934), 4–5.

in a manner, useful are nevertheless based upon different and outmoded values."[47]

Hence, while black historians like Carter Woodson attempted to glorify the Negro's history in this country, Johnson was perplexed because the Negro still had not escaped that past. He looked at contemporary southern sharecroppers and saw unstable families, lack of "approved" moral codes, illegitimacy, low economic status, habits of dependence, slovenly work habits, and belief in their own inferiority.[48] This was the real heritage of the Negro's slave past still existing in the present. It was not an inspiring legacy, but a burden—something from which the Negro must seek to escape.

Johnson happily observed that many Negroes had escaped that heritage when they migrated to the city. Like Frazier, he believed that "the northward migration with all its shock and initial disorganization has, on the whole, tended to advance the general culture of the group." The cosmopolitan atmosphere and the closer proximity to the dominant society had "brought a greater knowledge and sophistication, and exposure to those standards implicit in the complexity of city life: schools, hygiene, newspapers, and the myriad tools by which one gains control over the forces of his civilization."[49] In the cities, Johnson thought, the Negro was shedding his obsolete folk heritage and conforming to the patterns of twentieth-century American life. This would facilitate his acceptance into the heretofore closed society.

After the migration to the cities, the next most important factor in bringing American Negroes into the twentieth century was modern education. While Johnson admitted that the curriculum of the Negro child should be geared to prepare him for the realities of

47. Johnson, "The Education of the Negro Child," 39.
48. Johnson and Weatherford, *Race Relations*, 287. Johnson most fully developed this theme in his study of Negro tenants and sharecroppers in Macon County, Alabama. See his *Shadow of the Plantation*, xxiv, 215.
49. Johnson and Weatherford, *Race Relations*, 456–57. See also Johnson, "The Education of the Negro Child," 39, 41, 61.

his experience in America,[50] he scorned attempts, such as Woodson's, to develop a separate system and philosophy of education
for Negroes.[51] Johnson always maintained that the purpose of education for Negroes should be to bring them into fuller participation
in American culture.[52]

During the depression, Johnson conceived of a more immediately
important function for education than "cultural advancement." He
thought that the black masses were as backward economically as
they were culturally. He observed that it was entertaining for some
people to indulge in the reflection that the Negro was naïvely
preserving the idyllic relics of a pastoral yesterday in the face of
the corrupting influence of mechanization. This was crass romanticism. "The Negro worker must yet live and draw his sustenance
in a competitive struggle with workers who have adjusted themselves to the exacting tempo of the machine." He called for stronger
emphasis upon a system of education which would accomplish
the "remaking of Negro labor to fit the exigencies of the new age."[53]
This labor education had nothing to do with inspiring a class
consciousness among Negro workers as the young radicals would
have had it. Johnson, like a latter-day Booker T. Washington, called
for labor education designed to instill "the development of a technique, a sense for accuracy, precision, craftsmanship and creative
art."[54] The principal difference between Washington's and Johnson's educational models lay in the fact that Washington wanted
Negroes to develop specific skills for handicrafts which were already obsolete, while Johnson wanted Negroes to develop tech-

50. See Johnson, "The Education of the Negro Child," 39; and his "On the Need
of Realism in Negro Education," 376–78. Also see Fullinwider, *Mind and Mood of
Black America*, 113–14.
51. See Johnson, *Preface to Racial Understanding*, 85.
52. See Johnson, *Shadow of the Plantation*, 209; his "The Education of the Negro
Child," 41, 61; and his "The Present State of Race Relations, with Particular Reference to the Negro," *Journal of Negro Education*, VIII (July, 1939), 331.
53. Charles S. Johnson, "The New Frontier of Negro Labor," *Opportunity*, X
(June, 1932), 169, 172.
54. Johnson, *Preface to Racial Understanding*, 87.

niques of accuracy and skill so that they might adapt themselves to any number of complex occupations in ever-changing mass scale industries.

Johnson felt that this type of education was imperative because of the racial discrimination which blocked the Negro's entrance into industrial society. If the Negro was to compete with the mechanized skills of the white workers, he would have to achieve "superior competence" in those skills. Johnson reasoned that "so long as he must win his bread in this age of competition with hands and minds geared to this new phase of the economic revolution, he must at least be equally equipped; and if he is to succeed he must be better equipped and recognize the necessity for it."[55] He believed that if the Negro could develop superior skills, then "economic laws" would force industry to employ Negroes. And, somewhat illogically, he reasoned that if blacks could demonstrate this greater skill, the white workers might then be willing to accept them into their presence. Like the young radicals, he hoped to see the alignment of white and black workers. Unlike them, however, he did not wish to see such a coalition established for the purpose of carrying on a class struggle. He saw it more as a necessity brought on by the fact that "the new age of machinery has rendered archaic and ruinous the dual and mutually exclusive chambers of 'white' and 'black' labor."[56] In economics, as in culture, Johnson wanted the Negro to bring himself up to date and into conformity with the existing system. He never called upon Negroes to change that system, but merely to become a part of it. It was on this issue that he drew the enmity of some of the young radicals.[57]

55. *Ibid.*, 86. See also Johnson, "The New Frontier of Negro Labor," 172; and his "On the Need of Realism in Negro Education," 382.

56. Johnson, "The New Frontier of Negro Labor," 173.

57. See for example Johnson's exchange of letters with E. Franklin Frazier, in *The American Journal of Sociology*, XL (September, 1936), 252–53, 254–55; and Frazier's scathing review of Johnson, Edwin Embree, and Will Alexander's *Collapse of the Cotton Tenancy* (Chapel Hill: University of North Carolina Press, 1935), entitled "Seventy Years too Late," *Journal of Negro Education*, 5 (April, 1936): 273–75.

Like the young radicals, Johnson cast an economic interpretation upon the origins of race prejudice. "Any summary of Negro status in American civilization is a story of attitudes," he commented, "of attitudes changing slowly with the steady movement of economic forces."[58] Johnson, however, never became a monist; he never completely ignored the presence of race conflict. While he agreed with the radicals that race was as yet an undefined abstraction and that urbanization and industrialization were rapidly transforming America from a caste to a class society,[59] he criticized them for seeing the Negro's problems simply as a part of the class problem. This was "merely another kind of psychological escape" on the part of the radicals. In an incisive review of Ralph Bunche's *A World View of Race*, he castigated the author's myopia: "The problem is not so seriously one of the Negroes considering themselves as a race as of other groups treating them as a race with all the special connotations presently inherent in the classification."[60]

Johnson was just as happy as the young radicals to see the recent shift away from a strict caste-structured society toward a rising integrated class structure. But he was pleased for some different reasons. The young radicals primarily saw the increased class solidarity of black and white labor in terms of the class struggle against the capitalistic exploitation of all workers. Johnson, however, had no quarrel with capitalism or with the class structure of society. He praised labor solidarity because it strengthened labor's bargaining position within the present system. But most important was the fact that "class interests and class solidarity have measur-

58. Johnson, *Preface to Racial Understanding*, 11. For the most complete statement by Johnson on this theme, see his "Race Relations and Social Change," in Edgar T. Thompson (ed.), *Race Relations and the Race Problem* (Durham, N.C.: Duke University Press, 1939), 271–303.

59. See for example, Johnson, "The Present State of Race Relations, with Particular Reference to the Negro," 331.

60. Charles S. Johnson, "A World View of Race," *Journal of Negro Education*, VII (January, 1938), 62.

ably relaxed racial tensions."[61] Johnson saw worker solidarity not in terms of the class struggle, but merely in terms of potential racial integration, and integration could only mean "advance" for black men.

Johnson not only supported class solidarity among black and white workers, he supported it among the black and white middle and upper classes. He believed that class differentiation within the Negro group might profitably change the character of race relations. "For, against the weight of social tradition, class interests tend to find elements in common across strictly racial lines." The faster whatever solidarity the Negro group possessed could disappear, the better.[62]

Although Johnson firmly believed that "economic improvement will bring adjustments in the race problems,"[63] he thought that action in other spheres was also important. The action he called for, such as dissemination of literature informing the general public about the "correctable handicaps, as well as the striking evidences of the cultural development of the Negro," was scarcely novel. In fact, on the one occasion when he set down a list of "projects" which would improve race relations, he titled it "Some Successful Precedents."[64] Johnson looked to the past for help.

Johnson's programs for action were just as conservative as those of the older leaders. Like them he praised the "step-by-step progress of race relations." He was guardedly optimistic about signs of improvement in race relations and thought that "a few years" might bring significant change. He had, however, a curious conception of time: "In spite of the persistence of many old and strongly held views of race, it is possible to see changes. It is difficult now, for

61. Charles S. Johnson, Foreword to Cayton anl Mitchell, *Black Workers and the New Unions*, vi.
62. Johnson, "Race Relations and Social Change," 295.
63. *Ibid.*, 291.
64. Johnson, *Preface to Racial Understanding*, 188–89.

example, to take seriously the beliefs which were current only a few years ago and which molded and prompted behavior and all our social relations. In the field of religion we no longer burn witches. In the field of medicine we no longer cure asthma with the lungs of foxes, or find healing power in the moss from a skull of a person violently killed."[65] According to such a time table race relations might become amicable after two or three hundred years. It is not surprising that Johnson praised more effusively than anybody else, the "realistic" Booker T. Washington. For Johnson, "the genius of this brilliant temporization," should set an example for the new generation of black leadership.[66]

It is relatively easy to label A. Philip Randolph as a race man with a radical economic philosophy and Charles S. Johnson as his opposite, but it is not so easy to categorize the thought of the black journalist, George S. Schuyler, during the 1930s. As a weekly journalist Schuyler was, as might be expected, habitually inconsistent. For example, he once protested that "Amos 'n' Andy are a part of the sinister movement to disparage the Negro race and . . . Negroes who laugh at the supposed Negro humor of the pair are 'laughing themselves into semi-slavery.'" Later he contradicted himself, asserting that "it was thus impossible for me to join in the erstwhile baiting of Amos 'n' Andy for their boresome asininities when I knew in my heart that such types as they portrayed were as common as gonococcus."[67] Schuyler's columns were replete with such lapses of memory and self-contradictions. However, if one looks at Schuyler's writings for the entire span of the decade, certain patterns do emerge.

Schuyler was one of the most interesting figures of the decade. His weekly "Views and Reviews" in the Pittsburgh *Courier* was perhaps the most popular column in the Afro-American press. One

65. *Ibid.*, 183.   66. Johnson, *Race Relations*, 539.
67. George S. Schuyler, "Views and Reviews," Pittsburgh *Courier*, May 24, 1930, and February 18, 1933.

of the chief reasons for his popularity was his sense of humor—a unique gift among Afro-American intellectuals. Comments such as the following earned him the reputation of a "black Mencken": "Some day, perhaps, when white America has reached a more sophisticated cultural stage, unfortunate Senegambians falling afoul of the Nordic mob, will be lynched with more colorful ceremony, and instead of the bodies being totally incinerated or cut up into souvenirs, they will be hauled to the nearest barbecue pit and prepared by competent cooks to fill the stomachs of the paupers and unemployed."[68] Schuyler reached the peak of his satirical talents with the publication of his novel, *Black No More* (1930). In this book he examined all of the chaos—among both white supremacists and race leaders—when a doctor invented a method by which black people could be transformed into white people. All of the problems were resolved, however, with the discovery that the process made Negroes just a shade lighter than Caucasians. For a few years after the publication of *Black No More*, Schuyler was able to maintain enough detachment to permit him to continue to throw his satiric darts. But as the decade drew to a close, an increasingly pessimistic Schuyler offered his readers fewer and fewer humorous sketches. This departure from satire indicated a significant ideological shift.

With his sense of humor intact, Schuyler entered the decade as a self-proclaimed radical and ardent opponent of all race nationalism and separatism. He had long been an active critic of the capitalistic system. Throughout the 1920s he served with A. Philip Randolph and Chandler Owen on the editorial staff of the *Messenger*, a black Socialist journal. So the crash of 1929 and the depression merely confirmed his radical economic views.

During the early 1930s he sounded very much like the young radicals, except that he was often even more apocalyptic in his rhetoric. Like the young radicals, Schuyler placed the blame for

68. *Ibid.*, October 28, 1933.

race prejudice "squarely on the shoulders of the owning class and its intellectual police." Bigotry flourished because it was "profitable to this class and flattering to the white proletariat."[69] He was not optimistic about the possibility of white and black labor solidarity, but he conceded that "necessity knows no law, and circumstances cause strange alliances. In a pinch, the white and black wage slaves may make a common cause."[70] He hoped to see black workers "in the labor unions fighting with our white fellow workers." Also like the young radicals, Schuyler stressed the fact that the black masses should fight for economic rather than political power: "Before democracy can really function for the masses, they must control the nation's wealth; and then democracy and politics will be unnecessary."[71]

Schuyler's rhetoric, however, sometimes went beyond the Amenia radicals. He denounced those Negroes who adhered to the passive resistance ideas of Ghandi: "Ghandism appeals to some of our superficial Negro thinkers like Mordecai Johnson because it seems to offer a chance to be revolutionary and secure at the same time, which is never possible . . . government is established by force and violence and it can only be overturned in the same manner." And in a reply to one of Kelly Miller's attacks on the young radicals, Schuyler exulted: "I glory in the existence of these radicals . . . because they are on the right road. They know that the cards are stacked against them and they have sense enough to know that the only remedy is to break up the game."[72]

While Schuyler sometimes adopted the violent rhetoric of the

69. George S. Schuyler, "Some Unsweet Truths about Race Prejudice," in Samuel Schmalhausen (ed.), *Behold America!* (New York: Farrar and Rinehart, Inc., 1931), 89.

70. George S. Schuyler, "A Negro Looks Ahead," *American Mercury*, XIX (February, 1930), 213.

71. Schuyler, "Views and Reviews," September 15, 1934, and November 28, 1931.

72. *Ibid.*, May 10, 1930, and September 22, 1934.

Communists, he was never really in sympathy with them. Early in the decade he maintained a wait-and-see attitude: he agreed with the Communists' aims, but not with their tactics. By late 1932–early 1933, however, he had declared all-out war on the Communist "phrasemongers." As with so many other black intellectuals, the event which triggered the break was probably the Scottsboro trial in which the International Labor Defense (Communist legal defense organization) jeopardized the lives of the nine black defendants by insulting the court and by publicizing the case in terms of the class war. Despite his radical sympathies, Schuyler scoffed that "anybody who is at all familiar with the Southern psychology knows that no class issues are involved save of the most remote and inconsequential kind. It is a race issue pure and simple." "Negroes will do well not to have much to do with these fanatics who call themselves Communists," warned Schuyler, "there is no use of Negroes giving the crackers two reasons to lynch them where now one is more than sufficient."[73] From that time forward, Schuyler was probably the most vitriolic black anti-Communist in the United States.

Hence, although he defended the young radicals from the criticisms of Kelly Miller, he became alarmed because of the number of young Negro intellectuals who had suddenly grown enthusiastic over communism. He accused those who joined the Party of being "basically yokel-minded" because "in many instances this decision was hastened by the white comrades' judicious use of flat-heeled, leather-coated lady Reds willing to sacrifice their All for the Cause."[74]

Despite Schuyler's bitterness toward the Communists, he continued to criticize American capitalism on through the middle of the decade. His own solution to the economic crisis, like that of

73. *Ibid.*, August 15, 1931, December 10, 1932, and April 22, 1933.
74. *Ibid.*, January 12, 1934, and April 2, 1938.

Du Bois, was collectivization based upon consumer cooperatives: "We must discard the profit motive in our business and become cooperators with all sharing in the benefits of consumption."[75] He organized the Young Negro's Cooperative League in 1930 and continued to boost such efforts throughout the depression.

Schuyler, the self-proclaimed cynic, became even more rhapsodic than the romantic Du Bois when he discussed the future under a cooperative system. He called such a system "anarchism in action" because under it government would cease to exist: there would be no police, because property would be spread out so that there would be no poverty; no armies, because there would be no trade competition; no treasury department, because there would be no business to tax nor any duties to collect since the cooperative movement would eventually be international. He assured his readers that this anarchistic system would not endanger order, discipline, or security. "On the contrary," he observed, "it means that there will be much more of each, for the simple reason that competition, contest and the hatreds and jealousies and animosities that they engender will necessarily be eliminated with the universal application of the principles of co-operation."[76] Like Du Bois, he never got down to specifics concerning how competition and jealousies would be "necessarily eliminated."

Although Schuyler had denounced the black chauvinism of Du Bois's economic program, when he himself discussed consumer cooperatives, he almost always spoke in terms of the Negro as a separate group. "We must learn to face the facts of our position. The white people started racial separation and now," he advised, "it is up to black people to learn how to profit en masse from it." Despite the fact that he always deprecated any form of racial separation, he repeated the hope that "organized co-operatively as consumers in the cities and producers on the farm, urban and rural

75. *Ibid.*, October 17, 1936, and July 5, 1930.
76. *Ibid.*, September 24, 1932.

Negroes could get together on an economic basis for the first time."[77] No matter how much he tried to deny it, what he was in reality advocating was a separate economic establishment very similar to the Du Bois model.

Schuyler's ambivalence in this instance was not an isolated example. Throughout the decade he consciously argued against any form of race separatism or chauvinism. In fact, he saw the ultimate solution to the race problem in the amalgamation of the races. And yet, almost simultaneously with his outbursts against chauvinism and separatism he would make appeals for blacks to be more race conscious.

Schuyler criticized Negroes for "hampering their improvement by an over-stressing of race, by fostering chauvinistic isolation, by developing exaggerated race patriotism and seeing the whole world and its problems through black spectacles." He thought that it was suicidal for Negroes to become chauvinists. Besides, Negroes were Americans before they were Negroes: "Our language, our culture, our training are not African or Negro, but American. There is more in common between the white and colored folk in America than there is between the colored folk here and the colored folk anywhere else."[78] In fact, Schuyler once remarked "The Aframerican is just a lamp-blacked Anglo-Saxon."[79] Even Charles S. Johnson would never have posited so bold an opinion.

To those advocates of a separate black state or nation within the United States, Schuyler wryly responded that the idea of a separate territory was nothing new—the Indians had had it for years, "much to their disadvantage." Because he was convinced that "there can-

77. See *ibid.*, February 17, 1933, and April 7, 1934. On rare occasions he claimed that the cooperatives were to be "neighborhood" set-ups, not necessarily Negro groups. See *ibid.*, September 15, 1934; George S. Schuyler, "Speaking Economically," Norfolk *Journal and Guide*, September 19, 1931; Schuyler, "Views and Reviews," January 30, 1932.

78. Schuyler, "Views and Reviews," September 15, 1934. See also *ibid.*, March 10, 1934.

79. George S. Schuyler, "A Negro Looks Ahead," *American Mercury*, XIX (February, 1930), 217.

not be TWO nationalisms in the same territory," Schuyler advised Afro-Americans to "become less Negro as rapidly as possible."[80]

"The most cordial and profitable race relations," he advised, "are sex relations." He frequently called for massive miscegenation as a cure to America's race problems: "I maintain that to the extent that an oppressed group becomes related by blood and association to an oppressing group, to that extent the troubles of the former will vanish." The depth of Schuyler's commitment to this theory can be measured by the fact that in 1930 he himself married the daughter of a white Texas banker. That same year he optimistically prophesied that "by 2000 A.D. a full-blooded American Negro may be rare enough to get a job in a museum, and a century from now our American social leaders may be as tanned naturally as they now are striving to become artificially."[81]

At the same time that Schuyler was condemning race chauvinism and trumpeting the virtues of amalgamation, he was also scolding Negroes for their lack of race consciousness and loyalty in the support of race organizations and institutions. Despite his critical attitude toward pan-Africanism, Schuyler lambasted Afro-Americans for their lack of "solidarity with their brothers across the sea" during the 1935 Italo-Ethiopian crisis. And eventually he even came around to the position that Afro-Americans should even feel an almost mystical kinship with an African motherland: "Africa is another world, a different world and I think a more satisfying world. At least I found it so . . . no *intelligent* Western Negro who has ever felt its soil and glimpsed at its forests and mingled with its bronze folk can ever be satisfied away from it, and certainly not in this expansive penitentiary we call America."[82]

80. George S. Schuyler, "The Separate State Hokum," *Crisis*, XLII (May, 1935), 148; Schuyler, "Views and Reviews," June 5, 1937.

81. Schuyler, "Views and Reviews," September 19, 1931, July 13, 1929. See also "Views and Reviews," February 18, 1933, September 15, 1934, March 16, 1935, and January 16, 1937. Schuyler, "A Negro Looks Ahead," 220.

82. See Schuyler, "Views and Reviews," May 17, 1932, October 6, 1934, December 7, 1935, February 26, 1936, November 11, 1939.

Earlier in the decade he had consistently called for black and white solidarity, but later he put more faith in a "Negro Chamber of Labor." He had finally decided that "the Aframerican cannot regard the white proletarian as his friend and comrade." In 1940, Schuyler, who ten years earlier had called the Negro a "lamp-blacked Anglo-Saxon," proudly reported to his readers the findings of the chauvinistic historian, Joel A. Rogers: "The Negro is not only the primary human stock, but the most virile. . . . He originated art, religion and science. Every one of the major religions were started by black men."[83]

Perhaps the most significant indication of Schuyler's heightened sense of race chauvinism during the second half of the decade was his attitude toward pending war. Typically, he meandered back and forth over the issue of whether the war could have any positive results. The only constant was his racial provinciality. As early as 1935, he was hopefully predicting a full-scale war in Europe which would be a "signal for the fretful millions of Africa to arise and massacre the handful of whites left there." With jubilation he informed his readers: "So I rear back on my haunches, puff my cigars, sip my ale and await with joy the inevitable, praying that 'It won't be long now.'" In 1937 he was still espousing essentially the same line, noting that "the last war jumped the Negro ahead twenty years." Schuyler had been asked to join an antiwar group in Harlem, but he thought that "about the oddest creature I can imagine is a member of the colored group who is a pacifist."[84]

By 1939, however, he had decided that perhaps pacifism was not such a bad idea. The Negro, after all, actually had been pushed

83. *Ibid.*, June 28, 1941. See also *ibid.*, May 29, 1937. George S. Schuyler, "Negroes Reject Communism," *American Mercury*, XLVII (June, 1939), 177. Characteristically, Schuyler said this in spite of the fact that in his July 1, 1939, "Views" (in a review of Cayton and Mitchell's *Black Workers and the New Unions*) he noted the vastly improved relations between white and black workers in recent years. On Joel A. Rogers, see Schuyler, "Views and Reviews," October 19, 1940. For more of such boasting, see Schuyler's "The Rise of the Black Internationale," *Crisis*, XLV (August, 1938), 255–57, 274–75, 277.

84. Schuyler, "Views and Reviews," July 27, 1935, June 12, 1937.

back during the First World War, and "I foresee that his treatment during the next war will be the same." He confided that he would probably make a pretense of loyalty, "but my actual feelings will be . . . indifference, if not a hope that our white folks will not do so well on the field of battle." During 1940 and 1941 the majority of Schuyler's columns were taken up with savage tirades against the "war-mongering" Roosevelt, the imperialistic British and French, and those Negroes such as William Pickens and A. Philip Randolph who were pro-Ally. His interpretation was the most racially chauvinistic to appear in the Afro-American press. "The current war," he suggested, "is a struggle between rival groups of white exploiters for the right to fleece a billion colored folk whose ONLY inferiority is military inferiority: i.e., inferiority in the ability to murder in the grand manner." Schuyler did join the Negroes Against War Committee, and right up to the eve of Pearl Harbor he was advising his readers that for their own best interests as Negroes they should join the isolationist "America First" Committee.[85]

While he had offered "skeptical" support to President Roosevelt as late as 1936, Schuyler had generally been a severe critic of the New Deal. At first he was critical of the New Deal liberals because they did not want to "move the country farther in the direction of collectivism." However, he became increasingly disappointed with the New Deal's failure to confront the problems of black Americans. Toward the end of the decade he had nothing but scorn for "St. Franklin the First" and the liberals who supported him.[86]

---

85. *Ibid.*, August 12, 1939. See also *ibid.*, April 29, 1939; October 7, 1939; and December 2, 1939. For examples of Schuyler's tirades on Roosevelt, see *ibid.*, March 2, 1940, September 21, 1940, October 5, 1940, October 12, 1940, and September 20, 1941, December 23, 1940, and November 8, 1941. See also a pamphlet written by Schuyler, *Why We are Against the War*, for the Negroes Against the War Committee, Schuyler vertical file, Schomburg Collection, New York Public Library.

86. Schuyler, "Views and Reviews," July 11, 1936, October 17, 1936, November 24, 1934, March 2, 1935, December 26, 1936, March 20, 1937, November 23, 1940, October 2, 1937, and April 2, 1938.

Thus, having been a caustic critic of Roosevelt and the New Deal, Schuyler joined the "America Firsters" in suggesting the conspiracy theory after the war had become a reality: "By 1936 it was apparent the so-called New Deal had run its course and . . . the most astute politician since Lincoln, Mr. Roosevelt saw lean years ahead and began to prepare to head them off by the tried and true, surefire device of getting the country into war."[87] The one-time self-proclaimed radical entered the 1940s in the company of the far right. The comparison with Mencken was, indeed, fitting in this instance.

Perhaps the basic elements for Schuyler's conversion to conscious conservatism had always been present in his pungent cynicism. However, earlier in the decade he was able to express it humorously. As the years passed his humorous sketches declined and were replaced by pieces characterized by an almost fanatical suspicion. He was suspicious of FDR and "big government." He was suspicious of the British. He was suspicious of those blacks who disagreed with his views. By the end of the decade his cynicism was unrelieved. Looking back on his radical days he scoffed: "Once upon a time I was full of zeal to save humanity from evil forces encompassing it. Now I frankly do not give a damn."[88]

Race spokesman William Pickens was often as inconsistent in his newspaper columns as was Schuyler. In addition to traveling all over the country in his capacity as director of branches for the NAACP, Pickens was a contributing editor of the Associated Negro Press. His articles appeared in more than one hundred Afro-American weeklies throughout most of the decade.

Born in South Carolina in 1881 and reared in Arkansas, Pickens had first gained attention by winning a Phi Beta Kappa key at Yale in 1904. Through World War I he was a teacher and administrator at various black colleges. During these years he moved from a position of support for Booker T. Washington and his philosophy to

87. *Ibid.*, December 13, 1941.   88. *Ibid.*, May 20, 1939.

one of insurgent militancy. In 1919 he went to work full time for the NAACP, which used his considerable oratorical talent to promote membership and fund-raising drives in the various branches of the organization around the country. During the years between the wars Pickens became probably the most popular black orator in the country.

He provided an indication of his inconsistency—some called it opportunism—during his first years with the NAACP. While publicly speaking out in support of the association's integrationist philosophy, he was simultaneously flirting with Marcus Garvey's separatist Universal Negro Improvement Association (UNIA). Despite the fact that he very nearly went to work for the UNIA, he eventually recanted and was instrumental in Garvey's downfall.[89]

Pickens' inconsistency was often expressed in his newspaper columns and journal articles during the 1930s. Sometimes he praised the Communist party and its philosophy of white and black worker solidarity as a realistic solution to race problems; other times he condemned the Party as a white man's organization with little real interest in the problems of black men. Although he was fairly consistent in his belief that race problems stemmed from economic causes, he argued both for a new collectivistic economic system and, at the same time, in support of small black business. In two things only was he consistent; his vociferous criticism of the New Deal and his stubborn demand for American entry into the war against fascism, insisting in the latter case, that black Americans had a very real stake in the outcome of the war. Apart from these positions, he seldom preached a consistent over-all strategy; he was generally content to suggest immediate solutions to each problem as it came up.

Pickens had been one of the race leaders who was criticized at

89. See Sheldon Bernard Avery, "Up from Washington: William Pickens and the Negro Struggle for Equality, 1900–1954" (Ph.D. dissertation, University of Oregon, 1970), 2, 4–35, 63–100.

Amenia for being too conservative. He was conservative to the extent that he did not believe that the NAACP should abandon its emphases on propaganda and on securing civil rights through the courts.[90] However, a long-time Socialist sympathizer, Pickens was just as convinced as the young radicals that the basic problems of race had economic causes. But unlike them, he could not dismiss "the incident of 'race and color.'" As early as September of 1929, he optimistically observed that "the white workers in America are learning, although slowly, that the most important 'kinship' in this changing world is not the kinship of racial stocks, certainly not of color, but the Blood-kinship of Economic-Class." Up to then, he claimed, capitalistic "exploiters" had succeeded in preventing white and black workers from recognizing this. But he concluded that all this was rapidly changing and that "the most important group consciousness will soon be economic-class group consciousness."[91] Although he would eventually become pessimistic about the immediate possibility of black and white labor solidarity, Pickens would continue to adhere to the position that racial problems "will not disappear until the economic interests of the masses of men are served by its disappearance."[92]

During the early years of the depression Pickens wanted to see the NAACP move into a closer alliance with other progressive and even radical groups in an attack on the inequities of the economic system. During the late 1920s he had enjoyed rather amicable relations with the Communists, many of his articles appearing in the Party's various journals. Thus, in April, 1931, when the Party's International Labor Defense (ILD) preceded all other organiza-

90. *Ibid.*, 197.
91. William Pickens, "Educating Europe on the Race Question," Chicago *Whip*, September 7, 1929; "Pickens Says—," Washington *Tribune*, November 24, 1936. For a discussion of Pickens' courtship with the far-left, including his trip to Moscow during the 1920s, see Avery, "Up from Washington," 164–84.
92. William Pickens, "Economics and Race Problems," *Opportunity*, XIX (May, 1941), 145. This article represented a summation of Pickens' thinking on the issue.

tions, including the NAACP, in taking up the defense of the Scottsboro boys, Pickens thought he saw a cause around which a united
front of liberal and radical organizations could be constructed. At
the time of the ILD's entry into the case, Pickens was visiting midwestern branches and was out of touch with the NAACP's headquarters and unaware of its official position which had not yet been
made public.[93] Never known for caution, Pickens immediately
wrote an open letter to the *Daily Worker* congratulating the ILD
for its bold efforts. "The promptness," he wrote, "with which the
white workers have moved toward defending these helpless and
innocent Negro boys, sons of black workers, is significant and
prophetic. The only ultimate salvation for black and white workers
is in their united defense, one of the other." He emphasized the
idea that "the one objective for final security is the absolute and
unqualified unity and cooperation of ALL WORKERS, of all the exploited masses, across all race and color lines and all other lines."
Finally, he observed—in what was an implied criticism of the
NAACP—that "in the present case the *Daily Worker* and the workers have moved, so far, more speedily and effectively than all other
agencies put together."[94] Pickens' columns in the Afro-American
press during the next week echoed these sentiments.[95] The Communists used Pickens' letter to embarrass the NAACP which was
interested in the Scottsboro case but not in working with the ILD.
The Board of Directors of the association censured Pickens for his
indiscretion and Secretary Walter White convinced him that the
Communists had no real interest in the fate of the nine youths
beyond their propagandistic value.[96]

By June of 1931 Pickens had reversed his position to one of complete opposition to Communist participation in the Scottsboro

93. Avery, "Up from Washington," 166–88.
94. William Pickens, letter to the *Daily Worker*, April 24, 1931.
95. See for example, "Pickens Says—," New York *Amsterdam News*, April 29,
1931.
96. Avery, "Up from Washington," 183–88.

defense. He was now certain that the ILD's chief interest in the affair was propagandistic and that its disruptive tactics would do more to inflame racial antagonism in the South than anything else. He charged that whatever "efforts are put forth by the NAACP to defend these cases must first wipe out the mischief-breeding impression already made by the Communists."[97]

Although he continued from time to time to profess the efficacy of white and black labor solidarity,[98] and although he did not completely repudiate the Communists and their aims (in fact, during the late 1930s he was affiliated with several anti-Fascist organizations which later proved to be Communist fronts),[99] his attitude in the race press was generally hostile. As if to atone for his apostasy, Pickens especially attacked the Party's involvement in the Scottsboro case. He began to sound less the interracial radical and more the race man calling for race solidarity when he asserted that the "Negro in America must not turn over the guidance of his destiny to any other group or leadership, not even to the 'white proletariat.' They have their own axes to grind; their immediate objectives will be found in conflict with the aims of American Negroes at many points." He concluded that this was true, despite the fact that "the ultimate aims of the 'downtrodden' of all racial elements may be the same." He pointed out that intelligent Negro leadership knew that if there was to be a class war in America, "it must not be started or conducted in any way that will cause it to take on the appearance of race or 'color line.' In such a struggle the enemy of economic and political progress would simply beat the ancient tom-toms of race hatred and race prejudice —and the Negro would be a swift loser." The Communists were using black men as cannon fodder. Wherever they stirred black men into militant class action, "it is the Negro that remains to do the dying and the languishing in jail, while his white Communist

97. William Pickens, in Chattanooga *Times*, June 8, 1931.
98. See for example, "Pickens Says—," Washington *Tribune*, November 24, 1936.
99. Avery, "Up from Washington," 200–203.

leaders escape from the scene."[100] After the Scottsboro debacle subsided somewhat Pickens became less vitriolic toward the Party, but he remained skeptical. He was convinced that communism could not eliminate racism and he was offended by the blind loyalty which the Party demanded of its members. He confessed that he could never become a member "because I just cannot allow a machine or a clique or a cause to put words in my mouth."[101]

While Pickens demonstrated a rather embarrassing inconsistency with regard to the Communists and Scottsboro, he never wavered in his opposition to Franklin Roosevelt's New Deal. Even before the election of 1932, he was advising Afro-Americans to vote for the Socialist candidate, Norman Thomas. If that were not possible he then advised that they vote either for nobody, Herbert Hoover, or the Communist William Z. Foster.[102] Pickens was skeptical of any Democrat because of the South's power within that Party. He called those Negroes who supported "Marse Roosevelt" "black henchmen" and claimed after the election that they should be ashamed of themselves for helping "to put the South back into the saddle." He prophesied that "the 'new deal' is likely to be, for the Negro the same old deal: Namely, 'Let the Negro be damned!' "[103] Instead of promising to directly attack the specific problems of black Americans, Roosevelt had merely made some vague statements about the Negro being "included" in his general program.

After the New Deal had been in effect for a few months, Pickens

100. "Pickens Says—," New York *Amsterdam News*, August 19, 1931. See also "Communists Made a Mess in Alabama, Pickens Declares," Norfolk *Journal and Guide*, August 8, 1931; "Pickens Says—," New York *Amsterdam News*, November 4, 1931; "Dreiser Gets Taste of What Negro Suffers, Pickens Says," Pittsburgh *Courier*, December 3, 1931; "The Scottsboro Case," Pittsburgh *Courier*, April 9, 1932; and "Pickens Says—," Louisiana *Weekly*, January 14, 1933.

101. "Pickens Says Loyalty to Radicals Is Too Binding," Baltimore *Afro-American*, January 25, 1936.

102. "William Pickens Says," St. Louis *Argus*, October 28, 1932; William Pickens, "Leaders Blossom Forth For Each Presidential Election," Philadelphia *Tribune*, October 20, 1932.

103. William Pickens, "Reflections," New York *Amsterdam News*, May 17, 1933; and his "Roosevelt and His Negroes!" *The Union*, April 13, 1933.

believed that his prophecy had been fulfilled. "This administration, with its extraordinary peace time powers," he concluded, "is even more disdainful of the claims of the Negro race than was the administration of Woodrow Wilson."[104] Pickens was one of the first black critics of the New Deal to point out that many of its policies were detrimental to black Americans. He called the National Recovery Act (NRA) the "Negro Removal Act," because it forced a minimum wage level on many industries which was higher than the scale being paid black workers. Most employers, rather than pay their black workers the higher wage, merely replaced them with white workers. Where this was not the case, the administration was often not doing anything to make employers pay black workers the minimum wage.[105]

Pickens was also critical of the New Deal because he thought that it was producing a dictatorship in this country, and "dictatorship is dangerous for any minority, but especially for a minority which popular prejudice places somewhat outside the pale. For there is always the certain danger that the dominant race or group will dictate to the dictator."[106] And in the case of the Democratic president, it was all too apparent that those doing the dictating were southerners. This was amply demonstrated in the failure of the NAACP to get the president's support for antilynching legislation. Roosevelt would not risk the possibility of alienating southern support for his other domestic programs.[107]

104. William Pickens, "I Told You So," Norfolk *Journal and Guide*, August 19, 1933.

105. William Pickens, "NRA"—'Negro Removal Act'?" *The World Tomorrow*, XVI (September 28, 1933), 539–40. See also his "One Hundred Years of Race Progress in America," Chicago *Defender*, August 18, 1934; and his "Does It Mean Slavery?" Chicago *Defender*, September 22, 1934. For an analysis of the effect of the NRA on black workers, see Wolters, *Negroes and the Great Depression*, 83–215.

106. Pickens, "One Hundred Years of Race Progress." See also his "I Am With Henry Ford," Louisiana *Weekly*, November 11, 1933.

107. See Robert L. Zangrado, "The NAACP and a Federal Anti-Lynching Bill, 1934–1940," *Journal of Negro History*, L (April, 1965), 106–17. For a more detailed analysis, see Zangrado, "The Efforts of the National Association for the Advancement of Colored People to Secure Passage of a Federal Anti-Lynching Law,

In 1936 Pickens once again advised his readers to support Norman Thomas. However, black voters did not heed Pickens' warnings and for the first time gave a majority of their votes to a Democratic presidential candidate. After the election Pickens chided his readers with the observation that a victory for Roosevelt certainly was not a victory for their interests. He believed that henceforth they should display a more intelligent racial solidarity in their voting habits; that would be the only way black people would get anything from any politicians. "Whatever their party affiliations," he concluded, "the black people of the United States must stand as one for all things affecting their collective welfare and their rights as a group."[108]

Pickens also attacked the New Deal because it did not eliminate laissez faire capitalism which he believed was the root cause of the depression. The NRA, for example, was nothing more, in his estimation, than a "sort of bastard socialization." He wanted to see a planned economy lead to a Socialist democracy.[109] Despite his socialistic pretensions, however, Pickens consistently supported the development of small black businesses. As in the case of Du Bois, this made his commitment to socialism rather suspect among the young radicals.

Pickens thought that the depression might be a blessing in disguise because "it is forcing the Negro to learn 'business'—small trades."[110] Sounding very much like Carter Woodson, Pickens sug-

---

1920–1940" (Ph.D. dissertation, University of Pennsylvania, 1963). For an example of Pickens' criticism of southern Democrats who blocked antilynching legislation, see "Humanity Will Never Honor a Judas," *The Southern Broadcast*, August 4, 1934.

108. "Pickens' Observations," Washington *Tribune*, July 14, 1936; Avery, "Up from Washington," 229; William Pickens, "Reflections on the Election," St. Louis *Argus*, November 13, 1936. For an analysis of the election of 1936, see Henry Lee Moon, *Balance of Power: The Negro Vote* (Garden City, N.Y.: Doubleday, 1948), 18; and especially James A. Harrell, "Negro Leadership in the Election Year, 1936," *Journal of Southern History*, XXXIV (November, 1968), 546–64. For a more detailed discussion of Pickens' opposition to Roosevelt in 1936, see Avery, "Up from Washington," 227–34.

109. Pickens, "I Am With Henry Ford"; Avery, "Up from Washington," 213–16.

110. "William Pickens Says—," St. Louis *Argus*, October 7, 1932.

gested that black Americans should hold successful black business-men up for emulation: "If we study these successful men, we will find that the one thing they all have in common is a foundation basis of honesty. They are not pretenders, 'limelighters,' four-flushers, charlatans and rogues. They are conservative and care-ful."[111] Like many of the more conservative race men, such as Woodson and Gordon Blaine Hancock, Pickens supported such campaigns as the "Don't Buy Where You Can't Work" boycotts of white businesses. And when employees of the *Amsterdam News* tried to form a labor union during the mid-thirties, he suggested that black workers should not join unions if they were employed in black business because their employers were struggling to de-velop race enterprise.[112]

Pickens generally seemed to be most comfortable in the role of a race man preaching a text of race solidarity. And yet, as war approached at the end of the decade he had drifted far from the camp of most race men who were calling upon the race to unite to demand democracy at home as a price for fighting for it in foreign lands. Pickens was one of the few Americans, and one of the very few non-Communist black writers, who advocated United States intervention against the Fascist powers.

When, in 1931, Japan had first invaded Manchuria, Pickens was critical of Japan's warlike methods but proud of the fact that "they are the first colored nation to refuse to take orders or to be bluffed by white Europeans and Americans in generations." The fact that " 'White Supremacy' was slain in Manchuria" was, he concluded, "almost, perhaps altogether, a compensation for the evil."[113]

111. "Confidence In Negro Business On Upward Trend, Says Pickens," Pitts-burgh *Courier*, June 3, 1933.

112. William Pickens, "Pickets and Patrons," New York *Amsterdam News*, Sep-tember 29, 1934; William Pickens, "The Boycott," Louisiana *Weekly*, January 19, 1935; Gavins, "Gordon Blaine Hancock," 74, 104–105; and Cayton and Mitchell, *Black Workers and the New Unions*, 377.

113. William Pickens, "Reflections," New York *Amsterdam News*, March 17, 1932; and his "Reflections," New York *Amsterdam News*, March 9, 1932. See also

His first response to the rise of Hitler in Germany was a "we shall see" attitude. He was diametrically opposed to Hitler's racial theories, but he agreed with his demand that Germany should be equally as powerful as the other European powers. However, it did not take long for Hitler's treatment of Jews and other minorities to convince Pickens that Nazi Germany represented a threat to minority groups everywhere. He became one of the first black writers in this country to staunchly oppose the spread of fascism in Europe. In 1934, he compared Nazi Germany with racist Alabama, concluding "I prefer Alabama." And after Italy's invasion of Ethiopia in 1935, the creation of the Rome-Berlin axis and its support of the Fascist forces in the Spanish Civil War, Pickens became convinced that American intervention was imperative. Even Japan, he decided, had "built up a veritable Frankenstein in its army." The Japanese were merely rapacious aggressors after all. "What they cannot get by votes or by parliamentary methods," Pickens admitted, "they take with the sword." During the summer of 1938 Pickens visited Barcelona, which was one of the last of the Spanish loyalists' strongholds. He wrote home: "It is our fight."[114]

Writing in the *New Masses* in 1939, he tried to explain why he thought black Americans should be concerned about the destruction of fascism. "We have a democracy," he wrote, "something worth fighting for. The American Negro's choice should be easy. Where there is liberty, there is hope." Pickens was not ignoring racial injustice in this country. "A sane man cannot love everything

"Pickens Says—," New York *Amsterdam News*, December 23, 1931. Many black Americans apparently derived vicarious satisfaction as the result of Japan's exploits. See Dalfiume, *Desegregation of the U.S. Armed Forces*, 110–11.

114. William Pickens, "Reflections," New York *Amsterdam News*, February 1, 1933; his "Free Speech in Germany—For Hitler and Goebbels," Louisiana *Weekly*, October 6, 1934. See also Pickens' "Hitler-Hates-Humans," Louisiana *Weekly*, September 9, 1933; "Hitler—'Shadow Boxing,'" Louisiana *Weekly*, November 18, 1933; and Avery, "Up from Washington," 250–51; "Pickens Tells Japan," Baltimore *Afro-American*, March 7, 1936; and Pickens, "What I Saw In Spain," *Crisis*, XLV (October, 1938), 321; Avery, "Up from Washington," 251–52.

in America," he admitted, "but he can come very near to a 100 per cent hatred of the very essence of fascism."[115]

While Pickens was arguing for intervention and a few, such as George Schuyler, were arguing against, most black writers were not debating the pros and cons of intervention; they were asking whether black Americans should give their support if the country did become involved in the war.[116] After December 7, 1941, most black spokesmen, the NAACP included, advocated a "two front" policy of supporting the war effort but continuing to militantly oppose all forms of racial discrimination in this country at the same time. This included segregation in all branches of the military.[117] However, Pickens, who in his new capacity as head of the Negro section of the War Bond Division of the Treasury Department was supposed to motivate patriotism in the black community, was willing to accept segregated training facilities for the armed forces. Winning the war was now the most important task at hand, and he favored a partial moratorium on protest against domestic racial injustice in the interest of national unity during the crisis. In an article criticizing the NAACP's unceasing militancy against discrimination in the Army training camps, Pickens admitted that such discrimination was "damned nonsense," but the Army was not in business to bring about social changes. "It is planning to win a war," he challenged, "in spite of segregation or of those who oppose segregation."[118] The NAACP Board of Directors voted to sever Pickens' relationship with the organization. He had, in their eyes, abandoned his role as a race man.

Throughout the war years, Pickens' voice continued to represent a small minority of black leaders, such as the arch-conservative

115. William Pickens, "Why the Negro Must Be Anti-Fascist," *New Masses*, XXXI (May 30, 1939), 12.

116. Dalfiume, *Desegregation of the U.S. Armed Forces*, 111–13.

117. *Ibid.*, 124–31. See the editorial in the *Crisis*, XLIX (January, 1942), 36.

118. William Pickens, "Pursuit Squadron," New York *Amsterdam News*, January 31, 1942; Avery, "Up from Washington," 269–71.

president of Tuskegee Institute, Frederick D. Patterson, who opposed racial militancy for the duration.[119]

Randolph, Johnson, and Schuyler generally remained aloof from
the debate between the older leadership and the young radicals.
Even Pickens, who had been one of the young radicals' targets at
Amenia, did not often publicly engage in combat with them. But
Pickens, like each of the other men discussed in this chapter continued to be deeply concerned with the very same issues which
had been said to divide youth and age at Amenia. And each of
these men offered his own alternative solution to the problems
which confronted black America.

As a labor leader and long-time Socialist, A. Philip Randolph
generally espoused the same radical economic program to which
the young radicals gave their allegiance. As a staunch race man,
however, he proposed a program which, had it been espoused by
one of the older established leaders, would have been labeled "black
chauvinism" by the young radicals. Randolph's alternative to the
approaches of the older race leadership and the young radicals
was to put into action a feasible plan of black power for the benefit
of the black masses. Where most of the black intellectuals spent
their time in endless theorizing, Randolph proposed a simple plan
and acted.

Charles S. Johnson shared an objective antichauvinism with the
young radicals. But he was essentially a conservative, both economically and socially. Like Kelly Miller and Carter Woodson, his
thinking was much influenced by Booker T. Washington. What set
him apart from Miller and Woodson was the fact that while they
attempted to impose Washington's specific programs—out-dated
even when he had set them forth—on the world of the 1930s,
Johnson borrowed much from his general philosophy and attempted to mold it to fit the realities of a mechanized and urbanized

119. Dalfiume, *Desegregation of the U.S. Armed Forces*, 125.

society. Johnson's primary alternative was an attempt to bring Washington up to date.

George Schuyler entered the 1930s as a humorously irreverent left-wing antichauvinist. Never adhering consistently to any specific philosophy, he skittered about, first to one position, then to its opposite, and then perhaps back again. Economic problems gained most of his attention during the early years of the depression. Although he repeatedly scorned any form of race chauvinism, his own program of consumer cooperatives was essentially the same as Du Bois's. As the possibility of war drew near Schuyler abandoned his radical economics, his antichauvinism and much of his sense of humor. He entered the 1940s making rabidly chauvinistic, often irrational appeals for black Americans to ignore the war and look only after their own provincial interests. And yet, the tone of his antiwar articles was often more anti-Roosevelt and anti-New Deal than it was pro-black man. The genesis of Schuyler's extreme right-wing conservatism dates from the late 1930s.

Although he had been criticized for his conservatism and provinciality at Amenia, William Pickens was really consistently guilty of neither. Sometimes, as in his opposition to the New Deal, his support of black business, and his early assessment of Japan's activities in Asia, he played the role of ardent race man. And yet, often at the same time, he preached a radical brand of economic determinism, the viability of black and white labor solidarity, and eventually the need for unquestioning loyalty of black Americans during the crisis of war. It was on this last issue that Pickens was expelled from the orbit of the race men. In fact, because the war tended to unify black leadership around the idea of a "two front" strategy, it left him virtually without allies. The ultimate alternative which he offered went largely unheeded.

IV

"The Truth from Our Point of View"

" 'Negro history,' " wrote Lawrence D. Reddick in 1936, "is quite different from the study of the Negro." The young black historian found that "Negro history" was forced to assume burdens beyond the mere discovery and recording of the role of African peoples in the world. Its function was also to awaken and "educate" the majority population concerning this role; and even more important, it sought to inculcate a "dynamic pride" in Negroes themselves. In short, concluded Reddick, Negro history was principally a "lever of racial progress."[1]

Although he was critical of this type of history, Reddick's observations were scarcely original. Black intellectuals and historians had long been calling for the same thing. In his manifesto, *Negro Americans, What Now?*, James Weldon Johnson had considered the study of Negro history an indispensable technique for the advance of the race: "A study of the African cultural background will give our youth a new and higher sense of racial self-respect, and will disprove entirely the theory of innate race inferiority."[2] Carter Woodson, who devoted his life to the "Negro history" movement, proclaimed that the Negro's very survival depended upon his

1. Lawrence D. Reddick, "A New Interpretation for Negro History," *Journal of Negro History*, XXII (January, 1937), 17. For a more generalized study of Negro historians, see Earl E. Thorpe, *Black Historians: A Critique* (New York: William Morrow and Co., Inc., 1971).
2. James Weldon Johnson, *Negro Americans, What Now?* (New York: The Viking Press, 1934), 48.

awareness of the race's past: "The American Indian left no continuous record. He did not know the value of tradition; he left nothing to stimulate his race; and where is he today? The Hebrew keenly appreciated these values as attested by the Bible itself. In spite of world-wide persecution, therefore, he is still a great factor in our civilization."[3] The theme of Negro history as a source of race pride and as a force in race advancement was repeated again and again during the 1930s, in the prefaces to history books, in essays, and in newspaper columns.[4]

The special responsibilities of Negro history imposed certain preconceptions upon its chroniclers. Although Negro historians always professed to be objectively seeking truth, they inevitably sought out black "heroes" and dwelt upon the "contributions" of black men to world civilization. They were also generally caught up with the idea of the black man's rise within—or sometimes outside of—that civilization. Thus they were limited by preconceptions of the black man's greatness and his "progress." Since they set out to prove black accomplishment and equality—even superiority—this was naturally what they found.

Among the functions of Negro history delineated by Reddick

3. Carter Woodson, "History and Propaganda," in Otelia Cromwell, Lorenzo Dow Turner, Eva B. Dykes (eds.), *Readings from Negro Authors* (New York: Harcourt, Brace & Co., 1931), 303. From an address delivered in Baltimore, Maryland, February 10, 1926.

4. See Merl R. Eppse, *The Negro, Too, in American History* (Chicago: National Publication, 1938), x–xi; Merl R. Eppse, *An Elementary History of America, Including the Contributions of the Negro Race* (Chicago: National Publication, 1939), v–vii; Carter G. Woodson, *The African Background Outlined, or Handbook for the Study of the Negro* (Washington, D.C.: The Association for the Study of Negro Life and History, 1936), v; W. E. B. Du Bois, *Black Folk, Then and Now: An Essay in the History and Sociology of the Negro Race* (New York: Henry Holt & Co., 1939), viii; Charles H. Wesley, "The Reconstruction of History," *Journal of Negro History*, XX (October, 1935), 411–27; Luther Porter Jackson, "Unexplored Fields in the History of the Negro in the United States," *Quarterly Review of Higher Education Among Negroes*, IX (April, 1941), 73–77. These essays and articles are too numerous to cite here. Many will be used in later sections of this chapter. For a recent analysis which distinguishes "Negro" history from "Black" history, see Vincent Harding, "Beyond Chaos: Black History and the Search for the New Land," Black Paper No. 2 (Atlanta, Ga.: Institute of the Black World, 1970).

the pre-eminent one during the 1930s was the inculcation of pride. The Negro historian's concentration upon achievements and heroes sometimes brought charges of "minority jingo" from white critics.[5] In reply William Pickens defended the "jingoism" of black historians as "but the defensive reaction of the minority to the less excusable chauvinism of the majority."[6]

Majority chauvinism had either ignored or distorted the black man's past. Where standard histories depicted the Negro at all, he appeared as a happy, docile slave before the Civil War, or as a shifty, sometimes vicious freeman afterwards. Charles H. Wesley echoed most of his colleagues when he charged that "racial propaganda has been so interjected into the writing of history in the United States that the search for truth, which is the main pursuit of historical work, has been almost entirely obscured."[7] Ideally, black historians were seeking "the truth"; in reality they often, quite understandably, merely substituted black chauvinism for white chauvinism.

The Negro history movement was by no means exclusively the preserve of formally trained historians. Essential to its success was the very basic problem of reaching the black masses. One of the men most successful in this endeavor was the self-educated Joel Augustus Rogers. In addition to numerous newspaper articles on great black men, the former confident of Marcus Garvey published a weekly feature, "Your History," in the national edition of the Pittsburgh *Courier*. This feature was a black facsimile of Ripley's

5. See Benjamin Stolberg, "Minority Jingo," *Nation* (October 23, 1937), 437–39.
6. William Pickens, "Retort to Jingo Snobbery," *Crisis*, XLIV (December, 1937), 360. For a similar opinion, see Horace Mann Bond, "The Curriculum and the Negro Child," *Journal of Negro Education*, IV (April, 1935), 159–68.
7. Charles H. Wesley, "Propaganda and Historical Writing," *Opportunity*, XIII (August, 1935), 244. See also, Wesley, "Education and Propaganda," *Journal of Negro Education*, IV (April, 1935), 261–65; Sterling-Brown, "Unhistoric History," *Journal of Negro History*, XV (April, 1930), 134–61; Lawrence D. Reddick, "Racial Attitudes in American History Textbooks in the South," *Journal of Negro History*, XIX (July, 1934), 225–65; and especially Chapter 17, "The Propaganda of History," in W. E. B. Du Bois, *Black Reconstruction in America, 1860–1880* (New York: Harcourt, Brace & Co., 1935), 711–29.

"Believe It or Not." Most often Rogers was concerned with revealing the "true" racial identity of certain great figures in history who had previously been thought to be white. For Rogers the purpose of Negro history and his own "Your History" feature was to counter the universal belief that the Negro race had never accomplished anything. "It is important also," he wrote, "because of the attempt made in certain quarters to suppress the true racial descent of certain great men who were long believed to be 'pure' white."[8]

During the 1930s Rogers published, at his own expense, two lengthy pamphlets which elaborated upon the themes presented in "Your History." *The World's Greatest Men of African Descent* (1931) presented "to individuals of African descent and chiefly the youth, the lives of some of the men and women of their 'race' who have risen to commanding positions in spite of adversities, sometimes far greater than theirs."[9] Typical of the men sketched was "Kafur the Magnificent" who rose from the status of a eunuch slave to rule all of Egypt. Like Horatio Alger, Kafur owed his success to perseverance, the will to learn, and loyalty.[10] All of Rogers' heroes rose in a similar manner. Character qualities counted; outside forces were ignored. In such a way, Rogers implied, his youthful readers might also rise. They must only follow the example of some of the characters in the book who, Rogers assured them, were "not only equal to Plutarch's finest but will have been found to eclipse some of them in achievement, that is, by the greatness of the difficulties they overcame."[11]

In 1934, Rogers published *100 Amazing Facts About the Negro: With Complete Proof: A Short Cut to the World History of the Negro*. This pamphlet perhaps best demonstrated Rogers' simplistic conceptualization of history. In it he presented a list of unre-

8. Joel Augustus Rogers, "J. A. Rogers Explains 'Your History' Feature in the Courier," Pittsburgh *Courier*, November 21, 1936.
9. Joel Augustus Rogers, *The World's Greatest Men of African Descent* (New York: J. A. Rogers, 1931), i.
10. *Ibid.*, 52–53. 11. *Ibid.*, 1.

lated, often dubiously documented "facts": "Beethoven, the world's greatest musician, was without a doubt a dark mulatto. He was called 'The Black Spaniard.' His teacher, the immortal Joseph Haydn, who wrote the music for the former Austrian National Anthem, was colored, too." Also of comparable significance was the "fact" that "an American Negro has twenty chances to a white American's one of reaching a hundred years and over."[12]

These pamphlets were mere compendiums of "facts" which evidently were supposed to speak for themselves. And perhaps, given the purpose of the pamphlets—instilling pride in the largely untutored black masses—analysis was unnecessary.

While remaining essentially dogmatic, Rogers attempted to become analytical in his book, *Sex and Race: Negro-Caucasian Mixing in All Ages and All Lands* (1940). He set out to demonstrate "from the most authentic facts available what and what and what have entered into the family trees of the 'superior' and 'super-superior' races; whether in the case of Aryans it may not be a case of the pot calling the kettle black."[13] The history of miscegenation through the ages was a provocative undertaking; but Rogers' indiscriminate use of evidence and simplistic analysis did not do justice to the subject.

One flagrant example of this was when Rogers cited two scientists as the basis for his belief that "the earliest Jews were in all probability, Negroes." From this point he took up the Bible as his authority. Apparently he considered science and the Bible of equal value in historical analysis. The following is an example of his method. "Only seventy Jews went to Egypt, but according to the Bible, 600,000 men left it, which must have meant an additional two or three million women and children. Since the Jews were

12. Joel Augustus Rogers, *100 Amazing Facts About the Negro* (New York: J. A. Rogers, 1934), 5, 17.
13. Joel Augustus Rogers, *Sex and Race: Negro-Caucasian Mixing in All Ages and All Lands* (New York: J. A. Rogers, 1940), 10.

slaves their women were undoubtedly concubines of the Egyptians and must have produced mixed offspring. After more than three centuries of slavery almost every trace of the first seventy Jews must have been lost, together with their culture. Thus Jewish culture was Egyptian culture. For instance, the Egyptians did not eat pork, and still do not eat it."[14] This naturally meant Christ was black.

As an analytical historian, Rogers was a failure. Most of his professional contemporaries scorned his work. But as a publicist for race pride—and this was really what the Negro history movement entailed—his success was probably far greater than that of most professionals. By 1943, *100 Amazing Facts About the Negro* was in its eighteenth edition and had become the prime source book for soapbox orators and lecturers throughout the country.[15] Scorn him as they might, the formally trained professionals were preaching essentially the same thing as Rogers—the equality, and often the superiority, of black men.

If Rogers had a rival in reaching a wide audience, he was Carter Godwin Woodson. Like Rogers, Woodson made strenuous efforts to publicize Negro history in the Afro-American press. As founder and director of the Association for the Study of Negro Life and History, he was also responsible for the development of Negro History Week which focused upon making black students aware of the race's past. Woodson was also editor of the association's publishing house and its organ, the *Journal of Negro History* (and after 1938, the *Negro History Bulletin*). In this capacity he encouraged black scholars to publish articles and books which might not have received consideration elsewhere. Although Woodson was a trained historian with a Harvard Ph.D. degree, his importance

14. *Ibid.*, 91.
15. Roi Ottley, *New World A-Coming: Inside Black America* (Boston: Houghton Mifflin Co., 1943), 102, 103.

during the 1930s was related more to his activities as a Negro history propagandist than as a serious scholar.

Woodson liked to remind his readers that he was a "scientifically trained" historian. He advised that "if the story of the Negro is ever told it must be by scientifically trained Negroes." Being a Negro took precedence over scientific training. Like many of his black colleagues, Woodson shuddered at the thought of white men writing Negro history, "for we expect to be misrepresented or slandered." Although many black historians felt the same way, Woodson went a step further in asserting that "in the case of presenting the real history and the status of the Negro, however, men of other races cannot function efficiently because they do not think black."[16] Woodson nearly always associated "efficient" and "scientific" history with "thinking black."

The falsification of Negro history was a key factor in what Woodson called the "miseducation" of the Negro. "The great trouble with the Negro today," concluded Woodson, "is that his history has been written by some one else who has perverted it."[17] Much of the American Negro's self-hatred had been imposed by white historians—"traducers" Woodson called them—who were intent on demonstrating the Negro's inferiority by showing that he had done nothing of merit in the past. Although Woodson professed to be a scientific historian, and occasionally called upon black historians to be unbiased,[18] the central purpose of Negro history was

16. Carter Woodson, "Too Much 'Hindsight' Insufficient Foresight," Boston *Chronicle*, June 18, 1932. See also Carter Woodson, *The African Background Outlined* (Washington, D.C.: The Association for the Study of Negro Life and History, 1935), v. Carter Woodson, "Negro History Week—February 11–18," New York *Age*, February 3, 1934. See also "Carter G. Woodson Flays White Publishers; Refuse to Publish Scripts Because They Tell the Truth," Pittsburgh *Courier*, January 27, 1940.

17. Carter Woodson, "$30,000 for the Suppressed Truth," Norfolk *Journal and Guide*, April 6, 1935.

18. Carter Woodson, "Varying Conceptions of Negro History," Louisiana *Weekly*, February 17, 1934. See also Woodson, *The African Background Outlined*, 321–22; and his "Some Imperfect Reasoning," Chicago *Defender*, February 10, 1934.

the resurrection of black pride as a springboard for social and economic advancement. Black historians must inform Negroes of "their past which is just as glorious as that of any other race."[19] Because white historians had ignored or denigrated his race, Woodson seemed to assume that their main purpose was the glorification of their own race. He thought of them as being essentially white propagandists. It is not surprising that he conceptualized the role of the black historian in a similar manner. Nor is it surprising that he could make such unequivocal comments in the black press on African contributions to world civilization as the following: "If the results of these forces were eliminated, from the so-called white man's civilization, the Nordics would still be in a state of nature, the one flying at the other's throat and boasting of drinking from the skull bones of their enemies."[20]

Besides chastizing the white man and delineating a "glorious" past for the Negro, Woodson's newspaper sketches of persons and events pointed up certain lessons. He was fond of prefacing his statements with "history shows" or "history teaches," as if he were quoting from Scriptures. Woodson looked to the past for solutions to present-day problems. The men he wrote about were all heroes, all achievers. They were men who overcame tremendous obstacles on their way to success.[21] Their lives pointed up important lessons for Woodson's contemporaries: "Inasmuch as they faced hardship and suffered from disabilities greater than those we encounter today, their careers may supply us with very much needed lessons in meeting present-day emergencies." Thus Woodson saw great value in a study of "successful Negroes in business before the Civil War," many of whom "owned more property than Negroes in those

19. Carter Woodson, "The Side-Show of the George Washington Bicentennial," Boston *Chronicle*, December 12, 1931.
20. Carter Woodson, "Comments on Negro Education," Louisiana *Weekly*, September 19, 1931.
21. See for example, Carter Woodson, "Forgotton Negroes," Louisiana *Weekly*, February 24, 1934.

very places have today."[22]An interesting message emerged from the "success" orientation of these newspaper sketches. It was well reflected in the title of one of them: "American Blacks of 200 Years Ago Bolder Than People of Our Day."[23] The principal purpose of Negro history was supposed to be the resurrection of black pride, and yet this constant harping on past glories in comparison with contemporary failure—though perhaps developed with the idea of prodding Negroes into effort—conceivably may have had an effect opposite to that which Woodson desired.

Almost as much as he was preoccupied with success and failure, Woodson was concerned with the presence of good and evil in history. His advice to young historians was that they "bring out the truth on both sides, balance it in the great scale of time and find out whether there is a preponderance of good or of evil." "Good" was whatever advanced the race; "evil" was whatever injured the race. "The race" was always the primary ingredient in Woodson's moralistic scheme of history. Thus he evaluated the "great men" in light of how much they had done for the race. The best men were those who contributed most to the rise of the race.[24] While generally limiting himself to rating "great" black men, since, by definition, not many whites could qualify, Woodson sometimes ranked great white historical figures solely upon their contributions to his race. "Considered from the point of view of the scientifically trained historian," Woodson observed, "George Washington should be given much higher rank than most of the so-called friends of the Negro today."[25] For Woodson, George Washington's freeing of his slaves at his death was the most important act of his life. The good of this act was, he thought, in marked contrast to the

22. Woodson, "Varying Conceptions of Negro History." See also his "Some Imperfect Reasoning."
23. Baltimore *Afro-American*, January 9, 1932. See also his "Varying Conceptions of Negro History"; and "Negroes More Outspoken a Century Ago than Today," Louisiana *Weekly*, January 23, 1932.
24. Woodson, "Some Imperfect Reasoning."
25. Carter Woodson, "George Washington," New York *Age*, February 29, 1936.

evil perpetrated by most white men in their relations with black men.

Woodson generally concerned himself very little with white historical figures except in their role as exploiters of the black race. As a rule, whites in his scheme of history were on the side of evil. And however much he aspired to impartiality, he always ended up "honoring the distinguished men of African blood."[26] Very few black traitors appear in Woodson's historical writings. To have written about "Uncle Toms" would have defeated the stated purpose of Negro history. Woodson set out to look for figures whom the black man could honor, and, not surprisingly, he found them.

Woodson's scholarly output for the 1930s was largely concerned with contemporary conditions and might be termed sociological.[27] Except as compilations of data, these studies were undistinguished and undoubtedly would have gone unpublished had it not been for the fact that Woodson owned 90 percent of the stock in Associated Publishers. In previous years, Woodson had produced such important historical works as *The Negro in Our History* (1922)— probably the best and most detailed general history of the black man produced until John Hope Franklin's *From Slavery to Freedom* in 1957; *A Century of Negro Migration* (1918); *The History of the Negro Church* (1921); *Free Negro Owners of Slaves* (1924); and *The Education of the Negro Prior to 1861* (1915).

During the 1930s Woodson produced very little that was original. His *Story of the Negro Retold* (1935) was little more than a condensation of *The Negro in Our History* and was designed as a text for junior and senior high schools. Another book, *African Heroes and Heroines* (1939), was also designed for the same audience.

26. Carter Woodson, "Proper Setting Is Outlined by Noted Historian," Norfolk *Journal and Guide*, February 15, 1936.

27. These works by Woodson included: *The Rural Negro* (Washington, D.C.: The Association for the Study of Negro Life and History, Inc., 1930); *The Negro Professional Man and the Community* (Washington, D.C.: The Association for the Study of Negro Life and History, Inc., 1934); and *The Miseducation of the Negro* (Washington, D.C.: The Associated Publishers, Inc., 1933).

As might be expected, Woodson demonstrated that these "leaders of a despised people measure up to the full stature of the heroic in the histories of other nations."[28] This book drew heavily upon the research for Woodson's most ambitious scholarly endeavor of the decade, *The African Background Outlined, or Handbook for the Study of the Negro* (1936).

Woodson's handbook, at least half of which was a detailed bibliographic guide to Negro history, set out to prove that "the Negro has achieved much," both in Africa and in the United States. He freely admitted that he was very selective in his sources: "The author has not even undertaken to direct attention to all works on Africa, for the large majority of such productions are too biased and unscientific to merit such attention."[29] This may very well have been the case, but Woodson's almost exclusive reliance upon the sympathetic writings of Maurice Delafosse for the sections on Africa indicates that his account also suffered from a heavy bias. In many instances Woodson quoted directly from Delafosse for more than a page.[30] The rest of his citations were largely taken from Woodson's own *Journal of Negro History*.

In his chapters on Africa, Woodson concerned himself almost exclusively with great kings and kingdoms. He almost totally ignored the aboriginal peoples of Africa. Woodson was much more interested in those African nations which had exhibited an ability for self-government, stability, and an accumulation of great material wealth. "Stability, however," he wrote, "had been shown by long reigns and long lives of the people and their rulers. Kingdoms had lasted as long as Greece, Rome and Britain."[31] Thus, he chronicled the rise, and sometimes the fall, of Ghana, Melle, the Songhay

---

28. From the preface to Carter Woodson's *African Heroes and Heroines* (Washington, D.C.: The Association for the Study of Negro Life and History, Inc., 1939).

29. Woodson, *The African Background Outlined*, v.

30. See, for example, *ibid.*, 9–10.   31. *Ibid.*, 72.

Empire, and other great nations—always feeling compelled to compare them favorably with the "great" civilizations of Western history. At a time when cultural anthropologists, following the lead of Franz Boas, were successfully challenging the old method of judging cultures by standards which were foreign to them, Woodson continued to assess African and Afro-American culture by criteria which were often irrelevant.[32]

The term *chronicle* is an apt description of Woodson's method of discussing these empires. He spent altogether too much time relating how this king took over from that king and how the next took over from him. He did not offer adequate analysis. Often he would admit that the origins of an empire were shrouded in legend. He would repeat the legend and continue his narrative without taking the trouble to inform his readers where the legend ended and fact began.[33]

When Woodson did finally get down to subjects which demanded analysis, he was brief and tended to over-generalize. For example, he devoted one 10-page chapter to the subject of African culture. His treatment, while sometimes interesting, gave the impression that a single culture pervaded all of black Africa. He was guilty of making many rather simplistic judgments, wholly unsupported by his evidence. For example: "Africans have never been known as naturally lazy people in the sense in which we have viewed the North American Indians and other belated peoples. The Africans as a majority are industrious for the reason that their social order requires labor of all members of the group."[34] Although he ignored such "evil" occurrences as the fact that black men sold their brothers into slavery, he dogmatically proclaimed—again without sufficient evidence—that "students of African life are

32. See Gossett, *Race: The History of an Idea in America*, 422–23.
33. See for example Woodson's remarks on the origins of the Massi States, *The African Background Outlined*, 74.
34. *Ibid.*, 150.

almost unanimous in saying that the Africans are 'the most just of all the people of the world.' "[35] "Thinking black" made evidence superfluous. What has been called here the idea of Negro equality-superiority was, for Woodson, a self-evident "truth," but, significantly, a truth which still needed stating.

The noble virtues of the African were important for Woodson because he believed that they had been inherited by black Americans. Belief in the presence of African survivals among Afro-Americans was essential for Woodson and others with black nationalist inclinations. It strengthened the bond among black men beyond the mere circumstance of skin color. Woodson wanted to strengthen the black American's identification with his "African brothers" past and present. Thus, at a time when sociologists like Frazier and Johnson were denying the idea of cultural carryover, Woodson was propounding what might be called an African germ theory of history.

Woodson could thus dogmatically assert, again without evidence, that "the industry of the Negro in the United States may be partly explained as an African survival. The Negro is a born worker." And he could rationalize and turn into a source of pride the docility which others either denied or condemned as a humiliation: "The Africans brought to the United States did not have to be made to work as did the unprofitable white indentured servants and the untractable Indians who could not live up to the tempo set by the exploiters of the New World."[36] Again, if Africans were the "most just" of all people, then it must also hold true with his American brother. "With the exceptions of those charged with infractions of the law resulting from impoverishment and social repression," Woodson proclaimed, "the Negroes constitute the most law-abiding element of our population. Because of the African's keen sense of justice he could not develop other-

35. *Ibid.*, 156.
36. *Ibid.*, 170, 171.

wise abroad."[37] Ironically, such chauvinistic assertions were probably expressed for the purpose of convincing the white middle
class that the black middle class was more than ready for integration. Besides his chauvinistic emphasis on black pride, Woodson's
historical lessons, intentionally or not, could be used to facilitate
integration.[38]

At the conclusion of the narrative text on the African background, Woodson summed up what he believed he had demonstrated. The statement, which in tone sounds very much like the
boasting of a nineteenth-century nationalist historian, was characteristic of his approach to Negro history: "We may say that the
African Negro, like the exterminated Mesopotamian, Greek and
Roman, deserves a high place in history. No other race has achieved
so much with such a little help from without as the Negro. No
other element of our population has risen to such heights in spite
of so many handicaps. While there have been few agencies to
help the Negroes in Africa or abroad, there have been hordes to
impede their progress. In spite of all difficulties, however, the
annals of this race read like beautiful romances in an heroic age."[39]
No matter how much he called for bringing out "the truth on both
sides" and balancing it "in the great scale of time," Woodson was
incapable of objectivity.

Considering the negative treatment traditionally accorded the
black man in standard histories, Carter Woodson should not be
harshly judged. His bias was merely a sometimes less sophisticated
antithesis to theirs—less sophisticated because, in reality, his cause
was more profound than the mere writing of objective history.
Given the first prerogative of Negro history—the stimulation of
race pride—Woodson's efforts might be adjudged heroic. As a
tireless advocate of Negro history he was unsurpassed.

37. *Ibid.*, 185.
38. See Harding's essay, "Beyond Chaos," for a fuller development of this idea.
39. Woodson, *The African Background Outlined*, 179.

The over-sensitivity and corresponding over-compensation of Woodson and other black historians is understandable when one remembers the theme of Claude Bowers' immensely popular and influential history *The Tragic Era: The Revolution After Lincoln* (Boston, 1929).[40] For Bowers the Reconstruction era was a period when southern whites were the victims of unrelieved viciousness and corruption. The ignorant and sometimes bestial Negroes in Bowers' history threatened to Africanize the great white southern civilization. Bowers' interpretation of the Reconstruction era was generally in conformity with what had come to be the standard view of the period among American historians. His book merely added venom to the scholarly conclusions of William Dunning and John W. Burgess. Although as early as 1932, Francis B. Simkins and Robert H. Woody had written a monograph, *South Carolina During Reconstruction*, which was substantially less critical of the events of the period, the majority of the historical profession would remain satisfied with the Dunning-Bowers interpretation until after Howard K. Beale's call for a revision in 1940.[41]

As might be expected, black historians rejected the majority view. By 1938, Alrutheus Ambush Taylor had published three narrative accounts of the constructive role of Negroes in three southern states.[42] Taylor's works were loosely written and developed no other major theses. They were essentially collections of

40. According to Kenneth Stampp, Bowers' book "has attracted more readers than any other dealing with this period." Stampp, *The Era of Reconstruction, 1865–1877* (New York: Random House, Inc., 1965), 4.

41. See Howard K. Beale, "On Rewriting Reconstruction History," *American Historical Review*, XLV (July, 1940), 807–27.

42. See Alrutheus Ambush Taylor, *The Negro in South Carolina During Reconstruction* (Washington, D.C.: The Association for the Study of Negro Life and History, 1924); his *The Negro in the Reconstruction of Virginia* (Washington, D.C.: The Association for the Study of Negro Life and History, 1926); and his *The Negro in Tennessee, 1865–1889* (Washington, D.C.: The Association for the Study of Negro Life and History, 1938). Taylor's essay, "Historians of the Reconstruction," *Journal of Negro History*, XXIII (January, 1938), 16–34, pointed out the unfairness of the "standard" histories.

facts. Horace Mann Bond had intelligently pointed out, within the context of several studies, some of the positive results of Reconstruction in education and social welfare.[43] The works of neither of these men, however, aroused the controversy that surrounded the publication in 1935 of W. E. B. Du Bois's mammoth *Black Reconstruction in America, 1860–1880.*

Although he did not consider himself essentially a historian, Du Bois had long championed the role of the black man in Reconstruction. His chapter on Reconstruction in *Souls of Black Folk* (1903), was perhaps the first revisionist study. He looked at the positive aspects of Reconstruction, especially applauding the role of the Freedmen's Bureau. In 1909, he read what must have seemed a heretical paper, "Reconstruction and Its Benefits," before the American Historical Association.[44] It was not until the relatively peaceful years following his retirement as editor of the *Crisis*, however, that he found time to finally assemble his *magnum opus* on the subject. The book was the first by a black writer which attempted to give a detailed, interpretive account of the significance of Reconstruction from the black man's point of view. In 1935, this was a much different interpretation than Du Bois would have set forth had he written the book in 1909.

Du Bois was not as involved with Negro history as were Rogers and Woodson. While he occasionally upbraided blacks because of their lack of historical consciousness, Du Bois was generally preoccupied with contemporary issues in his newspaper pieces. Even

43. See Horace Mann Bond, *The Education of the Negro in the American Social Order* (New York: Prentice-Hall, Inc., 1934); his *Negro Education in Alabama* (Washington, D.C.: Associated Publishers, Inc., 1939); and his "Social and Economic Forces in Alabama Reconstruction," *Journal of Negro History,* XXIII (July, 1938), 290–348.
44. See W. E. B. Du Bois, "Reconstruction and Its Benefits," *American Historical Review,* XV (July, 1910), 781–99. For another discussion of Du Bois as a historian, see Herbert Aptheker, "The Historian," in *W. E. B. Du Bois: A Profile,* ed. Rayford Logan (New York: Hill and Wang, 1971), 249–73.

though he did not make strenuous efforts to publicize Negro history, he understood its considerable value as a force in social uplift.[45] And, as a scholar, his bias was a conscious one of "thinking black." A few years after the publication of *Black Reconstruction*, he admitted, "I do not for a moment doubt that my Negro descent and narrow group culture have in many cases predisposed me to interpret my facts too favorably for my race; but there is little danger of long misleading here, for the champions of the white folk are legion."[46] Du Bois carried his preoccupation with contemporary ideologies and issues, as well as his black bias, into his historical writing. He first combined them in *Black Reconstruction*. Like Rogers and Woodson, his loyalty to the race was never in doubt, but unlike them, Du Bois's writing also showed the definite influence of contemporary thought.

For Du Bois, Reconstruction represented a squandered opportunity; he saw it as "one of the most extraordinary experiments of Marxism that the world, before the Russian revolution, had seen." Far from being the villains or ignorant tools of Bowers' account, black men were the heroes of this noble experiment. They attempted to establish an "agrarian democracy" in the South, based upon a dictatorship of the proletariat. They were betrayed in this experiment by northern big business and by the poor whites of the South. During this brief period democracy had an opportunity to become a living reality, but, "Democracy died save in the hearts of black folk." Du Bois dramatized Reconstruction in simple, Manichean terms, as the clash of ideas between "abolition-democracy based on freedom, intelligence and power for all men" and "indus-

---

45. See for example, Du Bois, "The Wide, Wide World," New York *Amsterdam News*, August 12, 1931. See Du Bois's preface to *Black Folk, Then and Now*, vii–ix. This book, which will not be discussed in this chapter, elaborates the themes presented in *Black Reconstruction*, but imposes them upon both African and American history. It was essentially a more sophisticated version of Woodson's *The African Background Outlined*.

46. Du Bois, *Black Folk, Then and Now*, ix.

try for private profit directed by an autocracy determined at any price to amass wealth and power."[47]

Du Bois thought that the Reconstruction experiment, like the Russian Revolution, had its origins in the violence of civil war. Contrary to the passive role which most historians had assigned to Negroes in that conflict, Du Bois contended that they had consciously played *the* decisive part in its outcome. "From the very beginning," Du Bois contended, "the Negro occupied the center of the stage because of very simple physical reasons: the war was in the South and in the South were 3,953,740 black slaves and 261,918 free Negroes." What was to be the relation of this mass of "workers" to the war? "What the Negro did was to wait, look and listen and try to see where his interest lay." Du Bois employed the term *Negro* as if Negroes represented a single, monolithic force. He maintained that as soon as "the Negro" saw that the Confederacy was doubtful of victory, he realistically entered upon a "general strike" against slavery. He estimated that approximately 200,000 Negroes participated as Union soldiers, "whose evident ability to fight decided the war." Another 300,000 ran away from the plantations to work for the Union cause: "It was also true that this withdrawal and bestowal of his labor decided the war." Those who remained on the plantations consciously performed shoddy work to help undermine the southern economy.[48] Hence, the Negro did not just passively accept freedom; he actively and rationally fought for it, just as he would fight for the democratic social revolution which the war made possible.

Du Bois believed that the occupation of the vanquished South by federal troops enabled the radicals to impose their experiment in "proletarian dictatorship." The plans for the experiment were drawn up by men such as Charles Sumner and Thaddeus Stevens

47. W. E. B. Du Bois, *Black Reconstruction in America, 1860–1880* (New York: Harcourt, Brace & Co., 1935), 358, 345–47, 30, 182.
48. *Ibid.*, 57, 67, 57, 80.

who believed that "freedom in order to be free required a minimum of capital in addition to political rights and that this could be insured . . . only by some sort of dictatorship."[49] Curiously enough these democratic radicals were temporarily joined in the support of such a program by northern big business which feared the possibility that a rejuvenated planter aristocracy might impede its takeover of the South. As long as northern big business—Du Bois always wrote of it as if it also was a monolithic force—blessed it, the experiment would continue.

Du Bois thought that the most important fruit of this "understanding" between northern industry and abolition-democracy was the Freedmen's Bureau. In the Freedmen's Bureau, the United States started upon a "dictatorship by which the landowner and the capitalist were to be openly and deliberately curbed and which directed its efforts in the interest of a black and white labor class." "In its essence," concluded Du Bois, "the bureau was a dictatorship of the army over property for the benefit of labor." He thought that if the idea behind the Freedmen's Bureau had been permitted to fully develop, the freedmen and poor whites would have been able to hold the balance of political and economic power, and "as soon as political power was successfully delivered into the hands of these elements, the Federal government was to withdraw and full democracy ensue." But, unfortunately, the power employed to begin this dictatorship was the military arm of a government which was in the hands of "organized wealth"; and organized wealth had, after a few short years, accomplished its objective of economic domination of the South. It had come to an "agreement" with the southern employing class "that profit was most important."[50] Reconstruction was no longer expedient. Indeed, it was becoming dangerous.

All that remained was for the employing classes to convince

49. *Ibid.*, 185.   50. *Ibid.*, 219, 227, 345, 347.

white labor that "the degradation of Negro labor was more fundamental than the uplift of white labor." Naturally, this was not a
difficult task. Du Bois was especially critical of white labor because
he thought that the downfall of Reconstruction and the Negro was
contingent upon the betrayal of the poor whites. This betrayal was
not just a part of Reconstruction history, it was a worldwide phe-
nomenon. "Thus the majority of the world's laborers, by the insistence of white labor," wrote Du Bois, "become the basis of a system
of industry which ruined democracy and showed its perfect fruit
in World War and Depression."[51]

After presenting this overall interpretation of Reconstruction,
Du Bois went on to briefly examine it in each of the southern states.
Relying almost entirely on secondary sources, such as Taylor, and
Simkins and Woody, he demonstrated that, contrary to the interpretations of Burgess, and Dunning and Bowers, Negro legislators
were no worse, and generally better, than the white.[52] They were
often the men who most strongly supported the experiment.

In his typically romantic fashion, Du Bois concluded that Reconstruction was a failure for the black man, but "a splendid failure"
because it had not failed where it was expected to fail. "It was Ath-
anasius contra mundum, with back to the wall, outnumbered ten
to one, with all the wealth and all the opportunity, and all the world
against him. And only in his hands and heart the consciousness of
a great and just cause; fighting the battle of all the oppressed and
despised humanity of every race and color, against the massed hire-
lings of Religion, Science, Education, Law, and brute force."[53] Du
Bois's greatest hero was not a triumphant individual black man, but
"the Negro," and "the Negro" in the end was a black sacrificial
lamb. Unlike most Negro historians, Du Bois was less concerned
in *Black Reconstruction* with the building of black pride than he

51. *Ibid.*, 347, 30. 52. See for example, *ibid.*, 417, 425.
53. *Ibid.*, 708.

was with indicting American civilization. For ultimately the failure of Reconstruction was the failure of an entire nation's professed commitment to democratic ideals.[54]

Although Du Bois's book did not receive attention from the major historical journals, it did stir up controversy elsewhere. Most Negro historians received it favorably. Rayford Logan doubted the general strike thesis, but praised Du Bois's treatment of the black man. He was pleased that Du Bois at least made an attempt to apply Marx.[55] Charles H. Wesley heartily acclaimed Du Bois's "impartial" treatment of the Negro's role, practically ignoring Du Bois's Marxist interpretations.[56] Carter Woodson, however, merely commented that the book was "from Du Bois's point of view," and that *the* history of Reconstruction was yet to be written.[57]

The young radicals were uniformly critical. They generally ignored the value of Du Bois's attempt to give the black man a past he could use and value. Though conceding that the contemporary generation of Negro intellectuals probably owed more to Du Bois than to any other man, Abram Harris was very critical of the authenticity of Du Bois's new Marxist orientation. Himself a specialist in Marxist economics, Harris charged that Du Bois was "a racialist whose discovery of Marxism as a critical instrument has been too recent and sudden for it to discipline his mental processes or basically to change his social philosophy." He believed that Du Bois's attempt to blend his racial chauvinism with Marxism merely produced ideological confusion.[58] Ralph Bunche concurred in Harris' appraisal of Du Bois's confused thinking, commenting that "his

---

54. See Harding, "Beyond Chaos," 11–12.
55. Rayford Logan, "Review of Black Reconstruction," *Journal of Negro History*, XXI (January, 1936), 61–63.
56. Charles H. Wesley, "Propaganda and Historical Writing," *Opportunity*, XIII (August, 1935), 244–46, 254.
57. Woodson, *The African Background Outlined*, 303.
58. Abram Harris, "Reconstruction and the Negro," *New Republic*, VII (August, 1935), 367–68.

racialism appears to be a much too virulent breed to permit successful crossing with Marxism."[59]

Harris' white collaborator in the writing of *The Black Worker*,
Sterling Spero, was also amazed at the "strange intellectual marriage" between the racialist Du Bois and Karl Marx. He incredu-
lously observed, "This is the central thesis of 'Black Reconstruction.'
A proletarian dictatorship resting on the military forces of victo-
rious industrial capital!" However, Spero recovered long enough
to make perhaps the most objective criticism of *Black Reconstruction:* it would have been an important contribution to historical
literature if Du Bois had been content to demonstrate that the
Negro had, indeed, been an important participant in both the positive and the negative aspects of Reconstruction.[60]

Du Bois's attempt to impose a Marxist interpretation on American Negro history was less impressive than Richard Wright's use of
it in his *12 Million Black Voices: A Folk History of the Negro in the
United States.* Not generally considered a historian—he was much
more famous as a novelist and a Communist—Wright produced the
most provocative history written by any black man during the
depression.

Giving special emphasis to the great migration northward from
the farms to the cities, Wright offered an impressionistic version—
and it was more convincing probably because it was impressionistic
—of black folk, past and present. The book contained a series of
evocative photographs and Wright's narrative; the photographs
served as his documentary evidence. Relying heavily on sociological
data, Wright was concerned with revealing the quality of life of
these people and the vast forces which shaped it. In dramatizing
this, he was more concerned with white (especially upper-class)
oppression than with black achievement. Nowhere in the book will

59. Ralph Bunche, "Reconstruction Reinterpreted," *Journal of Negro Education,*
IV (October, 1935), 568.
60. Sterling Spero, "The Negro's Role," *The Nation* (July 24, 1935), 108–109.

the reader find the telling expression "as good as." Wright, unlike so many of the historians, had gotten beyond the comparative frame of mind and could tell the story on its own terms. He was definitely not pleading in the interests of the Negro middle class.

Wright generally employed the present tense in his history because the experiences of the black folk in the past continued as present reality. Like Charles S. Johnson, but unlike most Negro historians, Wright tended to see the past unfortunately living in the present.

The primary forces which molded the lives of the black folk in the South, according to Wright, were the soil and the "Lords of the Land." And after the machine had forced the black folk northward, the city of "steel and stone" and the "Bosses of the Buildings" came to have the dominant influence in their lives.

Life in the South was dominated by fear and violence. "Two streams of life flow through the South, a black stream and a white stream, and from day to day we live in the atmosphere of a war that never ends . . . when there are days of peace, it is a peace born of a victory over us; and when there is open violence, it is when we are trying to push back the encroachments of the Lords of the Land." The lords of the land used black slaves to subdue the poor whites and thus created an unnatural and often violent enmity between white and black workers. "And the irony of it is that both of us, the poor white and the poor black, are spoken of by the Lords of the Land as 'our men.' "[61]

And yet, in their relatively naïve state, the black folk of the rural South have found happiness within their own community, in their warm and "irreducibly human" relationships. These relationships, thought Wright, stood above the claims of law or property. "Our scale of values differs from that of the world from which we have been excluded; our shame is not its shame, and our love is not its

61. Richard Wright, *12 Million Black Voices: A Folk History of the Negro in the United States* (New York: The Viking Press, 1941), 46, 57, 16–17, 47.

love."[62] The black folk of the South were untainted by capitalistic culture.

But this simple, close-to-the-soil existence is jeopardized by a new force introduced by the lords of the land who have increasingly come under the influence of the bosses of the buildings. "Adding to our confusion is the gradual appearance of machines that can pick more cotton in one day than any ten of us. How can we win this race with death, when our thin blood is set against the potency of gasoline, when our weak flesh is pitted against the strength of steel, when our loose muscles must vie with the power of tractors?" The only answer seemed to be migration to the cities of the North. "Perhaps never in history," wrote Wright, "has a more utterly unprepared folk wanted to go to the city . . . we, who had known only relationships to people and not relationships to things." It is the "beginning of living on a new and terrifying plane of consciousness."[63]

In a brief paragraph Wright eloquently reconstructed the impact of the industrial city upon the migrating black folk: "It seems as though we are now living inside of a machine; days and events move with a hard reasoning of their own. We live amid swarms of people, yet there is a vast distance between people, a distance that words cannot bridge. No longer do our lives depend upon the soil, the sun, the rain, or the wind; we live by the grace of jobs and the brutal logic of jobs. We do not know this world, or what makes it move. In the South life was different; men spoke to you, cursed you, yelled at you, or killed you. The world moved by signs we knew. But here in the North cold forces hit you and push you. It is a world of things."[64] Wright observed the ambivalence that the black folk felt toward their new urban environment. They had escaped from the fearful realm of the lords of the land, but had encountered the strange new, impersonal machinelike city. They soon discover that

62. *Ibid.*, 61.   63. *Ibid.*, 49, 93, 99.
64. *Ibid.*, 100.

it is the bosses of the buildings who are the force which "makes it move." The bosses decree and exploit the black ghetto. Wright skillfully utilized the kitchenette as a symbol of the oppressive ghetto:

> The kitchenette is our prison, our death sentence without a trial, the new form of mob violence that assaults not only the lone individual, but all of us, in its ceaseless attacks.
> The kitchenette is the seed bed for scarlet fever, dysentery, typhoid, tuberculosis, gonorrhea, syphilis, pneumonia, and malnutrition.
> The kitchenette is the funnel through which our pulverized lives flow to ruin and death on the city pavements, at a profit.[65]

The bosses of the buildings are responsible for the kitchenettes, and like the lords of the land in the South, they have "so ordered the structure of the lives of both black and white that it is only through a heroic effort of will that either of us can cast off this spell of make-believe and see how artificial and man-made is this enmity between us, to see that our common lives are bound by a common cause." Speaking for the first generation of urban migrants, Wright concluded that "the city has beaten us; evaded us." But he held out some hope for the future. Just as E. Franklin Frazier had noted the rapid acculturation of second- and third-generation urban blacks, Wright observed that social barriers were not as firm in the flux of the city. Working-class unity was more a possibility. A few fortunate blacks, such as Wright himself, had discovered this already. "In this way we encountered for the first time in our lives the full effect of those forces that tended to reshape our folk consciousness, and a few of us stepped forth and accepted within the confines of our personalities the death of our old folk lives, an acceptance of a death that enabled us to cross class and racial lines, a death that made us free."[66]

Unlike most of the Negro historians, Wright did not look to the past for guidance. Though admitting that the past had its value in its own time and place, he was pleased to see black men "shed our

65. *Ibid.*, 106–107, 109.   66. *Ibid.*, 122, 136, 144.

folk swaddling clothes." He would not go as far as Frazier and ask the Negro to attempt to be a carbon copy of the twentieth-century white man. But if black men were to survive, they had to become a part of the twentieth century. Like other young radicals, he thought that this would be achieved through working-class unity.

Wright accomplished something which Du Bois attempted, but failed to do convincingly in *Black Reconstruction*. He went beyond the provincialism which had characterized Negro history. He told the story of the black folk in relation to broader forces which affected all men. This may have been possible for Wright because his objectives were quite different from those of most Negro historians. They were writing Negro history, while he was trying to escape from it. Wright did not have to prove that black men were equal to all other men because he took it for granted. Hence, Wright did not have to glorify the great men. He could depart from the Negro history tradition and write of the common folk.

Wright's impressionistic history fit most of the new criteria which Lawrence Reddick established in his thoughtful essay, "A New Interpretation for Negro History." Reddick would not go so far as to repudiate the venerable Carter Woodson and the other older men who dominated the profession, but he did call upon black historians to depart from their provinciality and their old "liberal" frame of reference which always regarded "Negro history" in terms of perpetual progress. Reddick also thought that too much attention had been given to the heroes and that "the historian may become more penetrating if he turns away a little more from the articulate professional classes to the welfare, feelings and thoughts of the common folk."[67]

During the depression era there were few, especially among the profession, who were willing to challenge the old guard Negro historians. A few, like Reddick, made respectful suggestions. And some, such as Doxey Wilkerson, a young assistant professor at

67. Reddick, "A New Interpretation for Negro History," 23, 26–27.

Howard, even challenged Woodson himself in a review of *The Story of the Negro Retold*. Wilkerson questioned "the appropriateness of an impassioned plea for historical objectivity in a text which, itself, so obviously negates that principle."[68]

But historical objectivity was perhaps an impossibility until the need for Negro history should disappear. None of the critics of Negro history appeared to be aware of the tragedy inherent in the mere fact that Carter Woodson felt compelled to say that the black man's history was as important as anybody else's. As long as black historians felt so compelled, "thinking black" would take precedence over so-called objectivity. Even many of the younger historians such as Charles Wesley, who wrote a reasonably objective monograph on the collapse of the Confederacy,[69] saw the need for Afro-America to "develop a reading public and channels of publication through which the truth from our point of view shall also have a hearing."[70]

68. Doxey Wilkerson, "A High School Text for Negro History," *Journal of Negro Education*, V (October, 1936), 628.
69. See Charles H. Wesley, *The Collapse of the Confederacy* (Washington, D.C.: Associated Publishers, Inc., 1937).
70. Charles H. Wesley, "Education and Propaganda," *Journal of Negro Education*, IV (April, 1935), 265.

V

The Old, the New, and the Newer Negro

The 1920s was the era of the so-called "New Negro" and the Harlem Renaissance. It was an exciting time for black writers, artists, and critics—an era, as Langston Hughes later observed, "when the Negro was in vogue."[1] Many critics, white and black, praised the art of young Negroes. White critics seemed most impressed with the "primitivism" they discovered in the works of black writers—and, indeed, the beating of tom-toms in black poetry became something of a cliché by the end of the decade. Many black critics, led by Alain Locke, applauded because the Negro artist was at last expressing pride in his own racial heritage—and, in doing so, was creating pride within the black community. During the 1920s only a few of the older generation of critics and those who expressed the sentiments of the black middle class were severely critical of the Renaissance. The New Negro's concern with "low life" offended their gentility.

1. Langston Hughes, *The Big Sea: An Autobiography* (New York: Alfred A. Knopf Co., 1940), 22. For analyses of the Harlem Renaissance, see Nathan Irvin Huggins, *Harlem Renaissance* (New York: Oxford University Press, 1971); Clare Bloodgood Crane, "Alain Locke and the Negro Renaissance" (Ph.D. dissertation, University of California, San Diego, 1971); S. P. Fullinwider, *The Mind and Mood of Black America: Twentieth-Century Thought* (Homewood, Ill.: Dorsey Press, 1969), 115–71; Gilbert Osofsky, *Harlem: The Making of a Ghetto* (New York and Evanston: Harper & Row, Publishers, 1966), 179–87; Robert A. Bone, *The Negro Novel in America* (2nd ed. rev.; New Haven and London: Yale University Press, 1965), 53–64; Harold Cruse, *The Crisis of the Negro Intellectual* (New York: William Morrow & Company, Inc., 1967), 22–53; and the entire issue of *Black World*, XX (November, 1970), which was devoted to a re-evaluation of the Renaissance.

But the voices of these genteel critics rapidly lost influence during the early 1930s, in part undermined by a group of younger writers and critics who were stridently critical of both the New Negro and the genteel mentality. In his bitterly satirical novel, *Infants of the Spring* (1932), Wallace Thurman—who had been among the New Negro group and who was to die at a tragically young age in 1934—wrote an unflattering obituary to the Renaissance. A few years later Richard Wright summed up the attitude of this younger group of critics toward both the genteel school of writers and many of the Renaissance writers when he wrote that their works were "prim and decorous ambassadors who went a-begging to white America. . . . They entered the Court of American Public Opinion dressed in the knee-pants of servility, curtsying to show that the Negro was not inferior, that he was human, and that he had a life comparable to that of other people. For the most part these artistic ambassadors were received as though they were French poodles who do clever tricks."[2] Wright and other young critics like Sterling Brown resented the fact that the genteel writers, in an effort to demonstrate the black man's humanity, had attempted to portray the black as a white man. These young critics also condemned many of the New Negro writers because they created black characters which just happened to fit the exotic stereotypes of white America during the 1920s. The characters of neither the genteel nor the New Negro writers possessed the universality and the reality which the young critics of the 1930s were desirous of stimulating. They did not see the need for proving the Negro's humanity; they assumed it. Nor during the harsh times of the depression could they find any relevance, any truth, in what they considered romantic primitivism. Their vehicle of expression was realism.

During the early 1930s the influence of the genteel critics was rapidly diminishing. Until at least the middle of the decade, how-

2. Richard Wright, "Blueprint for Negro Writing," *The New Challenge*, I (Fall, 1937), 53.

ever, they continued to exert the dominant influence in the Afro-American press and to hold the most prestigious positions in Negro universities. More often than not, critics writing for the black press attacked the recent emphasis by black writers on what they condescendingly termed "low life." While the white reviewer of the New York *Times* raved over the "pagan color" of Arna Bontemps' *God Sends Sunday,* a novel of low life in New Orleans and St. Louis,[3] Dewey R. Jones, book reviewer for the Chicago *Defender,* characterized the story as nothing more than "dirt."[4] Commenting on the same novel for the Norfolk *Journal and Guide,* Alice Dunbar-Nelson lamented that "a sour taste is left in the mouth after reading the novel. The characters are low, loose in morals, frivolous in principles, and in many instances even criminal." She conceded that "Bontemps, undoubtedly, has portrayed some conditions of Negro life, especially of the rural districts and customs of the South, but in my opinion Negro literature is not benefited thereby."[5] Negro literature had not benefitted because Bontemps had not made his characters conform to "acceptable" standards of beauty.

Aubery Bowser, who reviewed books for the New York *Amsterdam News,* believed that recent Negro writers had "gotten off on the wrong foot." Like the others, he was distressed because black writers now almost inevitably selected "the sickliest characters they can find." Bowser reflected the general attitude of his class of critics when he made a call for a romantic literature: "This is called the age of realism or naturalism in literature, and the Negro is not ready for it. An age of realism requires many preceding ages of epical, heroic, romantic literature. . . . All the white nations started in with their heroes and are just now coming around to their unheroic types. To put it plainly, a healthy, grown man can stand a few drinks of

---

3. Unsigned, "A Negro Jockey," New York *Times,* May 5, 1931.
4. Dewey R. Jones, "God Sends Sunday," Chicago *Defender,* August 8, 1931.
5. Alice Dunbar-Nelson, "Book Chat," Norfolk *Journal and Guide,* May 16, 1931. For a similar attitude, see also T. R. Poston, "New Book," Pittsburgh *Courier,* April 18, 1931.

whiskey, because his constitution has been built up against any in-roads they might make; but giving whiskey to a small child is quite another matter."[6] Bowser's comments were closely akin to those of the Negro history advocates. Such an attitude was antithetical to what the younger critics of the 1930s would propose.

The attitudes of these critics were very similar to those of W. E. B. Du Bois. In the pages of the *Crisis* he also condemned Bontemps' novel because none of the characters had any 'redeeming quali-ties."[7] He could not totally condemn Langston Hughes's *Not With-out Laughter* because, although "it touches dirt . . . it is not dirty and it ends with the upward note."[8] For Du Bois, these novels were not projecting the proper image of the Negro. As with history, Du Bois could never disassociate art from propaganda. "All art is pro-paganda," he wrote, "and without propaganda there is not true art."[9] He conceded, however, that in most cases propaganda could not be considered art.

For Du Bois the Catfish Row of Du Bose Heywood's *Porgy* lacked any value as propaganda or art because of its concern with low life. He was certain that the characters depicted by Heywood were in no sense typical American Negroes. He wanted instead, "the story of real, ordinary people, black and white." The "ordinary people" whom Du Bois wanted to see depicted, he found in Jessie Fauset's novel *Plum Bun*, an insipidly romantic dramatization of the black upper middle class. In explaining the reasons behind his admiration for the novel, Du Bois revealed the bias which made the young rad-icals skeptical of his self-proclaimed radicalism. "'Plum Bun,'" wrote Du Bois, "talks about the kind of American Negroes that I

6. Aubrey Bowser, "Book Review," New York *Amsterdam News*, February 13, 1929.
    7. W. E. B. Du Bois, "The Browsing Reader," *Crisis*, XL (September, 1931), 304.
    8. *Ibid.*, XXXIX (September, 1930), 321.
    9. W. E. B. Du Bois, "Dramatis Personae," *Crisis*, XXXVIII (May, 1930), 162.

know. I do not doubt the existence of the debauched tenth, but I cannot regard them as characteristic or typical."[10]

But Du Bois, as a literary critic, did not bear the brunt of the attack from younger critics. Instead, they leveled their scorn upon Benjamin Brawley, chairman of the English Department at Howard University. For them the term "Brawleyism" became synonymous with gentility, mediocrity, and race chauvinism. Interestingly enough, the most publicized attack on Brawley was launched by a white radical critic, Benjamin Stolberg, in the pages of *The Nation*. In his review of Brawley's book, *Negro Builders and Heroes*, Stolberg criticized his bourgeois bias, his racial chauvinism—"minority jingo"—and his "intellectual tawdriness."[11] Stolberg's pungent remarks brought a flood of defensive retorts from many black intellectuals, including William Pickens and Alain Locke.[12] But some of the younger critics received Stolberg's comments with gratitude. Loren Miller, a young man closely associated with the Communists, congratulated Stolberg "for saying some things that we younger Negro critics should have been saying." Miller attributed the paucity of sound criticism against Brawleyism to the "lack of organs to publish it; our journals are committed to Brawleyism."[13]

Miller was not quite right. There were several journals which were receptive to the younger radical critics, such as *Race, Challenge*, and *New Challenge*, all short lived, and two which were open to all opinions, the *Journal of Negro Education* and *Opportunity*.

10. W. E. B. Du Bois, "The Browsing Reader," *Crisis*, XXXVIII (April, 1929), 125. For a similarly laudatory review of Jessie Fauset's works by another of the genteel critics, see William Stanley Braithwaite, "The Novels of Jessie Fauset," *Opportunity*, XII (January, 1934), 24, 26–28. Braithwaite considered Fauset among the front rank of women novelists in America, the "Jane Austen of Negro literature." Braithwaite was wrong.

11. Benjamin Stolberg, "Minority Jingo," *The Nation*, October 23, 1937, p. 437.

12. See William Pickens, "Retort to Jingo Snobbery," *Crisis*, XLIV (December, 1937), 360; and Alain Locke, "Jingo, Counter-Jingo, and Us," *Opportunity*, XVI (January, 1938), 8.

13. Loren Miller, "Letters to the Editors: Brawleyism," *The Nation*, November 20, 1937, p. 571.

Nor was Stolberg the only man who had tilted with Brawleyism. The young black poet-critic, Sterling Brown, had long been engaged in such an effort.

Brown, who served under Brawley in the English Department at Howard, reviewed Brawley's books very critically, and in much the same terms that Stolberg employed. Brown was most disturbed, however, with his "academic gentility." Brawley's "critical generalizations," he wrote, "arise from a genteel, academic position. Professor Brawley tosses off debatable dogmas, but seldom adduces evidence. . . . Following Matthew Arnold, Professor Brawley recognizes poetry by using 'touchstones,' the test of the 'magic phrase.' . . . Unfortunately, these tell more about the critic than about the poetry."[14] Brawley could only weakly defend himself in replying to Brown's charges with the indignant remark that "I had supposed that reviewing in *Opportunity* was on a higher plane."[15]

Like most of his genteel colleagues, Brawley was strongly critical of the Harlem Renaissance. He considered its emphasis upon low life and the exotic as "one of the most brazen examples of salesmanship in the history of the United States." He was appalled by the emphasis on free verse rather than on standard literary forms. He condemned jazz and all other impulses which "annihilate form." Moreover, he felt threatened because "in the face of this, culture or reticence meant nothing." He was pleased that the stock market crash had brought the passing of the flighty Renaissance. "The day of inflation, of extravagance, of sensationalism is gone, and we must now come back to earth and to a truer sense of values."[16] Brawley never comprehended the futility of attempting to come back.

14. Sterling Brown, "The Literary Scene," *Opportunity*, XV (July, 1937), 216. See also Sterling Brown, "Book Reviews," *Opportunity*, XV (September, 1937), 280–81.
15. Benjamin Brawley, "Correspondence," *Opportunity*, XV (August, 1937), 248.
16. Benjamin Brawley, "The Promise of Negro Literature," *Journal of Negro History*, XIX (January, 1934), 54–56.

In addition to his role as a literary critic, Brawley was also a historian in the tradition of Negro historians. Most of his attempts at writing history appeared before the 1930s, and, as Stolberg commented, "each of Brawley's books is a rewrite of his last."[17] Brawley's histories were oriented toward heroes and successful men of color. Always, he told the story of the Negro in terms of steady advance.[18] The same criteria held true with his work in literature.

His two most important productions in the field of literary criticism during the 1930s were *Paul Laurence Dunbar: Poet of His People* (1936) and *The Negro Genius: A New Appraisal of the Achievement of the American Negro in Literature and the Fine Arts* (1937). In both books he promised more than he could deliver. In his biography of Dunbar, Brawley wanted to study the poet in relation to the age in which he lived. He also wanted to emphasize Dunbar's uniqueness within that context. He did not really attempt the first, and was largely unsuccessful in the second. As Sterling Brown accurately observed, Brawley's account came "uncomfortably close to Horatio Alger. What Dunbar was like as a person, essentially, escapes even more careful reading."[19] Brawley saw Dunbar's life as a success story.[20] As for Dunbar's prose and poetry, Brawley could do little but applaud. Brawley praised Dunbar as a writer for being in line with his times—for not speaking out. (Brown found this intolerable because "the greater writers often confront their times with the truth, however unpalatable."[21] As a critic, Brawley was uncritical.[22]

The Negro Genius was essentially an updating of Brawley's 1918

17. Stolberg, "Minority Jingo," 437.
18. See for example, Benjamin Brawley, *Negro Builders and Heroes* (Chapel Hill: University of North Carolina Press, 1937); and his *A Short History of the American Negro* (3rd ed. rev.; New York: The Macmillan Co., 1931).
19. Brown, "The Literary Scene," 216.
20. For a capsulized version of Brawley's study of Dunbar, see Chapter 24 of his *Negro Heroes and Builders*, 158–66.
21. Brown, "The Literary Scene," 217.
22. Alain Locke, "God Save Reality!" *Opportunity*, XV (February, 1937), 42.

study, *The Negro in Literature and Art*. In addition to some new material on recent writers, Brawley expanded the introductory chapter, "The Negro Genius," an attempt to define "Negro genius." He explained that "behind the achievement of the race is temperament, and that of the Negro has been shown to be pre-eminently imaginative and sensuous." Ignoring contemporary anthropology, he felt that every race had its own peculiar genius, and that the Negro was destined to achieve his greatest heights in the arts. The Negro's artistic temperament "would be seen first of all," he wrote "in the folklore."[23] In the chapters that followed, Brawley was little concerned with folklore and made no attempt to examine its influence on more recent writers. He set forth the interesting theory that "no people can rise to the heights of art until it has passed through suffering," and offered the Russians as a case in point. Considering the Afro-American's past, Brawley concluded that "the same future beckons the Negro."[24] This is another interesting theme which, apart from his success-in-the-face-of-overwhelming-odds biographies, he failed to develop in the body of the book.

Finally, Brawley pronounced a racialist thesis which made younger critics like Brown furious.[25] Brawley asserted that "such distinction as the Negro has won in the arts is due primarily to the black rather than the mixed elements in the race." He conceded that people of mixed ancestry had been the college presidents, the administrators, and the government employees, "but the blacks are the singers and seers." He claimed that black slaves had produced the spirituals, while "modern composers of a lighter hue transcribe them." Modern authors had reproduced in verse the sermons of the old black preachers, but they would hardly be capable of preaching

23. Benjamin Brawley, *The Negro Genius* (New York: Dodd, Mead & Co., 1937), 2.

24. *Ibid.*, 6. This idea also appeared in Brawley's "The Promise of Negro Literature," 57–58.

25. See Brown, "Book Reviews," *Opportunity*, XV (September, 1937), 280–81.

them. "In other words," he concluded, "the mixed element in the race may represent the Negro's talent, but it is upon the black element that he must rely for his genius."[26] Brawley, who could probably have passed as white, defended this provocative thesis by ignoring it in his critical study. He wrote about the talent, and not the so-called genius of the race; and but a few black faces appeared among this group. The body of the book was essentially the same conventional treatment of the same stock figures—such as Phillis Wheatley, Dunbar, et al.—whom Brawley had written about so many times over the past twenty years.

When he came to the contemporary scene, he chastised Countee Cullen for not wanting to be considered a Negro poet. He praised the poetry of Claude McKay, but thought that his low-life fiction was "metal of a baser hue." McKay had definitely sold out to the white public. He accused the "Hughes school," which condemned the old bourgeois stereotypes, of creating but another stereotype— the low-life stereotype. He was unhappy with all of the new realists because of their "preference for sordid, unpleasant, or forbidden themes." Although he was critical of the "Hughes school," he praised Langston Hughes as a poet for "employing the racial idea."[27] He ignored the fact that Hughes had also written considerable radical, class-oriented poetry. He was at least consistent in this; in *Negro Builders and Heroes* he had ignored A. Philip Randolph and other "radical" labor leaders. The realists and those involved in labor struggles were little concerned with beauty. Brawley sought beauty and wanted to "get back." In doing so he was forced to close his eyes to the present.

Alain Locke, Brawley's colleague at Howard, shared some of his attitudes. But Locke always made an attempt to keep an open mind to contemporary trends in literature and art. Although he never completely accepted the artistic orientation of the young realists of

26. Brawley, *The Negro Genius*, 8–9.   27. *Ibid.*, 235–37, 224, 14, 233, 247.

the 1930s, he at least tried to understand them. In fact, he gave the realists valuable support when the genteel critics were condemning them.

Locke was a professor of philosophy at Howard. Born into an upper-class Philadelphia family in 1886, he was a Harvard Ph.D. (1918) and had the distinction of being the first Negro Rhodes scholar. But he gained his greatest fame as editor of *The New Negro* (1925) and as the chief publicist of the New Negro movement.[28]

In *The New Negro* Locke praised the accomplishments of young Negro writers and artists and what he thought was their attempt to find a new group soul, a true race consciousness, and a "fresh spiritual and cultural focusing." In light of what he saw, he was optimistic enough to proclaim that "this deep feeling of race is at present the mainspring of Negro life."[29] Above all, he was pleased because they had found beauty in themselves, in their "instinctive love and pride of race."[30] Beauty, for Locke, as for Brawley, was the ultimate goal of the artist.

Some of the Renaissance writers were not always reciprocal in their appreciation of Locke. In his *Infants of the Spring*, Wallace Thurman caricatured Locke as a pretentious, romantic racialist. In the person of Dr. A. L. Parkes, Locke was presented at one of the gatherings of the Harlem literati as "a mother hen clucking at her chicks."[31] In his autobiography, Claude McKay, who thought that

28. For a more comprehensive analysis of Locke, see Crane, "Alain Locke and the Negro Renaissance." Also see Fullinwider, *Mind and Mood of Black America*, 115–22; Eugene Holmes, "The Legacy of Alain Locke," in John H. Clark (ed.), *Harlem: A Community in Transition* (New York: Citadel Press, 1964), 43–56; Eugene Holmes, "Alain Locke—Philosopher, Critic, Spokesman," *Journal of Philosophy*, LIV (February 28, 1957), 113–18; and Horace Kallen, "Alain Locke and Cultural Pluralism," *Journal of Philosophy*, LIV (February 28, 1957), 119–26.

29. Alain Locke, *The New Negro: An Interpretation* (New York: A. & C. Boni, 1925), 11. For a similar attitude expressed during the 1930s, see "Alain Locke Sees New Race Spirit as Culture Develops," Philadelphia *Tribune*, April 14, 1932. Nathan I. Huggins, *Harlem Renaissance* (New York: Oxford University Press, 1971), 56–60.

30. Locke, *The New Negro*, 52–53. Huggins, *Harlem Renaissance*, 202.

31. Wallace Thurmond, *Infants of the Spring* (New York: The Macaulay Co.,

the idea of a New Negro school of writers was preposterous and who had long been feuding with Locke, described him as "a perfect symbol of the Aframerican rococo in his personality as much as in his prose style." As a critic, McKay thought that Locke's artistic outlook was reactionary "due to its effete European academic quality."[32] While there was some truth in both observations, Thurman and McKay were unfair. They made no provision for Locke's sincere and sometimes successful efforts to understand them.

Locke carried many of his Renaissance attitudes with him into the depression era. Some of them bore close resemblance to those of the genteel critics. Like Brawley, Locke asserted that "the main line of Negro development must necessarily be artistic, cultural, moral and spiritual."[33] He thought that these characteristics were generally lacking "in a practical and efficient but emotionally sterile land."[34] Although he often sounded like Brawley when he wrote of "race genius," he did not believe that it was an inherent racial trait, but that it was environmentally induced. Nor did he believe in the idea of African cultural survivals. Whatever its origin, he prophesied that as this "race genius" matured and gained momentum, the Negro might find a new role in American life "as an artist class, as a social re-agent, and as a spiritual leaven."[35] A cultural pluralist, Locke believed that the "artistic, cultural, moral and spiritual" qualities of black America could harmoniously complement and perhaps even beneficially blend with the "practical and

---

1932), 233–35. Not surprisingly, Locke panned the novel in his review of it. See Alain Locke, "Black Truth and Black Beauty," *Opportunity*, XI (January, 1933), 16.

32. Claude McKay, *A Long Way from Home* (New York: Lee, Furman, Inc., 1937), 312–14. Locke also bitterly attacked this book for its lack of race loyalty in his review, "Spiritual Truancy," *New Challenge*, I (Fall, 1937), 81–85. See Crane, "Alain Locke and the Negro Renaissance," 129–32, for a discussion of this feud.

33. Alain Locke, "Negro Contributions to America," *The World Tomorrow*, XII (June, 1929), 257.

34. "Status of the Negro on Ascent—Locke," Pittsburgh *Courier*, September 19, 1931.

35. Locke, "Negro Contributions to America," 257. For a discussion of Locke's environmentalism and denial of African cultural survivals, see Crane, "Alain Locke and the Negro Renaissance," 119–23.

efficient" attributes of white America.[36] For the present, the all-important prerequisite to this cultural reciprocity would be the perfection of the race's "genius."

Locke assumed that the great suffering of the race in this land was one of the principal motivating factors in the development of this race genius. Through it "the Negro has been made the most sensitive spiritual medium in the land."[37] Even after he had accepted the "saving grace of realism," Locke always thought that Negro writers should reveal what he called the "spiritual essences" of Negro life. It was just this preoccupation with the search for vague spiritual values and Locke's inclination to romanticize such things as suffering that brought the scorn of many of the younger writers.

In addition to regenerating America—both black and white—Locke thought that the Negro artist had a primary role in the advance of the race. Like so many others among the older group of critics, he thought that the artistic success of blacks would bring about a favorable re-evaluation of the Negro by white Americans, "beginning, of course, with the cultured minority, but spreading gradually through the whole body of public opinion." In this his ideas bore rather close resemblance to those which many of the Negro historians imposed upon their craft.[38]

Locke published several books during the 1930s, including *The Negro and His Music* (1936) and *Negro Art: Past and Present* (1936), in which he, unlike Brawley, gave consideration to the in-

36. Alain Locke, "The Contribution of Race to Culture," *The Student World* (October, 1930), 349–53; and Crane, "Alain Locke and the Negro Renaissance," 16–21.

37. Locke, "Status of the Negro on Ascent." S. P. Fullinwider thoughtfully develops the concept of suffering among many of the older intellectuals and relates it to the Christ-like myth. See his *Mind and Mood of Black America*, especially Chapters I and II.

38. Locke, "Status of the Negro on Ascent." See Crane, "Alain Locke and the Negro Renaissance," viii; and Vincent Harding, "Beyond Chaos, Black History and the Search for the New Land," Black Paper No. 2 (Atlanta: Institute for the Black World, 1970), 6–8.

fluence of the folk upon Negro culture. But Locke's most significant efforts as a critic were probably his annual reviews in *Opportunity* of the advance of literature by and about Negroes. In these essays Locke demonstrated just how far he had moved from his Renaissance ideas and simultaneously how much he was still a captive of them.

Throughout the decade of the 1930s Locke alternated between a defense of the Renaissance and an admission of its failings. As early as 1929, he felt that it perhaps had been a fad,[39] and by 1931 he conceded that "the much exploited Negro renaissance was after all a product of the expansive period we are now willing to call the period of inflation and overproduction." But he did not consider this a cause for gloom. A perpetual optimist, Locke proclaimed in his typically hyperbolic manner: " 'Let us rejoice and be exceedingly glad.' The second and truly sound phase of the cultural development of the Negro in American literature and art cannot begin without a collapse of the boom, a change to more responsible and devoted leadership, a revision of basic values, and along with a penitential purgation of the spirit, a wholesale expulsion of the moneychangers from the temple of art."[40] He considered the present period to be the Reformation which would reinforce the achievements of the Renaissance.[41] He felt that the principal fault of the New Negro movement thus far had been its lack of any deep realization of "what was truly Negro," and what was merely superficially characteristic.[42] Just as he had during the Renaissance, Locke would spend the rest of the decade encouraging Negro writers to achieve this realization. But his advice was always vague because he never really defined "what was truly Negro."

39. Alain Locke, "1928: A Retrospective Review," *Opportunity*, VII (January, 1929), 8.
40. Alain Locke, "This Year of Grace," *Opportunity*, IX (February, 1931), 48.
41. *Ibid.*, 51. See also "Harlem: Dark Weather-Vane," *Survey Graphic*, XXV (August, 1936), 457; and "The Negro: 'New' and Newer," *Opportunity*, XVII (January, 1939), 6.
42. Locke, "This Year of Grace," 48.

An example of vagueness can be seen in his review of Langston Hughes's *Not Without Laughter*. Unlike many of the genteel critics who had been offended by its low-life subject matter, Locke was pleased because "its style palpitates with the real spiritual essences of Negro life."[43] But he failed to explain what these "essences" were.

During the early years of the decade Locke reoriented himself to some extent. He continued to think of the period in terms of a reformation following a renaissance—all part of one, long continuum. He continued to see racial consciousness as the basic ingredient for black writers.[44] But like many of the younger writers he also began to put more emphasis on the value of a broader perspective. Noting the seriousness of the times, he observed that the race's problems could not really be solved without reference to "other more fundamental social, political and economic problems of our day."[45] He asked black writers to look "beyond the narrow field of Negro life itself for our most significant explanations and more basic causes."[46] He was calling upon Negro writers to make themselves universally relevant.

And yet, in the same review Locke gave evidence that he was still seeking his old Renaissance goals. He saw in recent literature more of the "bitter tang and tonic of the Reformation than the sweetness and light of a Renaissance." He concluded that it was probably necessary to seek "the sober, painful truth before we can find the beauty we set out to capture." Sweetness, light, beauty, and truth remained Locke's principal artistic goals. He found the current association of truth and ugliness as necessary, but temporary. Truth and beauty, the goals of the old Renaissance, would someday be fused together. "In the end," he wrote, "we shall

43. *Ibid.*, 49.
44. See Alain Locke, "The Saving Grace of Realism," *Opportunity*, XII (January, 1934), 8.
45. Alain Locke, "We Turn to Prose," *Opportunity*, X (February, 1932), 41. See also Locke, "Black Truth and Black Beauty," 15, 17; and Alain Locke, "Deep River: Deeper Sea," *Opportunity*, 14 (January, 1936), 7.
46. Locke, "Black Truth and Black Beauty," 17.

achieve the promise that was so inspiring in the first flush of the Negro awakening,—a black beauty that is truth,—a Negro truth that is purely art."[47] But again he was vague.

As he advanced further into the 1930s, Locke gave increasing support to realism in literature, although his conception of it always remained somewhat vague. In 1932 he had lavishly praised Jessie Fauset's ultra-romantic novel of black middle-class life, *The Chinaberry Tree,* as a "mature" expression, "one of the accomplishments of Negro fiction."[48] But by 1934, he criticized Miss Fauset's irrelevance, noting that "the style is too mid-Victorian for moving power today, and the point of view falls into the sentimental hazard." Meanwhile, he was praising Claude McKay's novel of peasant life in Jamaica, *Banana Bottom,* and Sterling Brown's realistic poems about black American peasants in *Southern Road.*[49] Unlike the genteel critics, Locke was not ashamed of the folk heritage. Indeed, he had consistently encouraged the exploration and dramatization of it since the earliest days of the Renaissance.

Although he noted the obvious possibilities for black writers to explore this folk background within the context of the currently popular proletarian art,[50] Locke was generally critical of proletarian writers because they were more concerned with propaganda than with art. He admitted the necessity for propaganda, but had always been critical whenever it took precedence. He disliked proletarian poetry because it was "drab, prosy and inartistic, as though the regard for style were a bourgeois taint and an act of social treason."[51]

Locke, however, saw one positive aspect to proletarian art's impact upon the black writer: it was providing him with a more uni-

47. *Ibid.,* 14. See also "Deep River: Deeper Sea," 7.

48. Locke, "We Turn to Prose," 43. For an analysis of Locke's conception of realism, see Crane, "Alain Locke and the Negro Renaissance," 111–12.

49. Locke, "The Saving Grace of Realism," 9; Locke, "Black Truth and Black Beauty," 14, 16–17.

50. See Locke's favorable comments on the play "Stevedore," in "The Eleventh Hour of Nordicism," *Opportunity,* XIII (January, 1935), 12.

51. Alain Locke, "Propaganda—or Poetry?" *Race,* I (Summer, 1936), 73.

versal perspective. Hence, with some ambivalence he observed in his 1936 review that "our art is again turning prosaic, partisan, and propagandistic, but this time not in behalf of striving, strident racialism, but rather in a protestant and belligerent universalism of social analysis and protest. In a word, our art is going proletarian." He went on to warn that "those who hope for the eventual golden mean of truth with beauty must wait patiently,—and perhaps, long. Just now, all the slime and hidden secrets of the river are shouldered up on the hard, gritty sand bars and relentlessly exposed to view." [52]

In calling for the Negro writer to employ a universal perspective, Locke was most definitely not advising him to drop his racial perspective. He wished rather to see the two blended together. But in the final analysis, "any larger social vision must be generated from within the Negro's race consciousness, like the adding of another dimension to this necessary plane of his experience." [53] As in his Renaissance criticism, Lock still gave precedence to race.

While Locke joined the young critics in attacking Brawley, he defended "minority-jingo" because it was "counter-jingo." "The real jingo," he reminded Stolberg, "is majority jingo and there lies the original sin." Locke regretted the fact that so "much of the cultural racialism of the 'New Negro' movement was choked in shallow cultural soil by the cheap weeds of group flattery, vainglory and escapist emotionalism." But he concluded, "That does not invalidate all racialism." [54]

Locke's increasing disillusionment with the achievements of the Renaissance was eventually replaced by his conviction that the young realists of the 1930s were actually "realizing more deeply the original aims of what was too poetically and glibly styled 'The Negro Renaissance.'" He disagreed with the "*enfants terribles* of today's youth movement," like Richard Wright, who thought of

52. Locke, "Deep River: Deeper Sea," 7.
53. Locke, "Propaganda—or Poetry?" 71.
54. Locke, "Jingo, Counter-Jingo and Us," 8–9, 11.

themselves as a counter-movement against the Renaissance. "These 'bright young people' to the contrary, it is my conviction that . . . the 'New Negro' movement is just coming into its own."[55]

To an extent, Locke was correct. The young realists had seized upon what had been the "low-life" and folk themes of the twenties and developed them much more effectively than the New Negro writers had. But they had employed a stark realism to do so, and Locke was never quite comfortable with this. As late as 1940, while supporting realism, he was still encouraging the development of a "poetic realism." He wanted a realism with beauty. Significantly, when Locke reviewed Richard Wright's *Native Son* in 1941, he praised it effusively; but he praised it more for its social than its artistic value. "Its bold warnings and its clear lessons, temporarily overshadow its artistic significance."[56] There was truth, but no beauty, in *Native Son*.

James Weldon Johnson was another who had been one of the most prominent boosters of the New Negro movement of the 1920s. Unlike Locke, however, Johnson did not harp on the importance of searching for beauty or vague spiritual values. And Johnson was even more vehement than Locke in his defense of the New Negro's choice of low-life subject matter. He thought there was a great deal of snobbishness in terming the less literate and less sophisticated classes of Negroes as "lower." "At least as literary material," he wrote, "they are higher. They have greater dramatic and artistic potentialities for the writer than the so-called higher classes. . . . It takes nothing less than supreme genius to make middle-class society, black or white, interesting—to say nothing of making it dramatic." Johnson praised those writers who attempted "to make

55. *Ibid.*, 9; Locke, "The Negro: 'New' and Newer," 4–5. See also Locke's comments to the 1937 National Negro Congress in "Cultural Session," *1937—National Negro Congress Official Proceedings*, pages unnumbered.
56. Alain Locke, "Dry Fields and Green Pastures," *Opportunity*, XVIII (January, 1940), 4–5; and his "Of Native Sons: Real and Otherwise," *Opportunity*, XIX (January, 1941), 4–5.

those masses articulate." Although his production as a literary critic declined markedly during the 1930s, he continued to advocate an emphasis upon the black masses and the folklore which derived from them.[57]

Johnson resented the restrictions placed upon the black writer by his double audience. If a black writer wanted to achieve financial success, he was forced to conform to the stereotyped conventions of his white audience. But if he did this he ran the risk of being labeled a traitor by his own community. And often enough, even if he attempted an honest, but perhaps critical portrayal of Negro American life—something the genteel critics called "showing the race in a bad light"—he was savagely rebuked. Johnson cleverly noted that Negroes did not resent criticisms from their preachers, "but these criticisms are not for the printed page. They are not for the ears or eyes of white America." Johnson had been one of the first to criticize the advocates of a stereotyped "*nice* literature."[58]

As he had with history, Johnson regularly urged the use of literature as a weapon for the advancement of the race. He had come to believe that the Negro's situation was becoming less a matter of dealing with what the Negro actually was and more a matter of dealing with what America thought he was.[59] Repeatedly, he advised that "just as these stereotypes were molded and circulated and perpetuated by literary and artistic processes, they must be broken up and replaced through similar means."[60] Johnson was not calling for Negro artists to create yet another stereotype to counter

57. James Weldon Johnson, "Negro Authors and White Publishers," *Crisis,* XXXVIII (July, 1929), 229; his *Black Manhattan* (New York: Alfred A. Knopf Co., 1930), 263; and his *Along This Way: The Autobiography of James Weldon Johnson* (New York: The Viking Press, 1933), 380–81.
58. James Weldon Johnson, "The Dilemma of the Negro Author," *American Mercury,* XV (December, 1928), 480.
59. James Weldon Johnson, "Race Prejudice and the Negro Artist," *Harper's Magazine,* CLVII (November, 1928), 775.
60. James Weldon Johnson, *Negro Americans, What Now?* (New York: Viking Press, 1934), 92–93. See also "Race Prejudice and the Negro Artist," 769, 775–76; and *Black Manhattan,* 283.

the already existing ones. Quite to the contrary, they "need not be propagandists; they need only be sincere artists."[61]

Johnson, like Locke, wanted black writers to strive for the universal in their art. And like Locke, he thought that black writers could best interpret universal themes by dramatizing their racial experience. Unlike Locke, however, Johnson did not advance this idea because he thought black writers possessed some vague and unique race spirit. Johnson was more realistic. In commenting on black poets, he did not want to criticize arbitrarily all the poetry not stimulated by a sense of race, but, quite simply, he thought that the best poetry written by black men up to that time had been inspired by the racial situation in America. All of this, he concluded, merely confirmed the axiom that "an artist accomplishes his best when working at his best with the material he knows best. And up to this time, at least, 'race' is perforce the thing the American Negro poet knows best."[62]

During the 1920s, Johnson's had been the most important voice supporting the artistic exploration of the Negro's folk heritage. Late in the twenties, the voice of the young poet-critic, Sterling Brown, joined Johnson's and became preeminent in the 1930s. Perhaps the leading Negro literary critic of the period, Brown was outraged by the manner in which the dominant literary tradition had distorted the Negro folk heritage into a caricatured stereotype. In contrast to the social scientists who wanted to escape from the folk heritage, he asked black writers to rediscover this heritage and to dramatize it truthfully.

Besides his duties at Howard, Brown, who was an authority on Negro folklore and culture, also served as directing editor of Negro materials for the Federal Writers' Project in Washington, D.C. He was the most prolific writer among the Negro critics of the 1930s.

61. James Weldon Johnson, Foreword, *Challenge: A Literary Monthly*, I (March, 1934), 2.
62. James Weldon Johnson, Preface to the Revised Edition, *The Book of American Negro Poetry* (2nd ed. rev.; New York: Harcourt, Brace & Co., 1931), 7.

In addition to his poetic works, he wrote many critical essays for leading journals and a monthly literary review for *Opportunity*. His two books on the Negro in American literature, both published in 1936, were the most competent studies yet produced.[63] Brown also served as a co-editor of *The Negro Caravan*, the most intelligent and comprehensive of the many anthologies of Negro writers which had appeared.

Brown liked to use analogies of how other "submerged groups" reacted to literary exploitation by the dominant groups. He noted that "one of the by-products of exploitation is the development in literature of a stereotyped character of the exploited, which guards the equanimity of the 'superiors' and influences even the 'inferiors' when they are unwary." Thus, just as the image of Sambo evolved in the United States, the image of Paddy, the happy Irishman, took root in eighteenth- and nineteenth-century England. Brown thought that the manner in which Irish writers reacted to such treatment was worthy of study by Afro-American writers.

Such writers as Yeats and Synge, Brown observed, worked under the assumption that "Ireland, a country largely of peasants, needed to have its peasantry understood rather than caricatured, explored rather than exploited." Many of these writers were misunderstood by their own countrymen because they refused to create plaster-of-paris saints to counter the English stereotypes. But they believed that the creation of an original literature was more their calling than the creation of propaganda. In the end, Brown concluded, they proved successful because they touched upon the universality of experience within their provincial themes. The world was forced

---

63. See Sterling Brown, *Negro Poetry and Drama* (Washington, D.C.: The Associates in Negro Folk Education, 1936); and his *The Negro in American Fiction* (Washington, D.C.: The Associates in Negro Folk Education, 1936). Two studies published by other young writers were: Nick Aaron Ford, *The Contemporary Negro Novel* (Boston: Meador, 1936); and J. Saunders Redding, *To Make a Poet Black* (Chapel Hill: University of North Carolina Press, 1939). Neither Ford nor Redding published much apart from these two books during the 1930s.

to see the Irish as people with the same triumphs, blunders, farces, and tragedies as the rest of humanity. Sadly, Brown added, "It is one of life's ironies that this humanity ever had to be pointed out."[64]

Like Johnson, Brown attacked both those whites who exploited the stereotype and those genteel blacks who, perhaps because of it, were ashamed of their true folk heritage. He pointed out that prominent white writers, from James Fenimore Cooper and Edgar Allan Poe right down to the currently popular Octavus Roy Cohen and Roark Bradford, thought that they knew *the* Negro. But besides the fact that *the* Negro was a sociological mirage, Brown observed that such "generalizations about *the* Negro remain a far better analysis of a white man than of the Negro."[65]

Brown was critical of anyone who dealt in stereotypes, whether they were hostile or friendly toward the Negro. An example of this was his review of the "friendly" Fannie Hurst's novel, *Imitation of Life,* which was made into a popular motion picture. Brown sarcastically asked: "Can one reader be forgiven, if during such passages, there runs into his mind something unmistakably like a wild horse laugh?"[66] In an indignant and condescending letter to the editor of *Opportunity,* Miss Hurst took Brown to task for being "ungrateful."[67] In his reply, after patiently re-examining the racial stereotypes in her book, Brown quietly concluded, "I cannot imagine what in the world I have to be grateful for."[68]

Brown was likewise critical of the Harlem Renaissance because

64. Sterling Brown, "A Literary Parallel," *Opportunity,* X (May, 1932), 152–53. See also Sterling Brown, "Negro Character as Seen by White Authors," *Journal of Negro Education,* II (January, 1933), 180–201.

65. Brown, "Negro Character as Seen by White Authors," 180–81. This essay was the most devastating attack on racial stereotypes to appear during the 1930s.

66. Sterling Brown, "Imitation of Life: Once a Pancake," *Opportunity,* XIII (March, 1935), 87.

67. Fannie Hurst, letter to the editor, *Opportunity,* XIII (April, 1935), 121.

68. "Mr. Sterling A. Brown," *Opportunity,* XIII (April, 1935), 121–22. The controversy continued into the May issue of the magazine. See "Correspondence," *Opportunity,* XIII (May, 1935), 153.

it too often merely exchanged one stereotype for another. "The cabin was exchanged for the cabaret," he wrote, "but Negroes were still described as 'creatures of joy.'" More important, at least for a man writing during the socially troubled 1930s, was the fact that the Renaissance writers ignored "all of these seeds that bore such bitter fruit in the Harlem riot" of 1935.[69]

Brown was equally unrelenting in his attacks on genteel critics like Brawley and "those among us whose gods are the gods of Babbitry." While these critics were condemning the low life of Hughes's *Not Without Laughter* and Bontemps' *God Sends Sunday,* Brown heartily praised these writers for their sympathetic identification with the black folk. Brown pointed out several fallacies in the criticism of the genteel group. He thought that they looked upon all works concerning Negroes as if they were sociological documents intended as representations of the whole race. To counter this they insisted that all works must be idealistic propaganda. Hence they were afraid of realism which they were incapable of accepting as real. Finally, Brown thought that they were irrelevant because they criticized from the point of view of bourgeois America. He lamented that "if these standards of criticism are perpetuated, and our authors are forced to heed them, we thereby dwarf their stature as interpreters."[70]

In reply to the genteel point of view, Brown observed that not all French women were like Emma Bovary though *Madame Bovary* was a great work of art, nor were all Russians like Vronsky, yet *Anna Karenina* was also a great book. Hence, wrote Brown, "books about us may not be true of all of us; but that has nothing to do with their worth."[71] He would be one of the few black critics who

---

69. Brown, *The Negro in American Fiction,* 148–49.
70. Sterling Brown, "Our Book Shelf," *Opportunity,* VII (May, 1929), 161–62; "Our Book Shelf: Not Without Laughter," *Opportunity,* VIII (September, 1930), 279–80; "Our Book Shelf: God Sends Sunday," *Opportunity,* IX (June, 1931), 188; and "Our Literary Audience," *Opportunity,* VIII (February, 1930), 43.
71. Brown, "Our Literary Audience," 44.

by 1940 could accept Richard Wright's characterization of the "bad nigger," Bigger Thomas, with some equanimity.[72]

Brown admitted that propaganda should be counter-checked by propaganda; but he thought it should be found in newspapers and books expressly propagandistic. He believed that the artist's major concern should be with truth: "Propaganda, however legitimate, can speak no louder than the truth. Such a cause as ours needs no dressing up." Like Johnson, he resented the fact that genteel critics thought of the folk—the black masses—as low, and felt that the only fit subjects for literature were the "better" classes of Negroes. "It is sadly significant," he wrote, "that by 'best' Negroes, these idealists mean generally the upper reaches of society; i.e., those with money." Wryly, he noted that if such an economic hierarchy held true in literature, "it would rule out most of the Nobel prize winners."[73] Brown was not demanding that all black writers limit themselves to folk themes; rather they should be free to deal with whatever themes to which they, as individual artists, could give significant interpretation.

Brown thought that in their desire to get away from the masses, the genteel writers were seeking to escape from reality. The crime, squalor, and ugliness in the lives of the black masses were reality; and to ignore reality in such perilous times, Brown thought foolhardy. He thought that given the times, if a writer ignored social realism his work would be irrelevant.[74]

Apart from the pressure of hard times, Brown thought that there was another reason for the increasing popularity of realism among young black writers. Older critics thought that these writers were

72. See Brown's review of *Native Son*, "Insight, Courage and Craftsmanship," *Opportunity*, XVIII (June, 1940), 185–86.
73. Brown, "Our Literary Audience," 43, 44. See also Brown's "The Negro Author and His Publisher," *Quarterly Review of Higher Education Among Negroes*, IX (July, 1941), 145–46. See also Brown's "Chronicle and Comment," *Opportunity*, VIII (December, 1930), 375; and "Concerning Negro Drama," *Opportunity*, IX (September, 1931), 284.
74. Brown, "Our Literary Audience," 46. See Brown's comments to the 1937 National Negro Congress, "The Problems of the Negro Writer."

merely trying to exploit the sensationalism of low life. But Brown possessed broader vision. The young writers were turning to realism because they were a part of the literary environment of America; and realism was currently predominant in that environment.[75] Unlike his older colleagues, Brown always viewed black writers as a part of the American literary tradition. Hence the title of his incisive literary history was *The Negro in American Fiction*. This was in contrast to the usual concern in such studies with the Negro's contribution *to* American literature.

In an important volume, *The American Caravan* (1941), which Brown co-edited with two other young critics—Arthur P. Davis and Ulysses Lee—the editors flatly rejected the existence of a racial literary tradition. "In spite of such unifying bonds as a common rejection of the popular stereotypes and a common 'racial' cause," they wrote, "writings by Negroes do not seem to the editors to fall into a unique cultural pattern. Negro writers have adapted the literary traditions that seemed useful for their purposes." They concluded that "the bonds of literary tradition seem to be stronger than race."[76] Unlike Brawley and Locke, they could not believe in *any* kind of race genius.

Nevertheless, he believed that "the final interpretation of Negro life must come from within."[77] Brown asked black writers to explore their own folk heritage because of its rich potential and because they had lived close enough to it to give it the realistic dramatization it needed. While he frequently praised white interpretations of Negro life, he agreed with Johnson's reasoning that the best dramatizations would come from black writers merely because they would be drawing from their own experiences. Brown always urged

---

75. See Brown, "Book Reviews," *Opportunity*, XV (September, 1937), 280.
76. Arthur P. Davis, Ulysses Lee, and Sterling Brown (eds.), *The Negro Caravan: Writings by American Negroes* (New York: The Dryden Press, 1941), 6–7.
77. Sterling Brown, "More Odds," *Opportunity*, X (June, 1932), 188. See also *Negro Caravan*, 4; "Negro Character as seen by White Authors," 200–201; and *The Negro in American Fiction*, 4.

black writers to strive for the best art; and he thought the best art was universal. But at the same time, he believed that the universal was rooted in the provincial.[78]

Although he eschewed their propagandistic emphasis, Brown sympathized with the ideology of the proletarian writers and praised their development of realistic techniques in fiction and poetry. These writers started from the basic beliefs that Negroes had been miserably exploited, that they were growing steadily more conscious of and restive under this exploitation, and that they could get nowhere without the white workers, nor the white workers without them. "These," commented Brown, "are all truths that do not guarantee good fiction, but they cannot be neglected without a falsity to Negro experience, and the contemporary American scene."[79]

Brown, who was a radical to the extent that Ralph Bunche was a radical, declared at the 1937 National Negro Congress that "the Negro artist who will be worth his salt must join with those who are recording a world of injustice and exploitation—a world that must be changed."[80] Such a dogmatic comment sounded more like one of the Communist critics than it did the usually open-minded Brown. While the attitude reflected in it found expression in a considerable portion of his poetry during the latter half of the decade, it was not typical of his criticism. It reflected his politics, and he was generally successful in divorcing politics from his critical standards. Such was not the case with most of the radical critics—at least not while they were writing as radical critics.

Like many of the young radicals, Brown sympathized with some of the goals of the Communists, but he never permitted this to dic-

78. See for example Brown's comments on Erskine Caldwell's *Kneel to the Rising Sun*, in "Realism in the South," *Opportunity*, XIII (October, 1935), 311. Brown, "Our Book Shelf," *Opportunity*, VIII (September, 1930), 280; "The Literary Scene," *Opportunity*, IX (January, 1931), 20; and "The Negro Author and His Publisher," 144.
79. Brown, *The Negro in American Fiction*, 180–81.
80. Brown, "The Problems of the Negro Writer," pages unnumbered.

tate his individual aesthetic standards. Those black critics who were close to the Party, however, demonstrated a nearly unanimous lack of individual critical standards while they remained within the orbit of its influence. They all considered the value of literature primarily in terms of its usefulness in bringing social, economic, and political change. They emphasized a Negro heritage of revolt. They condemned the "New Negro" and all subjectivism and "middle class individualism." They demanded a proletarian literature that would encourage white and black solidarity.[81] Unlike Brown, who sought to free the black artist, they imposed narrow, dogmatic standards. One could inevitably predict the content of their essays before reading them.

Until Richard Wright gained prominence late in the decade, the darling of the Communist critics was the poet-novelist and close fellow traveler, Langston Hughes. In evaluating his work, Eugene Clay noted that "he has not followed in the retrogressive paths of his 'New Negro' renaissance colleagues." Instead, he thought that Hughes had evolved "an anti-bourgeois-intelligentsia outlook." Clay praised Hughes's radical, class-conscious poetry and fiction. But he either ignored those many works which did not fit the proletarian formula, or he described them as "retrogressions." But, he was quick to add, "these are allowable in the career of the fellow traveler."[82]

Clay's critical approach to Hughes's book of short stories, *Ways of the White Folks,* was typical. He was displeased because not all of the stories were "realistically anti-bourgeois or revolutionary." So in his criticisms he ignored all the stories but the few, such as

81. For a typical summation of this creed, see Langston Hughes's brief address to the 1935 American Writers' Congress, "To Negro Writers," in Henry Hart (ed.), *American Writers' Congress* (New York: International Publishers, 1935), 139–41. See also Eugene Gordon, "Social and Political Problems of the Negro Writer," *ibid.*, 141–45; and Eugene Clay, "The Negro in Recent American Literature," *ibid.*, 145–53; and Clay, "The Negro Writer and the Congress," *New Masses*, XIX (March, 1935), 22.

82. Eugene Clay, "The Negro and American Literature," *International Literature: Organ of the International Union of Revolutionary Writers*, 1935. No. 6, p. 79.

"Father and Son," wherein "the author states his belief that the union of white and black workers will be the single force which will smash American capitalism."[83] He added that Hughes's stories "would be greater than they are if they had to do with share-croppers, peons, convicts, factory-workers, sailors and stevedores."[84] It did not seem to matter whether these types of people had been a significant part of Hughes's experience. Clay ignored Hughes's blues poetry—in fact all of his poetry concerned with race—and all of the subjective elements that could be found in much of his work. Instead he praised what could only be described as Hughes's revolutionary sloganeering.

One Marxist critic who had difficulty submitting to Party discipline was Richard Wright.[85] He wrote some criticism which was totally "acceptable," such as his review of Arna Bontemps' historical novel, *Black Thunder*. Wright praised the novel as proletarian literature because it was "the only novel dealing forthrightly with the historical and revolutionary traditions of the Negro people." He was especially impressed because Bontemps had endowed his proletarian hero, the eighteenth-century black insurrectionist Gabriel Prosser, with "a myth-like deathless quality." His characters were more than human.[86] It is significant that in his own fiction, Wright very seldom tried to make his characters in such monumental dimension. But transforming proletarian heroes into great mythic figures was characteristic of proletarian writers, and critical praise of such figures was "acceptable." In later pieces Wright, who be-

83. Clay, "The Negro in Recent American Literature," 148.
84. Clay, "The Negro and American Literature," 80.
85. Another who displayed independence was Ralph Ellison, who was just starting his career in the late 1930s. Never a Party member, Ellison was an enthusiastic fellow traveler. See for example, Ellison's "Creative and Cultural Lag," *New Challenge*, I (Fall, 1937), 90–91; and especially his "Recent Negro Fiction," *New Masses*, I (August, 1941), 22–25. For insight into Wright's rebelliousness within the Communist party, see his essay, "I Tried to Be a Communist," in Richard Crossman (ed.), *The God That Failed* (New York: Harper & Row, Publishers, 1949), 103–46.
86. Richard Wright, "A Tale of Folk Courage," *Partisan Review and Anvil*, III (April, 1936), 31.

came increasingly rebellious within the Party, went beyond the customary criticism—a little beyond at first, and unacceptably beyond later.

Wright's first major critical essay, "Blueprint for Negro Writing," appeared in 1937 in the first and only edition of *New Challenge*. This journal, of which Wright was one of the editors, was established as an organ for young radical writers.[87] In his own essay Wright heaped abuse upon the previous generations of black writers for the bourgeois perspective and consequent alienation from the black masses; for their narrow, "devious" brand of black nationalism; and for their humble attempts at "begging the question of the Negroes' humanity."[88]

Wright thought that it was the black writer's duty to mold the consciousness of the black masses along class lines. He insisted that black writers must throw off their sterile relationship with the parasitic bourgeois society and learn "to stand shoulder to shoulder with Negro workers in mood and outlook."[89] By implication, if black writers accepted the humanity of the black masses and then identified with them, they could then assume their own humanity and not have to waste effort attempting to prove it. At any rate, Wright thought that they would gain a vital relevance which the pathetic black bourgeoisie lacked.

Unlike many of the young Negro radicals who condemned all black nationalism as "black chauvinism," Wright followed Communist party dogma and endorsed a vague nationalism. He recognized that this nationalism was reflected both in various Jim Crow institutions and in Negro folklore. "Negro writers," he reasoned, "must accept the nationalist implications of their lives, not in order to encourage them, but in order to change and transcend them. They must accept the concept of nationalism because, in order to

---

87. See "Editorial," *New Challenge*, I (Fall, 1935), 3–4.
88. Richard Wright, "Blueprint for Negro Writing," *New Challenge*, I (Fall, 1935), 53–56.
89. *Ibid.*, 55.

transcend it, they must *possess* and *understand* it." Wright's nationalism was one carrying the "highest possible pitch of social consciousness," one that "knows that its ultimate aims are unrealizable within the framework of capitalist America." In the end Wright wanted black writers to use their nationalism to create a "consciousness of the interdependence of people in modern society."[90] In other words, he professed a black nationalism which was anticapitalist and self-destructive.

Once the black writer had identified himself with the black masses, he was in a position to "create the values by which his race is to struggle, live and die." As a molder of consciousness he had to create a meaningful picture of the world. "Many young writers," said Wright, "have grown to believe that a Marxist analysis of society presents such a picture." And naturally Wright counted himself in this group of young writers, commenting that it was "through a Marxist conception of reality and society that the maximum degree of freedom in thought and feeling can be gained for the Negro writer." He thought that anybody without a definite theory about the meaning, structure, and direction of modern society was "a lost victim of the world he cannot understand or control."[91] By 1940, after he had completed *Native Son,* Wright would himself be a "lost victim" who would seek artistic freedom outside of any externally imposed theories.

But even in 1937, Wright would not accept theory alone. Marxism was his starting point, but, he wrote, "no theory of life can take the place of life." Life was a complex experience and no theory could explain all of it. Awareness of this was what separated the artist from the propagandist. Wright did not advocate conscious propaganda, but rather that complex reality should be viewed through a Marxian perspective. This was a universal perspective,

90. *Ibid.,* 58. For a recent critique of Wright's vague brand of nationalism, see Cruse, *The Crisis of the Negro Intellectual,* 181–89.
91. Wright, "Blueprint for Negro Writing," 59–60, 61.

concerned with the struggle of oppressed people everywhere. Wright concluded his 1937 essay by observing that "we live in a time when the majority of the most basic assumptions of life can no longer be taken for granted."[92] This was a thought which would have much more meaning for him by 1940.

Wright published *Native Son* in 1940. The book was much acclaimed by critics, but there were a few, black and white, who bitterly attacked it as blatant sensationalism and as the "preaching of Negro hatred of whites."[93] With the exception of Communist critics, who viewed it in class terms, none of the critics interpreted the novel beyond its racial context

Wright answered the attacks on his novel and in so doing also attempted to demonstrate that a novel by a black man could have implications far wider than race.[94] In "How Bigger Was Born," which was probably the most important critical essay written by a black man to that date, Wright assumed the role of critic of his own work. He explained how the character of Bigger Thomas was derived from his observations of various types of bad black men he had met during his years in the South. It was not until after he had journeyed north and become active in the Communist party that he discovered that "Bigger Thomas was not black all the time: he was white, too, and there were literally millions of him everywhere."[95] He saw that "the Bigger Thomas conditioning" was not just the result of southern racial oppression, but that there were

92. *Ibid.*, 60, 65.
93. See the review of the black critic, Theophilus Lewis. "The Saga of Bigger Thomas," *Catholic World*, CLIII (May, 1941), 201–206; and the white critics David L. Cohn, "The Negro Novel: Richard Wright," *Atlantic Monthly*, CLXV (May, 1940), 659–61; and Burton Rascoe, "Negro Novel and White Reviewers," *American Mercury*, L (May, 1940), 113–16.
94. See Richard Wright, "Rascoe Baiting," *American Mercury*, L (July, 1940), 376–77; his "I Bite the Hand that Feeds Me," *Atlantic Monthly*, CLXV (June, 1940), 826–28; and his "How Bigger Was Born," *Saturday Review*, June 1, 1940, pp. 3–4, 17–20.
95. Wright, "How Bigger Was Born," 4, 17.

larger forces which had a similar effect on people the world over. He was fascinated by the "emotional tensions of Bigger in America and Bigger in Nazi Germany and Bigger in old Russia." Bigger Thomas became, for Wright, a universal symbol of what man might become—or even perhaps what he already was. In the most important statement of his essay he explained the larger significance of Bigger Thomas. "All Bigger Thomases, white and black, felt tense, afraid, nervous, hysterical and restless. From far away Nazi Germany and old Russia had come to me items of knowledge that told me that certain modern experiences were creating types of personalities whose existence ignored racial and national lines of demarcation, that these personalities carried with them a more universal drama element than anything I'd ever encountered before; that these personalities were mainly consequent upon men and women living in a world whose fundamental assumptions could no longer be taken for granted; a world ridden with national and class strife; a world whose metaphysical meanings had vanished; a world in which God no longer existed as a daily focal point of men's lives; a world in which men could no longer retain their faith in an ultimate hereafter. It was a highly geared world whose limited area and vision imperiously urged men to satisfy their organisms, a world that existed on a plane of animal sensation alone."[96] The significance of this eluded critics in 1940, but it made *Native Son* a work significant even to those who lived in places where racial diversity was nonexistent.

The Communist critic, Samuel Sillen, claimed that before Bigger went to die in the electric chair, he found in the two Communists Max and Jan "a conception of man's fate which will enable him to die."[97] The Party was trying to get as much publicity out of the novel as it could. Wright, however, concluded that Bigger ended

96. *Ibid.*, 17–18.
97. "Richard Wright's *Native Son*," *New Masses*, March 5, 1940, p. 24.

up "accepting what life had made him."[98] And life had made him a lonely outsider, a man without any gods.

Although he was at odds with the Party by 1940, Wright had been troubled by the official Party reaction to his interpretation of Bigger. But he resolved his worries. "Though my heart is in the collectivist and proletarian ideal, I solved this problem by assuring myself that honest politics and honest feelings ought to be able to meet on common healthy ground without fear, suspicion, and quarreling. Further, and more importantly, I steeled myself by coming to the conclusion that whether politicians accepted or rejected Bigger did not really matter; my task as I felt it was to free myself of this burden of impressions and feelings, recast them into the image of Bigger and make him true."[99] This was Wright's own declaration of independence. He was committed to a personal interpretation of truth. No longer would he conform to other men's theories.

Truth, always an important concept in literary criticism, had been altered considerably since the easy days of the Harlem Renaissance. During the 1920s and into the 1930s the genteel critics clung to their demand that the truth be interpreted in terms of their own tiny and highly romanticized existence. In essence, they denied the existence of what Du Bois so unfortunately termed "the debauched tenth."

Alain Locke, arch-defender of the New Negro, always really wanted a "black truth" which he believed would make a valuable "spiritual" contribution to a culturally pluralistic society. Unlike the genteel critics, he thought that this truth could be dramatized in the lives of the black masses. But for Locke, and here he concurred with the genteel group, the concept of truth in art was always associated with beauty. In his search for beauty and for "spiritual essences" he was often as romantic as the genteel critics.

For the young realists the idea of truth with beauty was a con-

98. Wright, "How Bigger Was Born," 20.
99. *Ibid.*, 18. See also Wright, "I Bite the Hand that Feeds Me," 826–27.

tradiction in terms. Truth was reality; and reality for black people during the 1930s was for the most part ugly. Social realism was the vogue of the 1930s. In their use of it, the young critics attempted to broaden the black writer's conception of truth. The most important truth for them was the fact that, in addition to racial persecution, the basic social forces which oppressed black Americans were universal. Unlike the genteel critics and the Negro historians, both of whom sought a truth which would reflect favorably on the race, young critics like Sterling Brown and Richard Wright sought truths which were not limited by the demands of race advancement. Richard Wright went even beyond the truth as stark social reality. He plumbed deeper into the psychological roots of truth. The truth he laid bare was, indeed, universal.

VI

◈◈◈◈◈◈◈◈◈◈◈◈◈◈◈◈◈◈◈◈◈◈◈◈◈◈◈

Weavers of Jagged
Words

In his annual reviews of literature by and about Negroes during the 1930s, Alain Locke inevitably complained that black poetry had dwindled both in quantity and quality since the era of the Harlem Renaissance. He attributed this to hard times: "Poets, like birds, sing at dawn and dusk, they are hushed by the heat of propaganda and the din of work and battle, and become vocal only before and after as the heralds of the carolling serenaders."[1] He was quite correct about the sparsity of poetic expression. Black writers produced less than one volume of poetry per year between 1929 and 1942. But Locke's judgment that significant poetry could not be inspired by "the din of work and battle" was only partially correct. True, much of the protest poetry, particularly that which was concerned with proletarian themes, was pure doggerel. But much of it was creditable. Locke's inability to appreciate the poetic value of the brutal experience which several socially conscious younger poets skillfully rendered indicates the distance between the generations. These younger writers were not seeking beauty, but reality. The cynically pessimistic Frank Marshall Davis called himself "a weaver of jagged words," and even the more optimistic Robert

1. Alain Locke, "The Eleventh Hour of Nordicism," *Opportunity*, XIII (January, 1935), 11. See also "Jingo, Counter-Jingo and Us," *Opportunity*, XVI (January, 1938), 11; and "Of Native Sons: Real and Otherwise," *Opportunity*, XVII (January, 1941), 9.

Hayden responded to all those who sought beauty in times of suffering:

> And know that all your beauty's pentecostal tongues
> Fall mute before the urgent fact of T. B.-riddled slums
> And bloody cottonbolls and justice klansman-eyed.
> *There is no beauty that can cry to me*
> *More loudly than my people's misery,*
> *No beauty that can bind my heart and they not*
>   *free.*[2]

With the exception of Langston Hughes and Countee Cullen, most of the prominent poets of the Renaissance were relatively silent during the 1930s. The depression era was essentially a time of nascence in black American poetry; a time when new voices emerged and dominated. Some of these younger writers, such as Sterling Brown and Frank Marshall Davis, created their most important poetry during the depression and were little heard from thereafter. Others, such as Robert Hayden, Melvin Tolson, and Margaret Walker, launched what would be long and fruitful careers. Though, like the New Negro poets, they were most often inspired by race, they rebelled against the provinciality and what they considered the shallow, romantic primitivism of so many of the poets of the twenties. Many of the Renaissance poets had romanticized the African past in order to give substance to the idea of the black man's natural innocence and goodness in the face of the repressive, crassly materialistic Western civilization. The poets of the depression looked back to the black man's past in this country, and with a more realistic eye. Generally speaking their attitude was that this past was something more to be exposed than romanticized, exposed both for the strength it could offer and for the lessons it could teach. For example, they dwelt upon the Afro-

2. Frank Marshall Davis, "Frank Marshall Davis: Writer," *I Am the American Negro* (Chicago: Black Cat Press, 1937), 69. Robert Hayden, "Essay on Beauty," *Heart-Shape in the Dust* (Detroit: Falcon Press, 1940), 29.

American's historic identification with Christ and attempted to demonstrate how this had been used to keep black men down.

Protest in the poetry of the Renaissance was almost exclusively racial and generally mild by comparison with that of the depression. The protest of the young black poets of the depression was bitter and strident and, as the years passed, became increasingly concerned with the problems of all of humanity and not just with the black portion of it. Many of them turned to themes of white-black labor solidarity and ironically became just as romantic as were the New Negro poets whom they were rebelling against. But others turned to themes of deeper, wider significance such as the plight of modern man in the city and the evil foolishness of war. The mode of expression of these younger poets was realism, their perspective was often universal.

Countee Cullen was perhaps the epitome for them of all that was wrong with the Harlem Renaissance. During the 1920s he had been widely acclaimed as a precocious talent. Indeed, he published his first volume of poetry, *Color* (1925), while still a college student. In the next few years he was prolific, producing *Ballad of the Brown Girl* (1927) and *Copper Sun* (1927), and editing a well-received anthology, *Caroling Dusk* (1927).

Born in 1903, Cullen had grown up in comfortable and sheltered circumstances as the adopted son of a prominent Harlem clergyman. He graduated Phi Beta Kappa from New York University in 1925 and received a Master's degree from Harvard the following year. He spent most of his rather short life—he died in 1946—as a public school teacher in New York.

Cullen's idol was John Keats after whom he tried to pattern himself as a writer. He never attempted innovation but seemed content to conform to the traditions of the Victorian romantics. Although his best poems were inspired by race, Cullen most emphatically did not want to be known as a Negro poet. He wanted, rather, to be recognized merely as a poet. Thus he addressed a poetic rebuttal

to those black critics such as Alain Locke who ridiculed his dis-
avowal of racial consciousness:

> Then call me traitor if you must,
> Shout treason and default!
> Say I betray a sacred trust
> Aching beyond this vault.
> I'll bear your censure as your praise,
> For never shall the clan
> Confine my singing to its ways
> Beyond the ways of men.
>
> No racial option narrows grief,
> Pain is no patriot,
> And sorrow plaits her dismal leaf
> For all as lief as not.
> With blind sheep groping every hill,
> Searching an oriflame,
> How shall the shepherd heart then thrill
> To only the darker lamb?[3]

In 1929, Cullen published *The Black Christ and Other Poems*,
which in style and content was much like those he had published
previously and those which would follow. The title poem, which
was some forty pages long, is most interesting because Cullen dealt
with some of the themes which were to become prominent during
the 1930s, and his manner of treatment offered a significant contrast
to the renditions of later poets.

---

3. Countee Cullen, *The Black Christ and Other Poems* (New York: Harper &
Bros., 1929), 63.
  For a more intensive analysis of all of Cullen's poetry, see Jean Wagner, *Les
poetes nègres des États-Unis: Le sentiment racial et religieux dans la poesie de
P. L. Dunbar a L. Hughes* (Paris: Librairie Istra, 1962), the English translation of
which, *Black Poets of the United States: From Paul Laurence Dunbar to Langston
Hughes,* trans. Kenneth Douglas (Urbana, Chicago, London: University of Illinois
Press, 1973), appeared as the manuscript of this study was being prepared for press.
Wagner's is the most complete critical analysis of black American poetry for the
first half of the twentieth century as yet published. For further analysis of Cullen,
see also Blanche E. Ferguson, *Countee Cullen and the Negro Renaissance* (New
York: Dodd, Mead, 1966), and Beulah Reimherr, "Countee Cullen: A Biographical
and Critical Study" (M.A. thesis, University of Maryland, 1960).

"The Black Christ" is a poem about lynching. During the 1930s many poets compared the crucifixion of Christ with the lynching of black men in the American South. But Cullen's poem is much longer, much less realistic and much more obscure than the creations of later poets. He set the theme down concisely enough:

> How Calvary in Palestine,
> Extending down to me and mine,
> Was but the first leaf in a line
> Of trees on which a Man should swing
> World without end, in suffering
> For all men's healing, let me sing.[4]

Then, assuming the role of narrator-participant, he sets down the story of his brother who was actually two brothers, "One of spirit, one of sod." As children they used to talk about the racial persecution from which they suffered. His brother had dark forebodings:

> "I have a fear," he used to say,
> "This thing may come to me some day.
> Some man contemptuous of my race
> And lost rights in this hard place,
> Will strike me down for being black.
> But when I answer I'll pay back
> The late revenge long overdue
> A thousand of my kind and hue.
> A thousand black men, long since gone
> Will guide my hand, stiffen the brawn,
> And speed one life-divesting blow
> Into some granite face of snow."[5]

The concept of retaliatory violence—in this case, the retaliation is motivated by history—would be quite common among the young poets of the depression era. But for them the idea of a young southern black speaking in poetic verse would be laughable.

4. Cullen, "The Black Christ," *The Black Christ and Other Poems*, 69.
5. *Ibid.*, 78.

After Cullen takes his reader through pages of such conversations, in which the two brothers and their mother discuss such diverse subjects as the harshness and beauty of the southern landscape and the apparent indifference of God to their plight, he finally comes to the point where the brother makes good his prophecy. Naturally he is lynched. But Cullen's lynching scene takes place off stage. The young poets of the 1930s would not be so squeamish about depicting violence and gore. It had too much dramatic and propagandistic value. Cullen brings his black Christ back into view after he has been mysteriously resurrected:

> For there he stood in utmost view
> Whose death I had been witness to;
> But now he breathed; he lived; he walked;
> His tongue could speak my name; he talked.[6]

The black Christ tells his brother to see that he did not die in vain. But Cullen leaves the meaning of this resurrection rather hazy, for apparently the only people who were redeemed were the mother and the brother-narrator.

> Somewhere in the Southland rears a tree,
>
> . . . .
>
> And those who pass it by may see
> Naught growing there except a tree,
> But there are two to testify
> Who hung on it . . . we saw Him die.
> Its roots were fed with priceless blood.
> It is the Cross; it is the Rood.[7]

Cullen could have made the suffering of his black Christ more symbolic of the suffering of black people as later writers would do. He also could have applied the idea of redemption to the whole race and, indeed to all of humanity—a black Christ suffering for the sins of humanity (he had alluded to this in the introduction). But Cul-

6. *Ibid.*, 107.   7. *Ibid.*, 110.

len, who remained aloof from contemporary affairs, was concerned with personal, not social, salvation. Cullen's noninvolvement in contemporary issues and his romanticism alienated him from other young writers and critics. The poetry he produced during the 1930s received little critical attention because it was essentially the same as he had offered in his first volume during the height of the Harlem Renaissance.[8]

Langston Hughes, on the other hand, was involved in contemporary affairs, and he was not averse to experimenting with new forms of expression. During the Renaissance Hughes had popularized the blues form in poetry. His first volume, *The Weary Blues* (1926), followed by *Fine Clothes for the Jew* (1927), won wide popular and critical acclaim. His poetry was popular because it could be read easily by people of all ages and backgrounds.

Born in Joplin, Missouri, in 1902, Hughes's life was also very different from Cullen's. As a child he moved around from city to city. After his parents separated he remained with his mother who could not offer him the comforts enjoyed by Cullen. Still, he was more fortunate than most black youngsters; he completed high school, and eventually college. As a young man, Hughes worked on freighters in the Atlantic trade and lived a bohemian existence in Paris for a short while. When his poetic talent was first discovered by Vachel Lindsay, he was working as a busboy in a Washington, D.C., hotel.

In his poetry, Hughes turned from his blues celebrations of Harlem life to protest poetry during the thirties. For most of the decade he was closely associated with the Communist party. Much of his poetry—most of it his worst—appeared in various Party organs. Much of Hughes's poetry from the 1930s is important, if for no other reason, because it indicates the extent to which Communist party influence could stifle a genuine poetic talent. He published

8. Volumes Countee Cullen published during the period included *The Medea and Other Poems* (New York: Harper & Bros., 1935), which is his translation of the classic; and *The Lost Zoo* (New York: Harper & Bros., 1940), a book of verse for children.

three volumes of poetry during the 1930s: *Dear Lovely Death* (1931), which was a small collection privately printed; and *The Dream Keeper* (1932), which was essentially a collection of his poems from the 1920s republished for a juvenile audience; and *A New Song* (1938), a collection of his proletarian verse which was published by the International Workers Order. Many of the poems published in these volumes first appeared in various periodicals, journals, and anthologies. In fact, most of Hughes's poetic production of the 1930s can be found in these scattered sources.

In the early years of the decade, Hughes was still writing poetry considered "decadent" and "unacceptable" by Communist critics. In 1930, he wrote with quiet respect:

> MA LAWD ain't no stuck-up man.
> MA LAWD, He ain't proud.
> When He goes a-walkin'
> He gives me his hand.
> You ma friend, He 'lowed.[9]

As he had in his blues poetry of the twenties, he was here speaking in the voice of the black folk. But he was also capable of expressing himself in more conventional fashion. For Communist critics "Dear Lovely Death" was the epitome of decadent bourgeois subjectivism.

> Dear lovely Death
>   That taketh all things under wing—
> Never to kill—
> Only to change
> Into some other thing
> This suffering flesh,
> To make it either more or less,
> Yet not again the same—

9. Langston Hughes, "MA LAWD," in B. A. Botkin (ed.), *Folk-Say: A Regional Miscellany* (Norman: University of Oklahoma Press, 1930), 283. For a much broader analysis of Hughes's poetry, see Wagner, *Black Poets of the United States*, 385–474; and James A. Emanuel, *Langston Hughes* (New York: Twayne Publishers, Inc., 1967), which contains a helpful annotated bibliography.

> Dear lovely Death,
> Change is thy other name.[10]

And when Hughes protested, it was still exclusively in terms of racial persecution:

> I am the fool of the whole world.
> Laugh and push me down.
> Only in song and laughter
> I rise again—a black clown.
>
> . . . .
>
> Cry to the world that all might understand:
> I was once a black clown
> But now—
> I'm a free man![11]

But by 1932, Hughes's protest poems began to show a new influence. In that year he published a pamphlet containing a few poems and a brief poem-play, all dedicated to the black youths on trial for the alleged rape of two white prostitutes in Scottsboro, Alabama. Much of *Scottsboro Limited* shows the influence of Hughes's Communist affiliations. Poems such as "Scottsboro" vacuously identify the young boys with a long list of revolutionary saints including John Brown, Nat Turner, and Lenin. The effect of some of the poems is to transform the boys into militant proletarian heroes, while in reality they were poor, ignorant pawns.[12]

The poem-play, "Scottsboro Limited," dramatizes the theme of persecution of poor whites and blacks alike by "de rich white folks."

> Yes, 'cause de rich ones owns de land,
> And they don't care nothin' 'bout de po' white man.

10. Langston Hughes, "Dear Lovely Death," *Opportunity*, VIII (June, 1930), 182.
11. Langston Hughes, "The Black Clown," *Crisis*, XLI (February, 1932), 52. See also "Three Poems by Langston Hughes," *Opportunity*, 8 (December, 1930), 371.
12. See Dan T. Carter, *Scottsboro: A Tragedy of the American South* (Baton Rouge: Louisiana State University Press, 1969).

You's right. Crackers is just like me—
Po' whites and niggers, ain't neither one free.

He also imposes the theme of Communist sympathy with the black
victims:

RED VOICES: We'll fight! The Communists will fight for you.
Not just black—but black and white.
3RD BOY: Then we'll trust in you.

As might be expected, the black boys burst their bonds and rebel
in triumphant unity with the white workers and Communists:

BOYS: Together, black and white,
Up from the darkness into the light.
ALL: Rise, workers, and fight!
AUDIENCE: Fight! Fight! Fight!
(*The curtain is a great red flag rising
to the strains of the Internationale.*) [13]

But Hughes's poetic talents in this collection were not completely
obscured by proletarian formulas. Such poems as "Justice" and
"Christ in Alabama" reflected a genuine bitterness and not the defiant posing of most formula-type proletarian poetry. "Christ in
Alabama" is particularly striking in its imagery, much more striking
than Cullen's black Christ:

Christ is a Nigger,
Beaten and black—
O, bare your back.

Mary is His Mother—
*Mammy of the South,
Silence your mouth.*

God's His Father—
*White Master above,
Grant us Your Love.*

13. Langston Hughes, "Scottsboro Limited," *Scottsboro Limited* (New York:
The Golden Star Press, 1932), pages unnumbered. For an excellent delineation of
the proletarian formula in the literature of the 1930s, see Leo Gurko, *The Angry
Decade* (New York: Dodd, Mead and Co., 1947), 63.

> Most holy bastard
> of the bleeding mouth:
> *Nigger Christ*
> *On the Cross of the South.*[14]

This poem offended many people. Aimee Semple McPherson called Hughes "a red devil in a black skin!" And Hughes later related the story, perhaps apocryphal, of how one southern sheriff thought the poet should be run out of town when he appeared for one of his readings: "Sure, he ought to be run out! It's bad enough to call Christ a *bastard*. But when he calls him a *nigger,* he's gone too far!"[15]

As offensive as "Christ in Alabama" was to respectable folk, it was another, less imposing poem which brought the wrath of many black leaders down upon Hughes. "Good-bye Christ" was first published in a European Communist publication, while Hughes, like so many other black intellectuals during the 1930s, was enjoying a triumphal tour of the Soviet Union. It was subsequently published in some of the Afro-American weeklies, in Nancy Cunard's *Negro Anthology* (1934), and in *A New Song*. As with most of the poems he composed for the Party press, "Good-bye Christ" was a proletarian-formula poem. It was labored and stilted by comparison with "Christ in Alabama." It was almost as if different men wrote the two poems.

> Listen, Christ,
> You did alright in your day, I reckon—
> But that day's gone now.
> They ghosted you up a swell story, too,
> Called it Bible—
> But it's dead now.

14. Langston Hughes, "Christ in Alabama," *Scottsboro Limited*, pages unnumbered.
15. For both anecdotes, see Hughes's essay, "My Adventures as a Social Poet," *Phylon*, VIII (Third Quarter, 1947), 205–12.

The popes and the preacher've
Made too much money from it.

. . . .

Goodbye
Christ Jesus Lord God Jehovah,
Beat it on away from here now.
Make way for a new guy with no religion at all—
A real guy named
Marx Communist Lenin Peasant Stalin, Worker, ME—
I said ME! [16]

Hughes had come a long way since "MA LAWD." Ministers and genteel critics condemned Hughes's blatant atheism.[17] But the young poet and teacher, Melvin B. Tolson, came to Hughes's defense. Himself a Christian, he pointed out that Hughes was merely demonstrating that pious Christianity had become meaningless for millions who were suffering *in* this world.[18]

Hughes himself later gave some insight into his interpretation. In "A New Song" he wrote optimistically that the days of humiliation and brutal persecution were past. In the past the white world had no pity.

And only in the sorrow songs
Relief was found—
Yet not relief,
But merely humble life and silent death

16. Langston Hughes, "Goodbye Christ," reprinted in the Baltimore *Afro-American*, December 31, 1932.

17. See for example, Charles M. Thomas, "A Reply to Langston Hughes' 'Good Bye Christ'," Washington *Sentinel*, January 14, 1933; and the venerable Francis J. Grimke, "Langston Hughes Crazy or Blurred," Baltimore *Afro-American*, February 18, 1933.

18. Melvin B. Tolson, "Langston Hughes' Goodbye Christ a Challenge and a Warning," Pittsburgh *Courier*, February 4, 1933. Years later Hughes published what amounted to an apology for the poem, commenting that he wrote it as a radical but that he was no longer capable of writing in such a vein. See "Let's Get It Straight," Chicago *Defender*, January 11, 1941.

Eased by a Name
That hypnotized the pain away—
O, precious Name of Jesus in that day!

That day is past.

I know full well now
Jesus could not die for me—
That only my own hands,
Dark as the earth,
Can make my earth-dark body free.[19]

The idea that Christ had been manipulated to keep black people down and that they must rely on themselves, rather than passively "trusting in the Lord," became a common theme among most of the young radicals and poets during the thirties. Unlike Cullen, Hughes thought that the times demanded social salvation before spiritual.

Not all of Hughes's protest poetry was necessarily connected with race. Some of it was quite effective.

This is earthquake
Weather:
Honor and Hunger
Walk lean together.[20]

But in other pieces he abandoned his poetic muse to preach politics and was much less convincing. "Roar China" was typical:

Break the chains of the East,
Little coolie boy!
Break the chains of the East,
Red generals!
Break the chains of the East,
Child slaves in the factories!
Smash the iron gates of the Concessions!
Smash the pious doors of the missionary houses!

19. Langston Hughes, "A New Song," *Opportunity*, XIX (January, 1933), 23.
20. Langston Hughes, "Today," *Opportunity*, XV (October, 1937), 310. See also his "Ballad of Roosevelt," *New Republic*, November 14, 1934; "Big City Prayer," *Opportunity*, XVIII (October, 1940), 308.

. . . .
Stand up and roar, China!
You know what you want!
The only way to get it is
To take it!
Roar, China![21]

These exclamatory lines resemble the slogans—all ending with ex-
clamation marks—which concluded most columns in Party newspapers like the *Harlem Liberator*. Indeed, it is the impersonal,
standardized quality which sets these poems so disadvantageously
apart from Hughes's customary work. The lines could have been
written by anyone. The thing that was most important to the Party
was that Hughes's name appeared above them.

Hughes was not the only talented black writer who usually
achieved miserable results when he attempted political poetry.
Richard Wright also wrote poetry for the Party presses with the
same anonymous quality. Wright was capable of creating poetry
of real power—such as "Between the World and Me" which was
the most graphic lynching poem published during the decade. Another of his poems, "I Have Seen Black Hands," effectively developed the image of black hands playing; black hands working and
being smashed to produce goods which the "bosses" warned them
"were private and did not belong to them"; and black hands reaching out in desperation to "beat fearfully at the tall flames that
cooked and charred the black flesh. . . ." In the last stanza black
hands are joined triumphantly with white hands in a sudden display
of black and white labor solidarity.

I am black and I have seen black hands
Raised in fists of revolt, side by side with the white fists
    of white workers,
And some day—and it is only this which sustains me—

21. Langston Hughes, "Roar China!" *New Masses*, February 22, 1938, p. 20. For
other examples, see Hughes's "White Man," *New Masses*, December 15, 1936, p. 34;
and his "Columbia," *International Literature*, No. 2 (1933), 54.

> Some day there shall be millions and millions of them,
> On some red day in a burst of fists on a new horizon! [22]

"I Have Seen Black Hands" was more effective than most proletarian poetry, but when Wright tried to praise Soviet Russia, he became banal and predictable.

> Gallop on, Big Timer, gallop on!
> If anybody asks you who your Ma and Pa were,
> Show your birth certificate signed by Lenin:
> uuuu! ssss! ssss! RRRR!
> And tell them you're a man-child of the Revolution . . .[23]

Wright also composed a poem, "I Am A Red Slogan," which, while not intended as such, can be interpreted ironically.[24] Both Hughes and Wright were more valuable to the Party as bywords than as poets.

Fortunately, neither Wright nor Hughes permitted political formulas to stifle their artistic impulses. Wright went on to produce the most significant fiction yet published by an American Negro. And when Langston Hughes's volume, *Shakespeare in Harlem*, appeared in 1942, none of the proletarian doggerel was included. There were some poems of protest, but they were more subtle, without the vacuous loudness of many of his depression era proletarian poems. More important, he renewed his interest in the actual lives of black urbanites. Throwing off the labored seriousness of the 1930s, he returned to the bittersweet reality of the blues which had characterized his pre-depression verse.

> Folks, I come up North
> Cause they told me de North was fine.

22. See Richard Wright, "Between the World and Me," *Partisan Review*, II (July–August, 1935), 18–19. Wright's "I Have Seen Black Hands" was originally published in the *New Masses* (December 15, 1934), 16.

23. Richard Wright, "Spread Your Sunrise," *New Masses*, July 2, 1935, p. 26.

24. See *International Literature*, No. 4 (1935), p. 35. Another example of Wright's slogan-choked proletarian poetry is "Transcontinental," *International Literature*, No. 1 (1936), pp. 52–57.

I come up North
Cause they told me de North was fine.
Been up here six months—
I'm about to lose my mind.

This mornin' for breakfast
I chawed de mornin' air.
This mornin' for breakfast
Chawed de mornin' air.
But this evenin' for supper,
I got evenin' air to spare.[25]

Like Hughes, Sterling Brown was at his best when he used folk material. But instead of writing of the urban folk, Brown focused on rural subjects. He was an accomplished student of southern Negro folklore, culture, and dialect.[26] His volume of poems, *Southern Road* (1932), was the most highly acclaimed by any Negro poet during the depression era.

Doubleshackled—hunh—
Guard behin'.
Doubleshackled—hunh—
Guard behin'.
Ball an' chain, bebby,
On my min'.

White man tells me—hunh—
Damn yo' soul.
White man tells me—hunh—
Damn yo' soul.
Got no need, bebby,
To be tole.[27]

25. Langston Hughes, "Evenin' Air Blues," *Shakespeare in Harlem* (New York: Alfred A. Knopf, 1942), 38–39.
26. Sterling Brown's "Genres and Media: The Blues as Folk Poetry," remains a minor classic. See Botkin (ed.), *Folk-Say: A Regional Miscellany*, 324–29. For a more detailed analysis of Brown's poetry, see Wagner, *Black Poets of the United States*, 475–503.
27. Sterling Brown, "Southern Road," *Southern Road* (New York: Harcourt, Brace & Co., 1932), 46–47.

Southern Road was not inspired essentially by protest motives. The white man and his brutality are only of secondary interest. Rather, Brown focuses sympathetically on the lives of the black folk. Earlier poets had exploited the folk idiom as a source of comic amusement. Brown used it to express both the comic and the tragic experiences of the black folk. He did not laugh at them. When he laughed, it was *with* them. Brown was interested in the impact of forces other than racial persecution on the lives of the folk. He expressed the fears of the people when the rivers began to rise to a dangerous level and the plight of the man chained to "Old King Cotton."

> Ole King Cotton,
> Ole Man Cotton,
> Keeps us slavin'
> Till we'se dead an' rotten.
>
> · · · · · · · · · ·
>
> Starves us wid bumper crops,
> Starves us wid po'.
> Chains de lean wolf
> At our do'.[28]

When Brown wrote about the city, he was generally concerned with its effect upon recent southern immigrants. Inevitably, he sketched their blues, their yearning to get away from urban confusion and back to their roots. For them the city remained a "City of Destruction"; it was not yet a "City of Rebirth" as E. Franklin Frazier hoped it would be.

> Leave 'is dirty city, take my foot up in my hand,
> Dis do-dirty city, take my foot up in my hand,
> Git down to de livin' what a man kin understand.
>
> · · · · · · · · · · · · · · ·
>
> I'm got de tin roof blues, got dese sidewalks on my mind,
> De tin roof blues, dese lonesome sidewalks on my mind,

28. Sterling Brown, "Old King Cotton," *ibid.*, 65. See also, in the same volume, "Children of the Mississippi," 67–69; and "Foreclosure," 73–74.

I'm going where de shingles covers people mo' my
kind.[29]

For Brown, getting back to roots was more than just returning
to the South; it was an understanding and acceptance of the folk
heritage. In "Children's Children" he scolded the urbanized descen-
dants of the southern folk, "with their paled faces, coppered lips,
and sleek hair cajoled to Caucasian straightness," for their derisive
attitude toward the folk:

> When they hear
> These songs, born of the travail of their sires,
> Diamonds of song, deep buried beneath the weight
> of dark and heavy years;
> They laugh.
>
> When they hear
> Saccharine melodies of loving and its fevers,
> Soft-flowing lies of love everlasting;
> Conjuring divinity out of gross flesh itch;
> They sigh
> And look goggle-eyed
> At one another.[30]

Instead, he believed that American Negroes should look to the
spirituals and blues, and the heritage from which they sprang, as
a source of strength. Thus he wrote of the great blues singer, Ma
Rainey:

> O Ma Rainey,
> Sing yo' song;
> Now you's back
> Whah you belong
> Git way inside us,
> Keep us strong . . .[31]

29. Sterling Brown, "Tin Roof Blues," *ibid.*, 105. For Frazier's sociological interpretation, see Chap. II above, pp. 50–51, 52–53.
30. Sterling Brown, "Children's Children," *Southern Road*, 107–108. Another
attack on this lack of historical consciousness is Sterling Brown, "Remembering Nat
Turner," *Crisis*, XLVI (February, 1939), 48.
31. Sterling Brown, "Ma Rainey," *Southern Road*, 63.

Folk heroes such as John Henry and the real-life fighter, Jack Johnson, had given blacks a symbolic heritage of manly endurance and strength. He thanked Jack Johnson because

> You used to stand there like a man,
> Taking punishment
> With a golden, spacious grin;
> Confident.
> Inviting big Jim Jeffries, who was boring in:
> "Heah ah is, big boy; yuh sees whah Ise at.
> Come on in . . .[32]

In poem after poem Brown also celebrated this strength in the common black folk of the South: "low life," as the genteel writers termed it; the sharecroppers, the stevedores, the prostitutes, and the weary old folks who awaited death with quiet strength and dignity. For these people mere survival was an act of heroism. For Brown their very lives represented heroic expressions of the blues philosophy. He once wrote that "truth to Negro experience must consider the Negro's ability to take it, to endure and to wring out of life something of joy."[33]

The most strident note of racial protest in the volume was ironically titled "Sam Smiley." Brown relates the story of a World War I veteran who, upon returning to the South, discovers that his woman has been raped and killed by a white man:

> The whites had taught him how to rip
> A Nordic belly with a thrust
> Of bayonet, had taught him how
> To transmute Nordic flesh to dust.
>
> And a surprising fact had made
> Belated impress on his mind:
> That shrapnel bursts and poison gas
> Were inexplicably color blind.

---

32. Sterling Brown, "Strange Legacies," *ibid.*, 95.
33. Sterling Brown, "The Negro Author and His Publisher," *Quarterly Review of Higher Education Among Negroes*, IX (July, 1941), 146.

. . . .

And he remembered France, and how
A human life was dunghill cheap,
And so he sent a rich white man
His woman's company to keep.[34]

Messages of defiance and retaliatory violence would dominate in much of Brown's poetry for the rest of the decade. There is little of the humor to be found in his later poetry which can be found in the "Slim Greer" poems of *Southern Road*. Slim was a tall-talking black man who roved the South in search of mischief. He was the "Talkinges' guy / An' biggest liar, / With always a new lie / On the fire." He once told of "How he in Arkansaw / Passed for white, / An' he no lighter / Than a dark midnight." He took up with a white woman and nobody suspected his racial identity until a cracker overheard him playing at the piano.

An' he started a-tinklin'
Some mo'nful blues,
An' a-pattin' the time
With No. Fourteen shoes.

The cracker listened and then informed the white woman "No white could play like that. . . ." But she indignantly ordered the informer out and then

Crept into the parlor
Soft as you please,
Where Slim was agitatin'
The ivories.
    Heard Slim's music—
    An' then, hot damn!
    Shouted sharp—"Nigger!"
    An Slim said, "Ma'am?"[35]

She screamed and Slim lit out, bound for other misadventures. In Atlanta, Slim discovered that the local white folks had laws "to

34. Sterling Brown, "Sam Smiley," *Southern Road*, 36–38.
35. Sterling Brown, "Slim Greer," *ibid.*, 83–85.

keep all de niggers from laughin' outdoors." They made them do all their laughing in a telephone booth. When he saw a hundred of them waiting in line to get into the booth,

> Slim thought his sides
>   Would burst in two,
> Yelled, "Lookout, everybody,
>   I'm coming through!"

He burst through the door and stayed in the booth laughing for four hours.

> Den he peeked through de door,
>   An' what did he see?
> *Three* hundred niggers there
>   In misery.—
> Some holdin' deir sides,
>   Some holdin' deir jaws,
> To keep from breakin'
>   De Georgia laws.[36]

Naturally Slim is forced back into the booth for yet another laughing spree.

Such humor was rare in Negro poetry, especially during the depression era. The only other poet to use it effectively was Frank Marshall Davis, who directed it more at the foibles of his own people than at the absurdity of the whites as Brown had done. Significantly, as Brown turned more and more to overt protest in his poetry after *Southern Road,* he abandoned humor. This was unfortunate, because as vehicles of protest his humorous poems were generally more effective than his serious efforts.

Brown's protest poems were somber, expressed generally in conventional English and usually not so impressive as the best of his *Southern Road* poems. His protest poetry was full of violence and defiant heroes—all of whom became lynch victims. One such proletarian hero was a black sharecropper who belonged to the Southern Tenant Farmers Union. When an angry group of land-

36. Sterling Brown, "Slim in Atlanta," *ibid.*, 88–89.

lords came to him and demanded to know the whereabouts of the next union meeting, he refused to tell.

> They lashed him, and they clubbed his head;
> One time he parted his bloody lips
> Out of great pain and greater pride,
> One time, to laugh in his landlord's face;
> Then his landlord shot him in the side.
>
> . . . .
>
> Then to the dark woods and the moon
> He gave up one secret before he died:
> *"We gonna clean out dis brushwood round here soon,*
> *Plant de white oak and de black oak side by side."*[37]

The defiance, the brutality, and the prophecy of black and white labor solidarity were the stock content of poems published in the *New Masses* and other left-wing periodicals of the 1930s. Brown's poetry, however, never descended to the level of the slogan as did much of Hughes's. Most of the protest poetry of the era was direct, blunt. Brown was able to maintain a degree of irony, as in his portrait of a young "Southern Cop."

> Let us forgive Ty Kendricks.
> It was in darktown. He was young,
> His nerves were jittery. The day was hot.
> The nigger ran out of the alley,
> And so he shot.
>
> . . . .
>
> Let us pity Ty Kendricks.
> He has been through enough.
> Standing there, his big gun smoking,
> Rabbit-scared, alone;
> Having to hear the wenches wail
> And the dying nigger moan.[38]

37. Sterling Brown, "Sharecropper," *New Masses* (November 17, 1936), 12. See also his "Let us Suppose," *Opportunity*, XIII (September, 1935), 281; "Transfer," *Partisan Review*, III (October, 1936), 20–21; and "Break of Day," *New Republic*, May 11, 1938, p. 10.

38. Sterling Brown, "Southern Cop," *Partisan Review*, III (October, 1936), 21.

Between *Southern Road* and the 1940 publication of Robert Hayden's *Heart-Shape in the Dust,* only one black writer published volumes of poetry. Frank Marshall Davis brought out *Black Man's Verse* (1935), *I Am the American Negro* (1937), and *Through Sepia Eyes* (1938).

Born in 1905, Davis spent his youth in Kansas. He studied journalism for three years at Kansas State College after which he moved briefly to Georgia in 1931 to help start the Atlanta *Daily World.* He spent most of the 1930s, however, working for the Associated Negro Press in Chicago. The midwestern metropolis would have a profound influence on his poetry.[39]

Davis' poetry was stimulating, often quite provocative. He was a cynic with a sense of humor. His imagery was generally sharp, striking. His words, as he himself put it, were "gruff, stout, big muscled words"; his most effective lines were economical. Davis was essentially an urban poet. Some of his strongest poetry described urban scenes, especially Chicago which he affectionately called "my city." He was interested in the contrasts he found even in the Southside, "Chicago's Congo."

> Across the street from the Ebeneezer Baptist Church
>   women with cast iron faces peddle love
> In the flat above William's Funeral Home
>   six couples sway to the St. Louis Blues
> Two doors away from the South Side Bank
>   three penny-brown men scorch their guts with
>   four bit whiskey
> Dr. Jackson buys a Lincoln
> His neighbor buys second hand shoes
> —the artist who paints this town must
> use a checkered canvas ...[40]

39. For biographical information on Davis, see *The Negro Caravan,* 391–92. David Cannon's *Black Labor Chant* was published posthumously in 1939 by the National Council on Religion in Higher Education, but his verse was amateurish.

40. Frank Marshall Davis, "Chicago's Congo," *Black Man's Verse* (Chicago: Black Cat Press, 1935), 17–19.

And he studied the haggard patrons of "Mojo Mike's Beer Garden."

> From her youngly rouged face fifty year old eyes
>   look out
>   like unwashed windows in a newly painted house . . .
>   this woman who sits alone tosses a promise through
>   her gaze to all male youths
>
> . . . .
>
> Before the long flat back of a brown stained bar
>   men and women laugh, talk, drink, sweat
>   swapping monotony for alcohol.[41]

But when Davis called Chicago "my city," he meant all of it. His interest in it went far beyond the ghetto. In "Five Portraits of Chicago at Night" he started out with loud bragging, à la Carl Sandburg.

> My city is a strong-backed giant of a farm boy. . . .
>   My city stands with head thrown back . . . shouting
>   . . . swearing . . . my city dares the weak sissy
>   cities to come out in the yard and fight . . . my
>   city is thick-muscled and big-boned

Davis obviously felt affection for Chicago, and yet the imagery in the remaining portraits is negative, conjuring ugliness and life-lessness.

> Streets are gray veins on the thick body of a drowsy
>   giant
>
> . . . .
>
> Lighted buildings stare motionless at black faces of
>   dark neighbors like pensive old women in church . . .
>   as the toothless mouth of a door gapes open men and
>   women passing out are phlegm coughed from a dwell-
>   ing's throat
>
> . . . .
>
> a mangy flivver growls along the avenue . . . surface
>   cars like fat rats prowl cautiously over the floor of

41. Frank Marshall Davis, "Mojo Mike's Beer Garden," *ibid.*, 36–37.

> Chicago streets . . . overhead the green caterpillars
> of L trains crawl horizontally
>
> · ·
>
> The breath of my drowsy giant reeks of gin and ashcans,
> gasoline and hamburger stands. . . .[42]

While Davis displayed an intelligent interest in such nonracial
subjects as the city and the impact of the machine on modern civilization,[43] the primary impulse in his poetry was racial. Some of
his most effective poetry in this sphere was humorous. He aimed his
barbs at black and white alike. In "Georgia's Atlanta" he mixed his
cynicism with humor and observed that "From a billion billion
spermatazoa / which might have produced a hundred geniuses /
there evolved 270,000." Davis goes on to delineate numerous de-
grading aspects of race relations on both sides of the color line in
Atlanta and concludes:

> Well
> all but a few
> of the one third black
> and two thirds white
> were at their zenith
> when spermatazoa . . .[44]

His poems in the series, "Ebony Under Granite," are ironical and
often humorous epitaphs of black people from various walks of life.
In "Robert Whitmore," Davis pokes fun at the black middle class.

> Having attained success in business
> possessing three cars

42. Frank Marshall Davis, "Five Portraits of Chicago at Night," *ibid.*, 42–43. See
also Frank Marshall Davis, "Chicago Skyscrapers," *Through Sepia Eyes* (Chicago:
Black Cat Press, 1938), 6–7. Another talented observer of the urban scene during
this time was Melvin B. Tolson. See his "Gallery of Harlem Portraits," *Arts Quarterly*, I (April–June, 1937), 27.

43. See Frank Marshall Davis, "Modern Man—The Superman," *I Am the American Negro*, 51–54. Besides being antimachine, this poem is antiwar and anti-Fascist.

44. Frank Marshall Davis, "Georgia's Atlanta," *Black Man's Verse*, 52–53. See
also portions of Davis' "Snapshots of the Cotton South," *New Challenge*, I (Fall,
1937), 40–46.

one wife and two mistresses
a home and furniture
talked of by the town
and thrice ruler
of the local Elks
Robert Whitmore
died of apoplexy
when a stranger from Georgia
mistook him
for a Macon waiter.[45]

Davis also wrote in a more serious vein. Like so many others he wrote a vivid account of a lynching in which the victim defies his executioners as he faces death.[46] He also wrote a poem on the black Christ theme which was as irreverent as Hughes's. The tone of Davis' poem was not really serious, but mocking. For him the Christ which the white men had been painting "as fair as another New White Hope" was a fake. Davis' Christ was "a better Christ and a bigger Christ . . . one you can put your hands on today or tomorrow," he was a "Dixie nigger black as midnight."

My Christ is a black bastard. . . . Maybe Joe did tell
the neighbors God bigged Mary . . . but he fooled
no body . . . they all knew Christ's father was Mr.
Jim who owns the big plantation . . . and when Christ
started bawling out back in the cabins Mr. Jim made
all three git

· · · · · · · · · · · · · · · · · · · ·

Remember this you wise guys
Your tales about Jesus of Nazareth are no-go with me
I've got a dozen Christs in Dixie all bloody
and black . . .[47]

In his long and disjointed drama-poem, "I Am the American Negro," Davis likens the attitude of the black man to Christ's submis-

45. Frank Marshall Davis, "Robert Whitmore," *Black Man's Verse*, 79.
46. See Frank Marshall Davis, "Lynched," *ibid.*, 25–29.
47. Frank Marshall Davis, "Christ Is a Dixie Nigger," *I Am the American Negro*, 28–29.

siveness and then demands: "Arm your Christ with a shot gun . . . if David had slung a prayer and a hymn Goliath would have chalked up another win." He conceded that peaceful means of advance were the most desirable, but if the whites continue their violent opposition, "let 'em have it, buddy . . . you can't live forever anyhow!"[48] He would turn the heretofore humble and submissive black Christ into a wrathful avenger—a true proletarian hero.

Such strident notes appeared more frequently in his poetry during the later 1930s. These protested both racial and class persecution. In fact, like so many of the young radicals, he linked the two together. The opening lines of his "Snapshots of the Cotton South" could well have served as a scenario for the typical proletarian drama.

> Listen, you drawing men
> I want a picture of a starving black
> I want a picture of a starving white
> Show them bitterly fighting down on the dark soil
> Let their faces be lit by hate
> Above there will stand
> The rich plantation owner, holder of the land
> A whip in his red fist
> Show his pockets bulging with dollars spilled
> From the ragged trousers of the fighting men
> And I shall call it
> "Portrait of the Cotton South."[49]

But, always the cynic, Davis did not end his poem with a flourish of drums and red flags announcing the triumphant unity of the white and black workers. It ended instead with a challenge to "You apostles of Social Change": try to do something about it. For Davis was skeptical that anything could be done. His skepticism was most concisely expressed in "Race."

48. Frank Marshall Davis, "I Am the American Negro," *ibid.*, 20.
49. Davis, "Snapshots of the Cotton South," *ibid.*, 40. For another bitterly anti-capitalistic effort, see Davis' "To Those Who Sing America," *Through Sepia Eyes*, 3–5.

Four puppets
one white
one yellow
one red
one black
amuse the gods.[50]

Although, like Brown, he celebrated the black man's history of endurance,[51] he did not see it as a cause for optimism. "I Am the American Negro" ends apocalyptically:

The low, satin-soft voice he heard is drowned out
by the rolling tumble of loose, crashing stones . . .
these stones that formed the temple of America's Social
System end the life and problems of the Negro giant as
they collapse.[52]

Robert Earl Hayden's voice was much more affirmative and optimistic than Davis' voice. Born in Detroit, Michigan, in 1913, Hayden was just beginning his long and productive career during the late 1930s. Like so many other black writers he worked on the Federal Writers' Project; he was in charge of research into Negro history and folklore for the Detroit area.[53] His interest in Negro history was reflected in much of his poetry. Like Sterling Brown he saw it as a source of inspiration and strength. And like Brown, he wrote of the strength of the black folk who in spite of a harsh existence were able to endure. They expressed this strength in the "songs your anguish suckled":

These are the vital flesh and blood
Of any strength we have; these are the soil
From which our soul's strict meaning came—where grew

50. Frank Marshall Davis, "Race," *Black Man's Verse*, 62.
51. See Frank Marshall Davis, "What Do You Want America?" *ibid.*, 21–23.
52. Davis, "I Am the American Negro," *I Am the American Negro*, 22.
53. For biographical information on Hayden, see *The Negro Caravan*, 404.

> The roots of all our dreams of freedom's wide
> And legendary spring.[54]

But for the young Hayden who, like so many of the young writers, possessed radical sympathies, Negro history was more than just the heritage of endurance; it was also a tradition of revolt. Symbolic of this tradition was the rebellious slave Gabriel who was hanged for plotting a slave revolt. Hayden recorded the great martyr's last wish:

> That rebellion suckle
> The slave-mother's breast
> And black men
> Never, never rest
> Till slavery's pillars
> Lie splintered in dust
> And slavery's chains
> Lie eaten with rust.

And he was confident that his spirit would be reborn when he prophesied:

> The blow I struck
> Was not in vain,
> The blow I struck
> Shall be struck again.[55]

Like the other young radicals, Hayden advocated white and black labor solidarity. He pleaded with the workers, black and white, to see their mutual exploitation by the ruling classes:

> Hear me, white brothers,
> Black brothers, hear me:
>
> I have seen the hand
> Holding the blow-torch
> To the dark, anguish-twisted body;

---

54. Robert Hayden, "We Have Not Forgotten," *Heart-Shape in the Dust,* 10. See also Hayden's "What is Precious is Never to Forget," *ibid.,* 52.
55. Robert Hayden, "Gabriel," *ibid.,* 23–24.

> I have seen the hand
> Giving the high sign
> To fire on the white pickets;
> And it was the same hand.[56]

But most of Hayden's protests were naturally aimed at elucidating the persecution of the black man. Like so many others, he used lynching as the primary symbol of that persecution. In "Diana," subtitled "(An exercise in Southern mythology)," he struck a new note of irreverence by casting aspersions upon southern white womanhood. A young black has been lynched for the attempted rape of a young white woman whom he came upon while she was bathing. Naturally all of the guilt was placed on the black man; no one questioned the motives of the white girl,

> Nor question
> the lewd
> "Come, take me, black boy,"
> in Diana's eyes.
> Nor report
> the eager invitations of her breasts
> and how her thighs—
> > before she screamed
> > surprised at the sight of you—
> were quivering towards him,
> imploring the hard, male touch of him.
>
> Cry sacrilege
> obscene, obscene.
>
> Flay, rend burn,
> O Keepers of the white rose:
>
> Save the chaste harlot
> her venereal virginity.[57]

---

56. Robert Hayden, "Speech," *ibid.*, 27. See also the conclusion of Hayden's "These Are My People," *ibid.*, 63.
57. Robert Hayden, "Diana," *ibid.*, 43.

Hayden, like Cullen, Hughes, and Davis, also identified the suffering of Christ on the cross with that of the black lynch victim.
Unlike Hughes and Davis, Hayden's tone was reverent.

> By every black man burned
> Upon the lyncher's tree,
> We know, Lord Christ, we know
> Thine agony.[58]

But Hayden did not leave his black Christ dead upon the cross. He
followed the analogy through to resurrection:

> O burned black body
> on the tree of pain,
> you shall be born,
> be born again.

And Hayden, unlike Cullen, made it quite clear that his Christ's
resurrection was a symbol for the resurrection of the whole race:

> O black man ploughing
> the American earth,
>
> . . . .
>
> listen to the voices
> like arrows flying,
> listen to the voices,
> crying, crying;
> You shall be free,
> you shall have new birth,
> you inherit the earth.[59]

This note of affirmation was often struck in Hayden's volume. He
observed impoverished black folk growing sunflowers in the midst
of their decayed slum, and wrote:

> Here phonographs of poverty repeat
> An endless blues-chorale of torsioning despair—

58. Robert Hayden, "Religioso," *ibid.*, 40. See also his "Brown Girl's Sacrament,"
ibid., 39.
59. Hayden, "These Are My People," *ibid.*, 62–63.

And yet these dark ones find mere living sweet
and set this solid brightness on the bitter air.[60]

Hayden was generally optimistic about the future of black men in
America. But because of events then transpiring in Europe he was
not so pleased with the prospects for humanity in general. Like
many other poets in the late 1930s, black and white, Hayden
loathed the prospects of war.

> The warrior's ghost leaned
> against a lamp-post
> hoping the young men would see him there,
> with his armor hacked away and bloody,
> his face a rebus of mangled flesh,
> an iron sword buried
> to the hilt in his heart.
> But the young men ran past unheeding.[61]

His "Poem in Time of War" was a plea not just for a generation of
black men, but for all men.

> Though I be cast by war unto the rot, the dark,
> Though nightmare horrors mark my generation's end,
> Now while I live I'll not acknowledge death
> As Fuehrer to which the will must bend.
>
> O poets, lovers, eager-lipped young men,
> Say with me now that life is worthy—O give
> It affirmation; bring largesse of living,
> Make urgent now the will to live.[62]

In her volume, *For My People* (1942), Margaret Walker was
much more limited in her interests than any of the other poets thus
far considered. Each of the others had included some poems concerned with love or war or other subjects not necessarily related

60. Robert Hayden, "Sunflowers: Baubien Street," *ibid.*, 12. See also his "To A
Young Negro Poet" and "These Are My People," *ibid.*, 14, 56–63.

61. Robert Hayden, "The Wind, The Weathercock and The Warrior's Ghost,"
ibid., 22. See also his "Spring Offensive," *ibid.*, 17.

62. Robert Hayden, "Poem in Time of War," *ibid.*, 20.

to race. But as the title implies, her volume was put together for *her* people: her poems were about them and designed to inspire them to action.

Born in 1915, Margaret Walker was the daughter of a Methodist minister in Birmingham, Alabama. She was educated at Northwestern University (B.A., 1935), and Iowa State (M.A., 1940). Like Hayden, she served her apprenticeship in the Federal Writers' Project. Perhaps best known recently for her Civil War novel, *Jubilee* (1966), she first gained recognition with *For My People* which won the Yale University Younger Poets competition in 1942. Hers was the only volume of poems published by a black woman since Georgia Douglas Johnson's volumes of the 1920s.[63]

The kaleidoscopic title poem sets the theme for the whole volume. In the opening lines she pays her respects to the humble dignity and strength of the folk:

> For my people everywhere singing their slave songs
>   repeatedly: their dirges and their ditties and
>   their blues and jubilees, praying their prayers
>   nightly to an unknown god, bending their knees
>   humbly to an unseen power;

She also sings eloquently of the hopes and the inevitable disappointment and bitterness of the black man:

> For the cramped bewildered years we went to school to
>   learn to know the reasons why and the answers to
>   and the people who and the places where and the
>   days when, in memory of the bitter hours when we
>   discovered we were black and poor and small and
>   different and nobody cared and nobody wondered and
>   nobody understood;

And, finally, the invocation in which she strikes the major theme which dominates throughout: the times call for more than just the enduring strength of the folk.

63. For biographical information on Walker, see *The Negro Caravan*, 409.

Let a new earth arise. Let another world be born. Let
a bloody peace be written in the sky. Let a
second generation full of courage issue forth; let
a people loving freedom come to growth. Let a
beauty full of healing and a strength of final
clenching be the pulsing in our spirits and our
            martial songs be written, let the
            Let a race of men now rise and

    olume is given over to exhorting her people
   th necessary to *take* freedom now and keep it.
   ect for her ancestors was primarily motivated by
   . In "Lineage" she compared the present generation
with those of the past:

My grandmothers were strong.
They followed plows and bent to toil.
They moved through fields sowing seed.
They touched earth and grain grew.
They were full of sturdiness and singing.
My grandmothers were strong.

. . . .
Why am I not as they? [65]

And yet, while she admitted an admirable toughness in the old
folk, most often she used the past as a symbol of humiliation, something from which the black man must escape.

How many years since 1619 have I been singing
    Spirituals?
How long have I been praising God and shouting
    hallelujahs?
How long have I been hated and hating?
How long have I been living in hell for heaven?

. . . .

64. Margaret Walker, "For My People," *For My People* (New Haven: Yale University Press, 1942), 13–14.
65. Margaret Walker, "Lineage," 25.

> When will I burst from my kennel an angry mongrel,
> Lean and hungry and tired of my dry bones and years?[66]

She asserted that "there is a new way to be worn and a path to be broken from the past."[67] The time for action was now. And her frequently violent imagery did not suggest that by action she meant more talk.

> We have been believers believing in our burdens and our
>   demigods too long. Now the needy no longer weep
>   and pray; the long-suffering arise, and our fists
>   bleed against the bars with a strange insistency.[68]

Miss Walker, like most of the other black poets, also devoted a large section of her volume to the celebration of folk heroes. But, significantly, each of her heroes or heroines was what is termed a "bad nigger," one who would not subserve himself to any white man. Poppa Chicken, who was a "sugar daddy pimping in his prime," was typical.

> Poppa lived without a fear;
> Walked without a rod.
> Poppa cussed the coppers out;
> Talked like he was God.[69]

Margaret Walker addressed only one poem to white America, and it took the form of a bitter, ominous warning. In "Today" she spoke to a white America "complacently smug in a snug somnolescence," to a people "bothered by petty personals—your calories and eyemaline, your henna rinse and dental cream, washing your lives with pity, smoothing your ways with vague apologies." To these she scornfully wrote,

> I sing of slum scabs on city faces, scrawny
>   children scarred by bombs and dying of hunger, wretched

66. Margaret Walker, "Since 1619," *ibid.*, 26.
67. Margaret Walker, "Delta," *ibid.*, 22.
68. Margaret Walker, "We Have Been Believers," *ibid.*, 16–17.
69. Margaret Walker, "Poppa Chicken," *ibid.*, 36–37.

human scarecrows strung against lynching stakes, those
dying of pellagra and silicosis, rotten houses falling
on slowly decaying humanity.
  I sing of Man's struggle to be clean, to be useful,
to be free; of need arising from our lives, of bitter
living flowing from our laughter, of cankerous mutiny
eating through the nipples of our breasts.[70]

The harshness of Margaret Walker's words set her apart from
any of her female predecessors. Georgia Douglas Johnson and Anne
Spencer had never written of "slum scabs" or of "cankerous mutiny
eating through the nipples of our breasts." Such were not considered appropriate subjects—or means of expression—for lady poets
in previous eras. But Margaret Walker was of a generation of writers who came of age during bitter times, times which compelled
them to grapple with reality. Her break with tradition was an exaggerated expression of the departure of all of the significant black
poets from the romanticism of the 1920s.

As the depression deepened, most Negro poets turned away from
the celebration of Harlem exotics and concerned themselves with
bitter reality and with social protest. Protest, of one form or another, had always been the keynote of black poetry; and at least as
far back as Claude McKay's "If We Must Die" (1919), the concept
of retaliatory violence had been consciously cultivated. But when
McKay and those who echoed him in the 1920s said it, it still
shocked. Among the poets of the thirties, it became commonplace.
They were preoccupied with violent themes. What many of them
added to the idea of retaliation was the concept that both black
and white workers should strike back in unity against a class per-
secutor. Quite ironically, many of the self-styled realists who developed this theme actually ended up creating highly romanticized
proletarian heroes.

Before the thirties most black poets had conceived the black

70. Margaret Walker, "Today," *ibid.*, 28–29. See also her "Memory," *ibid.*, 56.

man's plight only in terms of racial persecution. But the depression era poets had a wider angle of vision. They became conscious of the universal impact of other forces, especially economic, on all men.

This broader perspective enabled them to look at things in their own terms, not necessarily in terms of race. Thus Frank Marshall Davis could examine the city without always seeing the ghetto, and Robert Hayden could despair of war because war is evil and not necessarily because the black man would or would not have a stake in it. Countee Cullen's attempt at a universal perspective looked backwards in time. The young poets of the thirties brought this perspective up to date.

And yet, granting this new perspective, these poets were still most concerned with the situation of their own race. And one theme was zealously reiterated by all of them: the black man must throw off his humble Christlike submissiveness and take freedom, forcefully if necessary. It was not a new theme, but never before had it been expressed with such unanimity. This militancy presaged the mood of black America during the war years.

VII

Black Reality and Beyond

Novels written by black writers during the 1920s were, for the most part, disappointingly shallow. For many readers the archetypal novel of the Harlem Renaissance was Claude McKay's *Home to Harlem* (1928). The Harlem which McKay depicted was the Harlem of cabarets and rent parties. His primitive-exotic hero, Jake, led a carefree life of parties, booze, and sex. The images McKay offered were essentially the same images which white thrill-seekers eagerly sought out as they invaded Harlem. They came to Harlem to be entertained, not to be exposed to unpleasant reality. For the thrill-seekers breezed into Harlem at night when the filth and decay, both of the tenements and of their human contents, were cloaked in darkness.

The principal alternative to the primitive-exotic image of the 1920s was the stereotyped middle-class paragon of virtue. Writers such as Jessie Fauset and Walter White attempted to demonstrate that middle-class Negroes were as morally upright as presumably were the "better class" of whites. Their lives differed very little from the lives of the idealized whites whom they imitated. They were generally light-skinned, extraordinarily refined, and financially secure. There was no valid reason that they should not be accepted into upper middle-class white society. They were the "prim and decorous ambassadors" whom Richard Wright so despised. The motives which had propelled these writers were similar to those

which had directed the Negro historians' emphasis on the heroic:
race pride and the hope for ultimate acceptance into the mainstream of American society. Significantly, one of the major themes
of these middle-class spokesmen was that of "passing." Their fiction
was excessively romantic and even more divorced from the reality
of the great majority of blacks than was *Home to Harlem*. Their
characters would have disdained contact with McKay's Jake because he was "low life." So were the black masses.

The novelists who came on the scene during the later 1930s
moved away from both stereotypes. They attempted to explore the
real lives of those ordinary black folk who lived in the tenements
or of their kinfolk who still scraped out a meager existence in the
South. They did not consider the black folk as "low," but as highly
important. Although they focused on the lives of the black masses,
even the more radical among them seldom relied on simplistic
proletarian formulas and stereotypes. Economic exploitation is
present in most of their fiction, but it is generally peripheral. Nor
did the novelists strike the note of white-black labor solidarity as
often as had the poets. The poets, many of them with radical inclinations, hoped for this unity, and hence often observed it when it
did not exist. The novelists—even the radical novelists—possessed
better vision. Perhaps the immense complexity of vision necessary
for the writing of a novel forced them to look a little harder at
reality. And as these young writers probed deeper and deeper into
the reality of black experience, the best of them evoked a universality which escaped most of the Renaissance writers; instead of
trying to romantically transcend reality, they immersed themselves
in it. Unlike the middle-class writers of the twenties, young novelists such as Zora Neale Hurston and Richard Wright did not think
they had to escape their blackness in order to dramatize themes of
genuinely universal significance.

It is difficult to classify these writers into specific groups or
schools because, unlike the New Negro writers of the 1920s who

lived and worked together in Harlem, these young novelists were scattered all over the country. It is almost impossible to discern any influence they may have had upon one another. But generally speaking, they were concerned with a social experience which was often violent and ugly, yet complex. Their characters were good, bad, happy, and pathetic. These writers were serious artists—trying neither to entertain nor to make a favorable impression, but to depict reality with honesty. The brooding and violent Bigger Thomas replaced the exotic and carefree Jake as the most memorable figure in Negro literature. Indeed, Bigger was the first black character created by a black writer to take his place among the most memorable figures in all of American fiction. This was so because while Bigger's experience was racially constricted, many of his deepest problems were those which confront all men in modern society.

Bigger Thomas' implications as a symbol for Americans were very different from Jake's. Although he symbolized a counterpoint to a sterile, materialistic civilization, it had been people like Jake, primitive creatures of joy, who had attracted the white slummers in search of entertainment. They would have been horrified had they been aware that people like Bigger were lurking in the darkness of the tenements they did not really see. As a symbol, Bigger was ominous, not entertaining.

With the exception of Langston Hughes's work, most of the fiction produced during the early 1930s continued to show the romantic influence of the Renaissance. The novels of Jessie Fauset, Countee Cullen, and Wallace Thurman displayed little social awareness of the problems of most black Americans. The novels of Claude McKay, though concerned with "low-life" blacks, were romantically oblivious to the difficulties facing black Americans during the depression. None of these writers' works indicated that they had been influenced by the hard times.

Jessie Fauset was one of the more prominent of the middle-class writers of the Renaissance. She published *The Chinaberry Tree:*

A Novel of American Life in 1931 and *Comedy American Style* in 1933. Both novels were the same kind of genteel melodrama which she had published during the 1920s. Her Foreword to the *Chinaberry Tree* announced her orientation. She first makes the statement that "to be a Negro in America posits a dramatic situation." But then she goes on to her major concern: "But of course there are breathing spells, in-between spaces where colored men and women work and love and go their ways with no thought of the 'problem.'" She has just taken *the* "dramatic situation" out of the formula. Indeed, the racial identity of the characters in *The Chinaberry Tree* is almost inconsequential. But this was precisely her point; she purposely depicted "something of the homelife of the colored American who is not being pressed too hard by the Furies of Prejudice, Ignorance, and Economic Injustice. And behold he is not so vastly different from any other American, just distinctive."[1]

The black middle class was not an invalid subject for fiction, but Miss Fauset's idealized treatment of it had little redeeming value. *The Chinaberry Tree* was much like the vapid romances that glutted the pages of the *Saturday Evening Post* during the 1920s and 1930s. For example, the beautiful (light-skinned) heroine, Laurentine Strange, who wants more than anything to be accepted by Negro society, muses to herself: "But she would always be kind, be courteous. 'Oh God, you know all I want is a chance to show them how decent I am.'"[2] Her young cousin, Melissa, sized up one of her suitors: "Asshur stood up, his hands in his pockets, looking rather wonderful in his brown, youthful perfection and again as on a former occasion she thrilled to his sheer masculinity. If only he weren't so set on becoming a farmer!"[3] And finally, another of Melissa's suitors, Malory Forten—who unbeknownst to them is actually her brother—woos her in the manner expected of a young

---

1. Jessie Fauset, *The Chinaberry Tree: A Novel of American Life* (New York: Frederick A. Stokes Co., 1931), ix–x.
    2. *Ibid.*, 36.   3. *Ibid.*, 91.

gentleman of color. "Every fellow does want his wife to be on a pedestal; he'd like to think of her as a little inviolate shrine that isn't ever touched by the things in the world that are ugly and sordid."[4]

Naturally, after floods of tears and heartache, Laurentine marries the handsome, brilliant young doctor and everyone ends up with his or her true love. The point is that instead of presenting a serious, realistic interpretation of middle-class black life, as she professed to do, Miss Fauset concocted a highly idealized romance. Her characters are not real human beings, they are idealizations of what the Negro middle class conceived itself to be. Ironically, this novel—along with Nella Larsen's *Passing* (1929)—is more effective for its unintended criticism, even satire, of the middle class's irrelevance than in demonstrating its potential for dramatic realization.

In his novel, *One Way to Heaven* (1932), Countee Cullen consciously satirized much of the black middle class which Jessie Fauset had satirized unconsciously. Cullen was particularly interested in the professional class which was a part of the Renaissance in Harlem. The novel is ostensibly about Sam Lucas, a one-armed itinerant panhandler who makes his living as a professional convert at revival meetings. At one such revival, Sam's dramatic conversion brought about the real conversion of an erstwhile doubter, one Mattie Johnson, who was so greatly impressed with Sam's conversion that she fell in love with and married him. The marriage lasts but a short while. Sam is a traveling man and he soon takes up with another woman. Mattie again becomes disillusioned. Sam returns to Mattie, but only after he has contracted a serious case of pneumonia. Aware of his impending death, he simulates yet another conversion for Mattie's sake. He thereby achieves real salvation for himself. Cullen contrasted Sam's charlatanry with that of Reverend Johnson, who was really as much a faker as Sam and a bit more hypocritical. These themes of doubt and salvation were

4. *Ibid.*, 265.

common in Cullen's poetry and were well developed in this novel even if the lives and character portraits of Sam and Mattie were not. But Cullen was more interested in Sam's spiritual salvation than in the reality of his life.

Although the story of Sam and Mattie was supposed to be the central theme of *One Way to Heaven*, Cullen devoted at least half of the novel to Constancia Brandon, a Harlem socialite whose soirees were a "must" for the fashionable crowd. Constancia's only relationship to the main plot of the story resided in the fact that Mattie was her maid. On this flimsy pretext Cullen was able to satirize the Negro middle class and much of the Harlem Renaissance. Although Constancia is shamelessly frivolous, she undoubtedly reflects Cullen's viewpoint. At her parties she observes various aspects of the Renaissance. At one such gathering she confronts one of the gawking white liberals who "discovered" the Negro during the 1920s. This is a Miss McGoffin, a missionary lady of abolitionist descent who was attempting to teach spirituals to her "African charges."

> "Of course they have never had the proper incentive for them over there, but you have no idea how they do rally to the mood and tempo. Sometimes as I shut my eyes over there in the African wilds and listen to them sing your songs that I have taught them in my poor way, I can fancy myself back in Georgia or Alabama or, or. . . ."
>
> "Or on Broadway?" suggested her hostess.
>
> "Why, yes, to be sure," Miss McGoffin was more than agreeable. "What I want to know is, are your people writing any more spirituals? I should like so much to carry back a brand new batch with me to show that civilization has not destroyed your creative instinct."
>
> "Indeed!" said Constancia with apparent emotion on the subject. "Indeed we *are*; we almost had run out of them for a while, but plans are under way for a fresh supply at any moment."
>
> "I am so glad," sighed the relieved Miss McGoffin.[5]

5. Countee Cullen, *One Way to Heaven* (New York and London: Harper & Bros., 1932), 159–60.

Nor did Cullen spare the exuberant New Negro. Always prominent at Constancia's parties was Mrs. De Peyster Johnson, a school teacher who prided herself as an inspirer of the New Negro. She was so taken with the movement that she had shunned the overtures of a relatively light-skinned professor so that she could marry a black man with whom she had nothing in common. Ironically, this union produced no black little New Negroes. As a teacher, she forced her pupils to study Negro literature in lieu of any other, praising even the poorest black poets effusively. Commented Constancia, "That's race pride with a vengeance for you, and self-criticism that isn't worth a penny."[6]

And yet, even Constancia chimes in with what was a typical Renaissance attitude. "I could go white if I wanted to," she explains, "but I am too much of a hedonist; I enjoy life too much, and enjoyment isn't across the line. Money is there, and privilege, and the sort of power which comes with numbers; but as for enjoyment, they don't know what it is. . . ."[7] For Constancia, blackness means a hedonistic style of life; it does not mean grinding poverty and ignorance. Her attitude is the same as that romantically expressed by Cullen in some of his Renaissance poetry.

It is significant that a novel in which the plot is concerned with the salvation of "low-life" figures, the most carefully delineated character is a middle-class socialite. Had Cullen attempted to contrast the world of Constancia with that of Sam and Mattie, there would have been sufficient rationale for his emphasis on her. But Cullen did not do this. Unlike the young realists who appear later in the thirties, he did not take a close look at the substance of "low-life" existence to give it the reality which he gave to Constancia's parties.

Cullen's satire of the Renaissance was gentle by comparison with that of Wallace Thurman. While Cullen satisfied himself with poking good-natured fun at various types of Renaissance figures, Thur-

6. *Ibid.*, 186.   7. *Ibid.*, 187.

man, in his bitter *Infants of the Spring* (1932), poured his scorn upon specific individuals. For example, Cullen is caricatured in the novel as DeWitt Clinton. Raymond Taylor, Thurman's principal mouthpiece in the novel, summons up "a vivid mental picture of that poet's creative hours—eyes on a page of Keats, fingers on a typewriter, mind frantically conjuring African scenes, and there would of course be a Bible nearby."[8]

Infants of the Spring was Thurman's second novel. In 1929, he had published *The Blacker the Berry*, a novel concerned with middle-class racial self-hatred. Although critics generally applauded his choice of subject, they panned his performance. They were quite right. Thurman could not even bring his main character to life. He was too obsessed with her hatred of her black skin to give her the human dimensions so important in skillful characterization.

Infants of the Spring was no improvement. It is warped by Thurman's bitterness over the failure of the Renaissance and, perhaps, over his own failure as an artist. Devoid of plot, the novel chronicles the aimless lives of the inhabitants of Niggeratti Manor —the Harlem intelligentsia and would-be intelligentsia who just seem to drift from party to party and drink to drink. The novel is flawed by the interminable discussions of these characters. The only two men who possess any real talent, Raymond and Paul, pontificate upon various issues of large import. They are little more than obvious mouthpieces for Thurman. In fact, Thurman is so overly concerned that each of his characters should reflect certain points of view that he never lifts them above stereotype.

Raymond and Paul consider themselves frustrated geniuses.[9] When they look within themselves they find only the mocking bitterness of their frustration, but never any of the cause for it. For

8. Wallace Thurman, *Infants of the Spring* (New York: The Macaulay Co., 1932), 236.
9. See Langston Hughes's appraisal of Thurman in *The Big Sea*. Hughes thought Thurman was one of the most brilliant men he had ever met. For a brief biographical sketch of Thurman, see Robert A. Bone, *The Negro Novel in America* (2nd ed. rev.; New Haven and London: Yale University Press, 1965), 92–94.

this they look outside themselves, to the literary movement of which they are a part. In their anger they lash out against almost everybody and everything. But in the end, Paul destroys himself.

Thurman lampooned those New Negroes, like Cullen, who achieved real prominence. He castigated the black middle class who "made themselves obnoxious striving to make themselves agreeable" to whites.[10] And he insulted white liberals whose influence he believed was stifling the real artistic expression of serious black writers. "I'm sick of all you goddamned whites," Raymond shouts, "you twentieth century abolitionists. You're a bunch of puking hypocrites. And that goes for reformers of your type and the lilly-livered bastards that come up here seeking thrills and pleasures."[11]

But Thurman's bitterest attack was against the whole idea of a Negro Renaissance. He thought that at one point it had perhaps been promising, but that promise had been corrupted by the "goddamned whites" and by untalented blacks. He believed that it had been a hoax, a fantastic publicity stunt. Hence, Paul in desperation to gain publicity for his novel, spreads the manuscript on his bathroom floor, gets into the bathtub and slashes his wrists. The water from the tub runs over and his manuscript is rendered illegible. The suicide which was designed to bring attention to the novel, prevents it from ever being read. Only the title page remains completely legible, and it represents Thurman's obituary for the Renaissance: "He had drawn a distorted, inky black sky-scraper, modeled after Niggeratti Manor, and on which were focused an array of blindingly white beams of light. The foundation of this building was composed of crumbling stone. At first glance it could be ascertained that the sky-scraper would soon crumple and fall, leaving the dominating white lights in full possession of the sky." Both of Thurman's novels failed because he was too deeply a part of them. The prob-

10. Thurman, *Infants of the Spring*, 183–84.
11. *Ibid.*, 202.

lems of his protagonists were his own problems. He never put himself at a great enough distance to look at them with some objectivity and wider perspective. One suspects that in writing of the failure of the Renaissance, he was really more concerned with his own.[12]

If *Infants of the Spring* possessed a major unifying theme, it was that "the more intellectual and talented Negroes of my generation are among the most pathetic people in the world today."[13] But Wallace Thurman could really only report the malady; Claude McKay went deeper and tried to dramatize the reasons. He found those reasons in the sterilizing influence of Western civilization upon the heretofore natural black man.

The character Jake in McKay's immensely popular *Home to Harlem* typified the popular image during the 1920s of the primitive-exotic black man whose life-style was uninhibited by a repressive civilization. McKay continued to be intrigued with the figure in his other two novels, *Banjo* (1929) and *Banana Bottom* (1933), and in his collection of short fiction, *Gingertown* (1932). Indeed, he was still singing the praises of the "natural man" in his controversial nonfiction account of Harlem in 1940.[14] Throughout the period McKay persisted in his belief that Afro-American intellectuals had been educated by the white man away from the simple and natural enjoyment of life which was the African heritage of the black masses. Though related to Carter Woodson's concept of miseducation, McKay's approach was definitely not bourgeois. McKay was as much a black nationalist as Woodson or Du Bois—although he was loath to admit it—but his black nationalism was more genuinely directed toward the glorification of the black masses.[15]

12. *Ibid.*, 284. See Bone, *The Negro Novel in America*, 93–94.

13. Thurman, *Infants of the Spring*, 225.

14. See Claude McKay, *Harlem: Negro Metropolis* (New York: E. P. Dutton & Co., Inc., 1940). For biographical accounts of McKay, see Bone, *The Negro Novel in America*, 67, 73–75; and James A. Emanuel and Theodore L. Gross (eds.), *Dark Symphony: Negro Literature in America* (New York: The Free Press, 1968), 85–88.

15. See Claude McKay, *A Long Way From Home* (New York: Lee, Furman, Inc., 1937); and *Harlem: Negro Metropolis.*

Banjo, correctly sub-titled *A Story Without a Plot,* is essentially an extension of *Home to Harlem,* except that it takes place on the teeming waterfront of Marseilles. The two principal characters are basically the same. Ray, the intellectual figure in *Home to Harlem,* is the same ambivalent Ray in *Banjo,* a man who knows that he is hopelessly trapped by his Western education into a sterile, life-denying civilization, while he yearns to be an instinctive, natural man. He marvels over Banjo, who assumes the primitive-exotic role of Jake in this novel and who represents "the happy irresponsibility of the Negro in the face of civilization."[16]

Banjo lives to drink, make music and love. He lives for the moment. He is the embodiment of hedonism. At one point in the novel, however, he loses his banjo and all of his money and is forced to go to work. McKay contrasts the drab, monotonous work of Banjo's essentially free spirit. But because he is unencumbered by the burden of an education, he is equipped to take such setbacks. His philosophy is that "life is a rectangular crossways affair and the only thing to do is to take it nacheral."[17] His constant advice to his friends is "to be nacheral."

Ray observes Banjo's life-style and covets it for himself. For him "it was hell to be a man of color, intellectual and naturally human in a white world." It was easy enough, he thought, for Banjo, "who in all matters acted instinctively. But is was not easy for a Negro with an intellect standing watch over his native instincts to take his own way in this white man's civilization. But of one thing he was resolved: civilization would not take the love of color, joy, beauty, vitality, and nobility out of *his* life and make him like one of the poor mass of its pale creatures."[18] But Ray never does really become a Jake or a Banjo for the very obvious reason that he always needs to rationalize the choice to do so. Ray's rationalizing and his

16. Claude McKay, *Banjo: A Story Without a Plot* (New York and London: Harper & Bros., 1929), 313.

17. *Ibid.,* 234.   18. *Ibid.,* 164.

incessant discourses with other figures over the great issues of the day take most of the drama out of the novel. Like Thurman, McKay here gives the impression that he was more concerned with using the novel as a platform from which he could deliver his chauvinistic philosophy and his views on various other topics than with using it as a vehicle for creative expression. In addition to this failing, McKay did not succeed in making Banjo a convincing human being. He was too much the stereotype of boundless joy. In this he rivaled Sambo.

Banana Bottom is a much more successful novel. McKay placed this story in Jamaica, the setting of his own boyhood. The protagonist is Bita Plant, a young black peasant girl who has been temporarily adopted and educated by a white missionary couple, the Reverend Malcolm Craig and his wife Priscilla. In this novel, McKay did not discuss the virtues of the peasants' primitive-exotic style of life; he merely let that style of life speak for itself. His peasants were happy, simple folk, content with living close to the fertile soil. McKay contrasted their uninhibited pastoral existence with the dour, sterile lives of the Craigs. The peasants had a healthy, honest attitude toward sex and were prolific; the Craigs who were embarrassed by sex had only one son, Patou, who was an imbecile.

Priscilla Craig sends Bita away to a school in England, hoping to civilize her, to educate her away from the loose peasant way of life. She thinks that after seven years "she would be English trained and appearing in everything but the color of her skin."[19] Her conception of education is repressive, designed "to make you see and do the correct thing almost automatically."[20] The "correct thing," for example, would be for Bita to marry the respectable divinity

19. Claude McKay, *Banana Bottom* (New York and London: Harper & Bros., 1933), 91.
20. *Ibid.*, 45.

student, Herald Newton Day, who has been completely educated to the white world's standards. Herald is attracted to Bita because she has been "trained like a pure-minded white lady."[21] But Bita is saved from this fate when "Herald Newton Day had descended from the dizzy heights of holiness to the very bottom of the beast. The rumor ran through the region that Herald Newton had suddenly turned crazy and defiled himself with a nanny goat."[22] In such a manner were the once-healthy instincts of a peasant boy perverted by the white man's education.

Unlike Herald Newton Day, Bita never completely succumbs to her English education. She appreciated it, but she did not permit it to destroy her natural instincts and identity. "Many young natives had gone to the city or abroad for higher culture and had returned aloof from, if not actually despising, the tribal life in which they were nurtured. But the pure joy that Bita felt in the simple life of her girlhood was childlike and almost unconscious. She could not reason and theorize why she felt that way. It was just a surging free big feeling."[23]

In the end, Bita deserts the "civilized" life of the Craigs and the "cultivated" Negroes and goes back to the peasant life. She marries Jubban who "was superior in one thing. He possessed a deep feeling for the land and he was a lucky-born cultivator."[24] Unlike Ray, Bita is a well-adjusted person. She uses her education to understand the things of the white world, but at the same time she instinctively remains what she really is.

McKay's novels are crudely Manichean: the totally sterile and repressive white civilization versus the idealized fruitful existence of the black man in his natural state. *Banana Bottom* was praised by many critics because of its realism, because McKay, at times, portrayed low life realistically. But he never really dealt with the

21. *Ibid.*, 100.
22. *Ibid.*, 175.
23. *Ibid.*, 41.
24. *Ibid.*, 291.

misery of low life. Just as Jake and Banjo were ideal types of the primitive-exotic, the pastoral life described in *Banana Bottom* was nostalgically ideal.

It is significant that all of McKay's major fiction was written while he was living either in Europe or in Morocco. Perhaps this accounts for his softening of the harsher aspects of reality. After nearly ten years of living the bohemian life abroad, he was out of touch with the violence and excruciating poverty that filled the lives of black men in the United States of the depression era. His celebration of black primitivism looked back into the "liberated" 1920s, but it simply was not relevant to the pressing reality of the 1930s.

In his 1930 novel, *Not Without Laughter*, Langston Hughes also touched upon the theme of the degenerating effects of white education on the lives of blacks. Tempy is one of three daughters of Aunt Hagar. She marries into the black middle class and soon assumes the artificial values of her husband who hated the blues and the spirituals because "they were too Negro." "Colored people certainly needed to come up in the world," thought Tempy, "up to the level of white people—dress like white people, talk like white people, think like white people—and then they would no longer be called 'niggers.'" [25]

Hughes contrasts Tempy's coldness with the joy and love to be found in Aunt Hagar's shanty. For his fifteenth birthday, Tempy gives her nephew Sandy a book, *The Doors of Life*, written by a white New England minister "who stood aghast before the flesh." Ironically, instead of teaching young men about love, Sandy found that "its advice consisted almost entirely in how to pray in the orthodox manner, and in how *not* to love." [26] In the end, Tempy denies even her mother.

---

25. Langston Hughes, *Not Without Laughter* (New York: Alfred A. Knopf Co., 1930), 240.
    26. *Ibid.*, 260.

But Hughes was less interested in dramatizing what white middle-class values had done to Tempy than he was with looking realistically into the lives of the common folk in a small Kansas town. There he found much pain and sorrow, and not a little bitterness; but he also found the humor and beauty as expressed in the blues sung by Sandy's father, and most of all the love and quiet courage of Aunt Hagar, Sandy's grandmother.

Aunt Hagar is a pious old washerwoman who because of her genuine Christianity is beloved by all folks in the community, black and white. In spite of her hard lot, and in contrast to Tempy, her constant advice—indeed, her way of life—is to love. "When you starts hatin' people," she tells Sandy, "you gets uglier than they is —an' I ain't never had no time for ugliness, 'cause that's where de devil comes in—in ugliness!"[27] Instead, she counsels, "there ain't no room in this world fo' nothin' but love."[28]

Although the novel centers about the growing years of young Sandy, it is old Aunt Hagar whom Hughes develops most completely and to whom he attributes heroic stature. For although she, like so many of the older Negroes, passively lays her fate in the hands of "de Lawd," she has also endured much and through it all has been able to find some beauty and some laughter in life. Late in the novel, after Hagar has died, Sandy comes to an appreciation of these qualities. He sees a group of haggard old black men laughing raucously. "That must be the reason, thought Sandy, why poverty-stricken old Negroes like Uncle Dan Givens lived so long—because to them, no matter how hard life might be, it was not without laughter."[29] Be it noted, however, that theirs was not the uninhibited, carefree laughter of a Jake or Banjo. It was the laughter which Hughes had captured so well in his blues poems.

Not Without Laughter was an important novel because it was one of the first by a black writer in which the life of the common

27. *Ibid.*, 177.   28. *Ibid.*, 182.
29. *Ibid.*, 251.

folk was examined on its own terms, not for its humor or propaganda value. Hughes achieved a realism lacking in the fiction of
other black writers until the middle of the 1930s because he
recreated the complexity of life in the black community. Unlike
McKay, he did not have to "jazz up" his characters to make them
significant or interesting.

Another of Hagar's daughters, Harriet, is interesting because she
expresses views which would receive more of Hughes's attention
as the decade passed. "Aw, the church has made a lot of you old
Negroes act like Salvation Army people," Harriet yells at her mother. "Your old Jesus is white, I guess, that's why! He's white and
stiff and don't like niggers!"[30] To young Harriet's way of thinking,
Aunt Hagar's religion has made her a "white folks' nigger." In his
short fiction, Hughes took up the theme of the ways in which whites
attempted to mold blacks into their conceptions of what they should
be. This is, in fact, the major unifying theme of his collection of
short fiction, *The Ways of the White Folks* (1934).

In a typical example, "The Blues I'm Playing," Mrs. Dora Ells-
worth attempts to make the talented young pianist, Oceola Jones,
into her own conception of the artist: a life-denying conception of
living for art and not for life. But "music to Oceola, demanded
movement and expression, dancing and living to go with it."[31]
Oceola will not docilely accept a way of life imposed from without.

Hughes strikes his most militant note in "Father and Son," the
story of a young black man's defiance against his white father.
When Negroes on the Norwood plantation become dissatisfied with
their conditions and start to say so, Colonel Norwood orders the
black Baptist minister to start a revival to drain off the unrest. He
knew that as long as they were singing and praying, they would
forget about the troubles of this world. "In a frenzy of rhythm and

30. *Ibid.*, 42.
31. Langston Hughes, *The Ways of the White Folks* (New York: Alfred A. Knopf
Co., 1934), 111.

religion," wrote Hughes, "they laid their cross at the feet of Jesus." Writing in the same vein as he had in his poems, "Good Bye Christ" and "A New Song," he continued, "Poor over-worked Jesus! Somehow since the War, he hadn't borne that cross so well. Too heavy, it's too heavy! Lately, Negroes seem to sense that it's not Jesus' cross, anyhow, it's their own. Only old people praise King James anymore."[32] Norwood's black son, Bert, tells the young people on the plantation "to stop being white folks' niggers" and the revival fails. Bert further proves his militance when at the certain forfeit of his own life he strangles his enraged landlord father.

This story was melodrama. Both the white landlord father and the militant young son were the ludicrous stereotypes endemic to proletarian fiction. But "Father and Son" was Hughes's most serious attempt at proletarian fiction.[33] It was the story always cited by Communist critics to prove Hughes's allegiance to the proletarian struggle. The most shocking message was that of black violence against the white oppressor. It had not appeared very frequently in previous Negro fiction, but it would become commonplace by the later years of the depression.

Like Hughes at his best, Zora Neale Hurston wrote about Negro folk life because of its own intrinsic value and interest. Radical critics like Richard Wright criticized her harshly for not demonstrating a political and social consciousness in her novels. For them her novels were insignificant. Indeed, she was perhaps less concerned than any other black writer during the period with the conventional problems of the Negro. Casting aside the problems of race relations, her novels are set entirely within the black community. And despite Wright's scorn, she did discover much of significance.[34]

32. *Ibid.,* 223.

33. See also Hughes's story, "The Negro in the Drawing Room," published in *Race,* I (Summer, 1936), 90–92.

34. For biographical accounts of Zora Neale Hurston, see her autobiography, *Dust Tracks in the Road* (Philadelphia, New York, and London: J. B. Lippincott Co., 1942); S. P. Fullinwider, *The Mind and Mood of Black America: Twentieth-Century Thought* (Homewood, Ill.: Dorsey Press, 1969), 169–71; Bone, *The Negro*

Zora Neale Hurston published two novels during the 1930s: *Jonah's Gourd Vine* (1934) and *Their Eyes Were Watching God* (1937). In *Jonah's Gourd Vine* she demonstrated a fine skill at transcribing the folk idiom and an intelligent understanding of folk life, but the novel suffers from a lack of plot and faulty structure. Miss Hurston's command of folk culture can be attributed to the fact that she grew up in the South, within its influence, and she came to an intellectual appreciation of it while a student of Franz Boas at Columbia. Her interest in the folk also resulted in the publication of two books of folklore, *Mules and Men* (1935) and *Tell My Horse* (1938).

Their Eyes Were Watching God is one of the better novels produced by a black writer during the 1930s and despite Wright's contention that it was shallow romance, lacking in protest value, Miss Hurston skillfully wove the romantic elements into a pattern of protest; not race or class protest, but feminine and individual protest. One of the major themes of the novel is expressed by the protagonist's grandmother: "De nigger woman is de mule uh de world so fur as Ah can see."[35] Her greatest wish is that Janie find a respectable husband with property. "Ah can't die easy," she warns Janie, "thinkin' maybe de menfolks white or black is makin' a spit cup outa you."[36]

Janie, still just a young and lonely girl, idealistically dreams of love and beauty in her search for a man. But she allows her grandmother to marry her off to an old farmer who owns sixty acres and a house. She finds in her marriage not beauty, not love, but respectability and drudgery. She soon discovers that her role called for her

---

Novel in America, 126. Another writer who set his novel entirely within the rural black community in the South was George Wylie Henderson. See his *Ollie Miss* (New York: Frederick A. Stokes Co., 1935). For a critical analysis, see Bone, *The Negro Novel in America*, 123–26.

35. Zora Neale Hurston, *Their Eyes Were Watching God* (Philadelphia and London: J. B. Lippincott Co., 1937); the selections following are from the paperback edition (Greenwich, Conn.: Fawcett Publications, Inc., 1968).

36. *Ibid.*, 21.

to be little more than her husband's slave. Like the livestock on the farm, her value seemed to be measured in terms of how much work she could do. It does not take long for Janie to resume her dreams and at this juncture in walks Jody Starks, an ambitious young man on his way to make his fortune in a small all-black community down in Florida. Jody is attracted by Janie's good looks and he promises to fulfill her dreams if she will run away and marry him. Janie becomes Mrs. Jody Starks.

Her new husband becomes mayor of the community and, as proprietor of the general store, its wealthiest citizen. He is egotistical and consumed by a desire for possessions. Janie becomes aware that her value to him is primarily that of a possession to be shown off. After a short while she finds almost no fulfillment in her marriage at all. "The spirit of the marriage left the bedroom and took to living in the parlor. It was there to shake hands whenever company came to visit, but it never went back inside the bedroom again." She becomes quiet and withdraws within herself, spending the next twenty years "saving up feelings for some other man she had never seen."[37]

While she works in the general store Jody bosses her around as if she were a child, and day after day she overhears his friends and him joking at the expense of women. Only twice does Janie steel up the courage to get back at the men. Her first rebuttal is in the feminist tradition and is directed toward men in general: "Sometimes God gits familiar wid us womenfolks too and talks his inside business. He told me how surprised He was 'bout y'all turning out so smart after Him makin' yuh different; and how surprised y'all is goin' tuh be if you ever find out you don't know half as much 'bout us as you think you do. It's so easy to make yo'self out God Almighty when you ain't got nothin' tuh strain against but women and chickens."[38] Her second rebuttal is directed toward Jody and the sham of their marital relationship. For him Janie has not been

37. *Ibid.*, 62, 63.   38. *Ibid.*, 65.

another human being, but a symbol for other men to see of his virility—a virility not much in evidence since the early days of their marriage. One day, in the presence of several customers, Jody ridicules Janie to the point that she finally breaks her silence with "when you pull down yo' britches, you look lak de change uh life."[39] This completely destroys Jody's spirit and he dies not long after. It is the beginning of Janie's rebellion.

Sympathetic neighbors counseled Janie that "Uh woman by herself is uh pitiful thing. . . . Dey needs aid and assistance. God never meant 'em tuh try tuh stand by theirselves. . . . You been well taken keer of, you needs uh man."[40] Janie knew that she needed a man, but not for the reasons defined by her neighbors. She had been living too long in conformity with the definitions of others. She wanted a man with whom she could share a warm physical and emotional relationship.

At this stage Tea Cake comes into Janie's life. Tea Cake is a happy, vibrant and perhaps irresponsible young man—at least fifteen years younger than Janie—who is attracted to Janie merely for herself. He makes her feel alive for the first time since her childhood. Much to the consternation of the community, Janie decides to run off with him. "So us is goin' off somewhere and start all over in Tea Cake's way. Dis ain't no business proposition, and no race after property and titles. Dis is uh love game. Ah done lived Grandma's way, now Ah means tuh live mine."[41] Janie and Tea Cake run off to a life of work and play as agricultural laborers. The life is hard, but they make the most of it, never letting *things* come between them.

Until his death two years later, Janie finds complete fulfillment in her relationship with Tea Cake. She feels heavy grief over his death, but she is comforted by something which she had once told him during earlier, happier days: "We been tuhgether round two

39. *Ibid.,* 69.   40. *Ibid.,* 77.
41. *Ibid.,* 96.

years. If you kin see de light at daybreak, you don't keer if you die at dusk. It's so many people never see de light at all."[42] For two years Janie has defined her own style of life and unlike her previous marriages, her relationship with Tea Cake has been one of two human beings who mutually enjoyed each other. Their life together represented an act of rebellion against outer-imposed definitions—against things as they are supposed to be. As Janie tells her friend, Pheoby, after returning from burying Tea Cake, "It's uh known fact, Pheoby, you got tuh *go* there tuh *know* there. Yo' papa and yo' mama and nobody else can't tell yuh and show yuh. Two things everybody's got tuh do fuh theyselves. They got tuh go tuh God, and they got tuh find out about livin' fuh themselves."[43]

Claude McKay's Bita rebelled against the identity which white society attempted to impose on her. McKay never really lifted her out of the black and white dichotomy. But Miss Hurston cast Janie's rebellion on a more universal level. First of all, she rebelled as a woman against masculine definitions. But finally, she rebelled against *any* outer-imposed definitions. At the end of *Banana Bottom*, Bita decides to be her black self; Janie, rather, decides merely to be herself. Miss Hurston was able to dramatize elements of universal significance while confining her story entirely within the reality of black experience.

Richard Wright condemned Zora Neale Hurston's novel because it was unconcerned with the race or class struggle or the revolutionary traditions of black people in America.[44] He used the same criteria in lavishly praising Arna Bontemps' *Black Thunder* (1936) as the first Negro proletarian novel. He thought that Bontemps had done a fine job of transforming Gabriel Prosser, the leader of a slave insurrection in Virginia, in 1800, into a great proletarian hero. "Bontemps endows Gabriel," he wrote, "with a myth-like death-

42. *Ibid.*, 131.   43. *Ibid.*, 158–59.
44. Richard Wright, "Between Laughter and Tears," *New Masses*, October 5, 1937, pp. 22, 25. See also W. A. Hunton, "The Adventures of the Brown Girl in Her Search for Life," *Journal of Negro Education*, VII (January, 1938), 71–72.

less quality," which transcended personal dignity and personal courage.[45]

In addition to being a proletarian novel, *Black Thunder* was a fine piece of historical fiction. During the 1930s the historical novel enjoyed a great vogue in the United States. It served two major and diametrically opposing functions during a period of severe crisis: providing escape and generating morale.[46]

All three of Bontemps' novels were historically based. The first of these, *God Sends Sunday* (1931), was concerned with the rise and fall of a Negro jockey, Lil' Augie, back at the turn of the century. Bontemps skillfully reproduced the environment of the sporting world of New Orleans and St. Louis, but his characters had much of the primitive-exotic about them. Of the two functions suggested, *God Sends Sunday* definitely falls into the category of escape.

Bontemps' later novel, *Drums at Dusk* (1939), recreates the successful slave revolt of Toussaint l'Ouverture in Haiti. This novel is full of romance and melodrama, somewhat similar to the fiction that would later make Frank Yerby famous. *Drums at Dusk* possessed a message of revolt, but it was clothed in such romance as to make its effect essentially that of escape.

Though still a romance, *Black Thunder* (1937) possessed a realism lacking in the other two novels. Bontemps spent three years in painstaking research for this novel. Some of his figures, such as Gabriel, are heroic, but humanly heroic. Their motivations and their failures are believable. Neither Gabriel nor any of the other conspirators are stereotyped proletarian heroes.

Unlike his other two novels, *Black Thunder* assumed the task of bolstering Afro-American morale and pride in the black heritage.

---

45. Richard Wright, "A Tale of Folk Courage," *Partisan Review and Anvil*, III (April, 1936), 31. For a brief biographical account of Bontemps, see *Dark Symphony*, 477–78.

46. See Leo Gurko, *The Angry Decade* (New York: Dodd, Mead and Co., 1947), 191.

The heritage Gabriel bequeathed to black men was one of manhood. *Black Thunder* was the first full-length novel to have black violence against white society as its major theme.

In the attempted revolt which Bontemps recreated, the blacks were to be unmerciful in their vengeance: "They ain't going to spare nothing what raises its hand—nothing."[47] On the night of the insurrection one of the slave rebels waits in ambush and thinks: "It was going to be like hog-killing day. Criddle had a picture in his mind; he remembered the feel of warm blood. He knew how it gushed out after the cut. He remembered the stricken eyes. Then more blood, thicker and deeper in color. Criddle knew."[48] "Hog killing," he thought, "wasn't a bad preparation for tonight's business." Such a note, although not uncommon in Negro poetry, was new in Negro fiction. It revealed the depth of bitterness which black men felt towards the white men and the course of action they might take should they become desperate enough in their frustration.

Although the revolt fails and Gabriel is eventually captured and hanged, he dies like a man—like a free man. For as he awaits his death he realizes that although his body is shackled, his act of rebellion has made him a free man: "I been free. And, Lordy, I's free from now on, too. . . . They know I'm a free man, me."[49] Such an attitude, thought Bontemps, could inspire oppressed black men everywhere. Like Carter Woodson, Bontemps sought glory in Afro-American history.

In his eloquent novel, *Blood on the Forge* (1941), William Attaway also delved into the history of the black man in America. But, like Richard Wright in his folk history of the migration, instead of dramatizing the exploits of a historic race hero, Attaway looked with the scrutiny of a sociologist at the brutal experience of the mass of blacks who migrated from the agrarian South into the industrial North at the time of the First World War. Like *Black Thun-*

47. Arna Bontemps, *Black Thunder* (New York: The Macmillan Co., 1936), 60.
48. *Ibid.*, 90.   49. *Ibid.*, 199.

der, Attaway's novel should be classed as proletarian fiction. In fact, the general structure of the novel conformed more closely to the typical proletarian novel than did Bontemps' because the setting was more contemporary and the exploitation of the workers was placed in an industrial environment. But Attaway's book was not the run-of-the-mill, artless formula-novel which was characteristic of so much proletarian fiction. For in addition to portraying the persecution and exploitation of the workers, black and white, Attaway also intelligently dramatized the erosion of the old southern folkways by the immense and impersonal force of the machine.

Blood on the Forge was Attaway's second novel. In 1939, he had published *Let Me Breathe Thunder,* a picaresque novel about two depression era hoboes. Perhaps the most interesting note about this novel is that its principal characters are white. Though in many ways Attaway's first novel is very effective, it relies too heavily on melodrama; his protagonists are just a bit too naïve and sentimental to be believable. Such is not the case with *Blood on the Forge* which ranks as one of the finest novels of the depression era.

Attaway's main characters are three brothers. Chinatown is lazy, hedonistic, and lives by outer symbols—his proudest possession is his golden tooth about which he explains "can't 'ford to lose this tooth."[50] Melody is introspective, intelligent, and sensitive—the music he makes on his guitar is expressive of his personality. And, finally, Big Mat, the oldest brother, is a physical giant who, in hopes of some day receiving a call to preach, reads his Bible every day. Wrote Attaway, "To almost everybody but his close kin he was a stupid, unfeeling giant, a good man to butcher hogs. . . . Melody alone knew him completely. Melody, from his dream world, could read the wounds in Big Mat's eyes."[51] The essential characteristic

50. William Attaway, *Blood on the Forge* (New York: Doubleday, Doran and Co., Inc., 1941), 49. See Bone, *The Negro Novel in America,* 133; and Edward Margolies, *Native Sons: A Critical Study of Twentieth-Century Negro American Authors* (Philadelphia and New York: J. B. Lippincott, Co., 1968), 54–55.
51. Attaway, *Blood on the Forge,* 14.

of each of the three men will be destroyed by the new machine environment.

All three brothers are tenant farmers in the green hills of Kentucky. They are forced to flee from those hills when Big Mat, pouring out the bitterness of years of humiliation and persecution, thrashes the white riding boss: "The riding boss fell to the ground, blood streaming from his smashed face. He struggled to get to his feet. A heavy foot caught him in the side of the neck. His head hung over his shoulder at an odd angle." Aside from the immediate necessity of escaping white retaliation, their flight has another level of meaning for Attaway. They are leaving the land because it has become infertile. It is worn out, incapable of sustaining the black folk any longer. "The land has jest give up, and I guess it's good for things to come out like this,"[52] observes Big Mat as they prepare to leave.

They meet an agent from a northern steel mill who gives them passage to the mill on board a freight car. The blackness of the boxcar is symbolic of a womb out of which they will be reborn into the industrial environment.[53] But it is also a coffin, symbolic of the impending death of the folk consciousness: "Squatted on the straw-spread floor of a boxcar, bunched up like hogs headed for market, riding in the dark for what might have been years, knowing time only as dippers of warm water gulped whenever they were awake, helpless and drooping because they were headed into the unknown and there was no sun, they forgot even that they had eyes in their heads and crawled around in the boxcar, as though it were a solid thing of blackness."[54]

When the new men arrive at the mills, Attaway contrasts them to the men who have already been conditioned to the sterile monotony of industrial existence: "Everything was too strange for the green men to comprehend. In a daze, they were herded to the mill

52. *Ibid.*, 33, 43–44. 53. See Margolies, *Native Sons*, 55.
54. Attaway, *Blood on the Forge*, 45.

gates and checked in. The night shift was getting off. They mingled for a few minutes at the mill gates. All of them were gray in the dirty river mist."[55] The idea that the green men will become gray men is skillfully developed by Attaway. He never deviates from the attitude that as bad as the feudalistic southern environment was, it was still alive; it was still characterized by very personal relationships between human beings, not the impersonal, mechanized quality of the northern environment. Social scientists like E. Franklin Frazier, looking toward long-range goals, had optimistically observed the destruction of the old folk culture as a positive development accelerating integration into the mainstream of American society. Attaway had carefully dramatized this process, but without the optimism of the sociologists. His artistic consciousness was much more sensitive to immediate suffering, and it told him that possibly something valuable was being destroyed.

It does not take long for the three brothers to become gray men, stripped of their folk identities by the mills. Melody finds that "the old music was going," and after an accident to his hand in the mills he ceases to play his guitar altogether. Chinatown is blinded by an explosion in the mills and he is no longer capable of seeing those outward symbols through which he had lived: "Now those symbols were gone, and he was lost."[56] Big Mat, because of his enormous strength, fares best in the competition with the monster machines. But even he succumbs eventually, losing his religion and becoming shamefully impotent—a mere hulk of the virile man he once was.

The last sections of the novel revolve around Mat and his efforts to regain his manhood. There is rising dissatisfaction among the workers at the mills and they decide to strike. Big Mat has no intention of joining the union. And through his attitude the author attempts to explain why black men were successfully employed as strike-breakers for so many years. "Big Mat was not thinking about

55. *Ibid.*, 64.				56. *Ibid.*, 190.

the labor trouble. Yet he knew that he would not join the union. For a man who had so lately worked from dawn to dark in the fields twelve hours and the long shift were not killing. For a man who had ended each year in debt any wage at all was a wonderful thing. For a man who had known no personal liberties even the iron hand of the mills was an advancement. In his own way he thought these things. As yet he could not see beyond them."[57] Mat is signed up as a company deputy and he regains his manhood through violence: "He had handled people, and they feared him. Their fear had made him whole." But this feeling of manhood is only temporary, it has no strength against feelings or ideas such as those behind the expression "nigger." He can maintain his manhood only through repeated violence.[58]

Attaway reintroduces the proletarian theme within the context of Mat's anti-union violence. He understands Mat's position, but clearly disagrees with it. Mat achieves proletarian consciousness only as he is being beaten to death by one of the union men. He suddenly suspects that he has taken over the role of the riding boss. "Maybe somewhere in these mills a new Mr. Johnson was creating riding bosses," realizes Mat, "making a difference where none existed."[59] Big Mat's sudden, intuitive realization rings perhaps the one false note in Attaway's novel.[60] The attempt to submerge race conflict within the context of class conflict was no more convincing when portrayed dramatically than when it was proclaimed by radical politicians and scholars.

The most famous black proletarian writer during the late 1930s was Richard Wright. In his collection of novellas, *Uncle Tom's Children* (1938), he employed a sharp realism to recreate the brutality of life under Jim Crow in the South. Each of the stories vividly emphasizes the violence that pervades southern life; in two of the

57. *Ibid.*, 208; Margolies, *Native Sons*, 59.
58. Attaway, *Blood on the Forge*, 255, 264.   59. *Ibid.*, 274.
60. See Bone, *The Negro Novel in America*, 139.

stories Wright creates lynching scenes effectively enough to induce a genuine feeling of nausea in the reader. His emphasis on violence was the most persistent and striking of any black writer to date.

But there is also another thread which ties these stories together. Each of the leading characters asserts himself in some way—usually with violence—in the face of Jim Crow repression. They are, after all, the children of Uncle Tom and like most children they have rejected the ways of their fathers. In asserting themselves they each overcome their brutal circumstances.

"Fire and Cloud" comes closest of any of the stories to falling into the proletarian formula. Dan Taylor, a Negro preacher, is at first mired down in the resignation of his religion. He imputes to God the responsibility for earthly salvation: "The good Lawd's gonna clean up this ol world some day!"[61] The poorer sections of the town in which Taylor lives are suffering from starvation. The officials of the city will offer no assistance. As a leader of the Negro community, Taylor is prevailed upon by agitators to lead his people in a protest march. He is also prevailed upon by the white power group to remain silent. His failure to assure them of his submissiveness gives them cause to have him severely beaten. This savage treatment, in addition to the prodding of his son—"We jus as waal git killed fightin' as t get killed doing nothin"[62]—determines the course which Taylor will pursue. He will step from behind his mask of docility.

Then, as so often occurs in proletarian fiction, he leads an all-too-successful march of poor blacks and poor white who triumphantly gain their demands. And Dan Taylor, now finally enlightened, like so many other proletarian heroes during the 1930s proclaims "Freedom belongs to the strong!"[63]

61. Richard Wright, *Uncle Tom's Children* (New York: Harper & Bros., 1940); the selections following are taken from the 1965 paperback edition, 131. This analysis of *Uncle Tom's Children* and of *Native Son* is taken largely from the present writer's M.A. thesis; see James Owen Young, "Richard Wright: A Study in Isolation," (M.A. thesis, University of Southern California, 1968), especially pp. 79–88.

62. Wright, *Uncle Tom's Children*, 134   63. *Ibid.*, 180.

Considered by many to be the masterpiece of the collection, "Bright and Morning Star" is a story in which the hero is a woman, a unique occurrence in Wright's fiction. At the outset of the story Aunt Sue is another figure who is trapped within the stifling confines of her apathetic religious orientation: "Long hours of scrubbing floors for a few cents a day had taught her who Jesus was, what a great boon it was to cling to Him, to be like Him and suffer without mumbling a word." Like Dan Taylor, she has left the task of earthly salvation to the action of a Higher Being. Her attitude is reflected in the expression "we gotta live in hope." But in addition to living "in hope," Aunt Sue also lives in perpetual fear. "As she had grown older, a cold white mountain, the white folks and their laws, had swum into her vision and shattered her songs and their spell of peace." [64]

Both of Sue's sons are arrested for Communist party organizing activities. The older son is sentenced to prison. When the younger son carries on the work of his brother, he is apprehended by an ugly mob. Living her entire life in docile submission, Aunt Sue is at last stirred to action by the threat to her child. Carrying a white sheet—ostensibly a shroud in which to place her son after the mob has done with him—she goes to the site of his agony. However, beneath the sheet she conceals a shot gun with which she intends to take revenge for the outrages endured by her son, and beneath her subservient mask she hides an unquenchable rage. After witnessing the almost unimaginable suffering to which her son is subjected, she makes her way into the middle of the mob and suddenly reaps her vengeance with blasts from the shotgun.

After this moment of heroic action she almost happily submits to the penalty she knows she must pay. In the seconds before she is obliterated, she achieves a sublime serenity: "And she was suddenly at peace; they were not a white mountain now; they were not pushing her any longer to the edge of life. It's awright. . . ." [65]

64. *Ibid.*, 184.   65. *Ibid.*, 213.

Ironically, she achieves salvation, not through turning the other cheek, but through violence. Like Frank Marshall Davis, Wright would have armed his Christ with a shot gun.

Although Wright's novellas represented the most brutally realistic fiction produced by any black writer up to that time, they were still very melodramatic. After he read the reviews of the collection he felt that he had made a naïve mistake in writing "a book which even bankers' daughters could read and weep over and feel good. . . . I swore to myself that if I ever wrote another book, no one would weep over it; that it would be so hard and deep that they would have to face it without the consolation of tears."[66]

So Wright created Bigger Thomas, an antihero, as the protagonist of *Native Son*. Bigger is no militant black proletarian hero struggling against the repressive forces of capitalism. Bigger is ignorant. He is bitter. He is mean. He is a coward. He is a murderer. His act of violent rebellion is unconscious. His murder of Mary Dalton is motivated by the fear of a black man that he will be caught alone with a young, drunken white woman in her bedroom. Although it was an accident, Bigger acknowledges to himself that "in a certain sense he knew that the girl's death had not been accidental. He had killed many times before, only on those other times there had been no handy victim or circumstance to make visible or dramatic his will to kill. His crime seemed natural; he felt that all of his life had been leading to something like this."[67] The fact that Bigger's victim is the daughter of wealthy white liberal philanthropists is quite significant. While considering themselves altruistic "benefactors" of black America, Mary's parents were extracting exorbitant rents

66. Richard Wright, "How Bigger Was Born," *Saturday Review*, June 1, 1940, p. 19.
67. Richard Wright, *Native Son* (New York: Harper & Bros., 1940), 101. The most helpful critical analyses of *Native Son* for the purposes of the present study are: Nathan A. Scott, Jr., "Search for Beliefs: The Fiction of Richard Wright," *University of Kansas City Review*, 23 (October, 1956), 19–24, and (December, 1956), 131–38; Bone, *The Negro Novel in America*, 140–52; Margolies, *Native Sons*, 65–86; and Fullinwider, *Mind and Mood of Black America*, 187–93.

from the rat-infested tenement in which Bigger and his family were entrapped. Bigger's murder of Mary Dalton is Wright's bitterly ironic comment on the failure of white liberalism in America—a liberalism in which men like Kelly Miller and James Weldon Johnson had placed so much faith. But even more important, Wright is indicting an entire civilization which produces misfits like Bigger who can only achieve a definition of his identity—who can only communicate his feelings—through violence. The murder gave Bigger his first opportunity to assert himself—to create an identity for himself—in his efforts to elude detection and capture: "Never had he had the chance to live out the consequences of his own actions; never had his will been so free as in this night and day of fear and murder and flight."[68]

Perhaps the most important aspect of Bigger's personality which Wright developed, but which was missed by contemporary critics who were too shocked by Wright's strident protest against racism, was the theme of human isolation. Bigger exists "behind a wall, a curtain" from which he never emerges.[69] He is incapable of communicating with anybody. Significantly, his girlfriend Bessie holds no attraction for him other than animal gratification. Living as two isolated individuals, there is no communication between them other than on a physical level.

Bigger probably comes closest to communicating with Max, his Communist lawyer. But even here, as sympathetic as he is, Max never really looks at Bigger as another fellow human. "Well, this thing's bigger than you, son. In a certain sense, every Negro in America's on trial out there today,"[70] he tells Bigger. In the end, Bigger goes to the electric chair realizing that he has never really related to another human being. His only effective means of communicating with the rest of the world has been violence. He has lived and will die an outsider.

68. Wright, *Native Son*, 225.   69. *Ibid.*, 14.
70. *Ibid.*, 340.

As Wright indicated in "How Bigger Was Born," modern man has failed to communicate on a universal level those inner feelings which might produce human unity. In one of the most significant images to be found in all of Wright's fiction, Bigger has a dream—it must be a dream because Bigger was not sophisticated enough to express it:

> He saw a dark and vast fluid image rise and float; he saw a black sprawling prison full of tiny black cells in which people lived; each cell had its own jar of water and a crust of bread and no one could go from cell to cell and there were screams and curses and yells of suffering and nobody heard them, for the walls were thick and darkness was everywhere. Why were there so many cells in the world? . . . Slowly he lifted his hands in the darkness and held them in mid-air, the fingers spread weakly open. If he reached out with his hands, and if his hands were electric wires, and if his heart were a battery giving life and fire to those hands, and if he reached out with those hands and touched other people, reached out through these stone walls and felt other hands connected with other hearts—if he did that, would there be a reply, a shock? Not that he wanted those hearts to turn their warmth to him; he was not wanting that much. But just to know that they were there and warm! Just that, and no more; and it would have been enough. And in that touch, response of recognition, there would be a union, identity; there would be a supporting oneness, a wholeness which had been denied him all his life.[71]

Bigger's dilemma is symbolic of the dilemma of modern man. His image of life as a "black sprawling prison full of tiny black cells" reflects Wright's bleak conception of life. Life is seen as a unified whole, and yet it is inhabited by isolated individuals. Men share a unity, and yet are unable, even on the basis of this unity, to see or understand each other. In reaching out his hands, Bigger is seeking to touch this unity in humanity as a basis for communication and compassion. Wright is certain that modern man lives completely apart from his fellow man. He hopes that there is a unity which,

71. *Ibid.*, 334–35.

when clarified, will draw men together. And yet Bigger never realizes his hope of finding a meaningful basis for communion with the rest of mankind. He goes to his death in hate, cynically believing in nothing except the nihilistic fact that "what I killed for, I *am*."[72] He was an ominous, and perhaps even prophetic, symbol to a nation—and a world—which was rapidly descending into the bloody anarchy of world war.

Wright went beyond the rather facile attempts of most young radical intellectuals to identify the black man's problems and his future with an economic class. Unlike them he saw that racism was too deeply woven into the fabric of American life for this to be a realistic possibility. Rather, he attempted to identify the metaphysical despair and aspirations of all men within the situation of an ugly black youth. It was precisely this depth and breadth of vision which set Wright apart from most of the other black intellectuals of the era.

72. *Ibid.*, 391–92.

Epilogue

Throughout the depression years the older race men had been preoccupied with strictly racial matters. Indeed, for some of them race seemed to be a means of escape from reality. Hence, romantic historians like Carter Woodson glorified the black past, and literary critics like Benjamin Brawley effusively praised many works of Negro literature which were at best mediocre. Other men, like Du Bois, losing faith in the struggle to gain access into American society, sought escape into an all black nation within a nation. In greater or lesser degree all of the race men expressed black nationalist sentiments. All of them employed a racial perspective in defining problems and solutions. They saw racism as the preeminent problem in American society. They very realistically based this judgment upon their own historical experience dating back to the late nineteenth century. As race men, they thought that black America's problems could ultimately be solved only when black Americans learned to organize themselves in their own interest. And yet here the agreement ended. If they were to successfully organize the race, an essential prerequisite would be a strong unanimity amongst themselves. Instead, they spent altogether too much of their time sniping at one another or at the young radicals. Perhaps the most striking example of this can be found in Du Bois's characteristically honest obituary for Kelly Miller in 1940: "If his mental brilliancy had been backed by power of concentration and hard continuous work, he might have left the world imperishable literary monuments. But Miller was not only intellectually lazy, but the very lightness and scintillating quality of his mind easily beguiled him from drudgery and left him satisfied with epigrams, keen thrusts, telling but too often superficial criticisms." Unforgiving, even to a dead man, Du Bois concluded that Miller had gained a "widespread reputation for instability of judgment and disloyalty to most causes."[1] This lack of unity, which was one of the most striking characteristics of black writers and spokesmen during the depression years, was perceptively described by William Pickens in his criticism of the young radicals' dream of a national Negro congress: "It is to be a miracle of God to make twelve Negroes pull in the same direction, it will be a miracle beyond God to bring all Negro and pro-Negro organizations under one direction."[2]

At the same time that the older race men were calling for organization, many of them were also preaching the virtues of rugged individualism. With the exception of a few men such as James Weldon Johnson, the standards and values of these men were rooted in the nineteenth century. In economics they advised that if black men would make sacrifices, if they would strive harder than white men, then they could succeed. Socially, they taught joyless respectability. Their literary tastes were genteel. Few of them ever really came to terms with the twentieth century.

Nor did they ever really come to terms with the experience of the common black man in the United States. Despite all of their race pride, the virtues which they trumpeted were the highly romanticized ideals of nineteenth-century middle-class white America. They were often ashamed of black life as it really was. Their

1. W. E. B. Du Bois, "As the Crow Flies," New York *Amsterdam News*, January 6, 1940.
2. William Pickens, "Ruminations While Driving a Ford," Louisiana *Weekly*, March 14, 1936.

escape from twentieth-century reality and into a romanticized race chauvinism isolated them from both the mainstream of modern society and the masses of black Americans.

Reacting against the provinciality of the older race men, the younger intellectuals who came to maturity during the 1930s sought to broaden their horizons. They attempted to view the black man and his problems objectively within the context of the larger society. The catastrophic depression of the 1930s convinced many of them, especially the academic radicals, that black America's principal problem was the same economic problem which faced the rest of the nation.

In their published writings at least, men like Ralph Bunche sometimes pushed this interpretation so far that they tended to ignore race altogether. They observed that the black masses were of the working class and went on to theorize that the basic problems facing black workers were therefore essentially class, not race problems. In contrast to the race men, whose black chauvinism they publicly denounced, they publicized the idea that the black masses should de-emphasize race consciousness in favor of working-class consciousness. Sociologist E. Franklin Frazier optimistically believed that the black folk's migration into the cities would accelerate this process. Like the older leaders, the young radicals thought that the black men should be organized, but more along class than race lines.

Just because these young academic radicals emphasized the uplift of the black masses does not mean that they identified with them any more than did Du Bois or Benjamin Brawley. Their understanding of the black folk was essentially theoretical. The real life of the black masses was just as "low" for them as it was for any of the older race leaders. It was low because most of them had never been a part of it. They had been born into the same black middle class as many of the older leaders.

Unlike most of the older men, many of these young academics

had been trained in the best graduate schools, learning the socio-logical theories of men like Robert Park, who taught that assimila-tion was the inevitable fate of all minority groups in this society. Never questioning the value of complete assimilation, the young academics looked about hopefully for increasing evidences of the disintegration of the anachronistic folk culture as black people mi-grated into the cities. The integration of black workers into the CIO's organizing campaigns also gave them cause for optimism. The organized labor movement could possibly help to accelerate the process of assimilation which their sociological theories told them was inevitable.

Their own experiences undoubtedly had an important influence upon their optimistic outlook. By the 1920s and 1930s racism was no longer intellectually respectable in academic circles, and young Negro scholars were being accepted into the company of their fellow white graduate students. In his autobiography, Horace Cay-ton observed that he was always more comfortable with the white "university crowd" than he was with most blacks.[3] Many of these young intellectuals were also warmly accepted into the company of white radicals during the 1930s. These experiences surely had an effect on their reorientation away from a narrowly racial per-spective.

Too often, however, this reorientation carried the young aca-demics as far away from reality as an out-dated provinciality had carried some of their elders. Just as the older race men often ad-vised an escape into race, these young radicals advocated escape—escape from the reality of race into a theoretical class. As both Du Bois and Miller had suggested, they should have studied the history of their fathers more closely.

The broader vision and attempted objectivity which was pursued by the young academic radicals was given a different expression by the young literary critics, poets, and novelists. True, many of

3. Horace Cayton, *Long Old Road* (New York: Trident Press, 1965), 208.

them frequently wrote in support of a class perspective, but they often went beyond this. Many of them successfully defined the universals of human experience within the complex reality of black experience. They did not deny the folk culture as Frazier did, nor ignore the reality of race as Bunche so often did. They frequently followed Richard Wright's advice that they must understand, use, and even embrace the racial implications of their lives, not necessarily to encourage them, but in order to finally transcend them.

Older critics like Alain Locke had frequently called upon black writers to strive for universality. But Locke seldom got beyond rather vague generalities. Young critics like Sterling Brown and Wright attempted to specifically define the universalities within the black experience. Unlike Benjamin Brawley and many of the other older critics, these young men were reasonably objective. They tried to judge a work of art for its artistic value, not its utility to race advancement. They also thought that it was time to judge works by black writers were to produce something really significant, it would criticism, and not merely in relation to other Negro literature. If black writers were to produce something really significant, it would have to be as good as anything produced by other writers.

Although their output was not as great in volume, the works of the young poets and novelists of the 1930s were often superior in quality to those of the Renaissance. In some instances their work compared very favorably with the best in contemporary American literature.

In poetry, Frank Marshall Davis and Robert Hayden demonstrated that black men could write effectively on important themes which were not necessarily related to race. In later years, Hayden would gain recognition—which Countee Cullen had always coveted—as a great poet and not necessarily as what had condescendingly been called a great *Negro* poet. Nevertheless, race continued to be the primary force in the works of black poets, and militant anger was now the predominant mood. The violent, often apoca-

lyptic, imagery in much of their verse presaged the events of the
war years in which the pent-up anger of black Americans would
finally boil over into bloody retaliation on military bases and in the
streets of Detroit and Harlem.[4]

Young novelists like Langston Hughes, Zora Neale Hurston, William Attaway, and Richard Wright were successful in their search
for universality within the reality of black experience. Unlike their
genteel and "New Negro" predecessors, they saw no need to make
their characters middle-class idealizations or primitive creatures of
joy in order for them to be significant or interesting. Instead, they
attempted to look objectively into the lives of the common black
folk. There, as Sterling Brown had predicted, they found beauty
and ugliness, strength and weakness, all of which provided rich
material for the dramatization of universal themes.

The most important expression of this broader perspective was
Richard Wright's *Native Son*. For Wright was able to portray Bigger Thomas on many levels. Bigger can be defined as a race victim,
and he can be defined as a class victim. Wright's protest on these
two levels was obvious and his frankness stunned everybody in
1940. But finally, Bigger can be defined merely as a human victim.[5]
It was Bigger's humanity which was ignored in 1940. People viewed
him merely as a symbol of social maladjustment—as a monster
created by a repressive environment. Not for several years did anybody see him as an individual human facing an isolation which
Wright believed had become the modern condition of man.

Possibly because *Native Son* was the first novel of its kind to
reach the best-seller lists, white Americans were most shocked by
Bigger's hatred of them. They had been smugly unaware of the
depth of such hatred. Wright had most effectively done what Wil-

4. Harvard Sitkoff, "Racial Militancy and Interracial Violence in the Second
World War," *Journal of American History*, LVIII (December, 1971), 668–75; and
Sitkoff, "The Detroit Race Riot of 1943," *Michigan History*, LIII (Fall, 1969),
183–206.

5. Margolies persuasively argues that there are three kinds of revolutionism in
Native Son: Communist, racial, and metaphysical. See Margolies, *Native Son*, 81–82.

liam Attaway and many of the poets had also tried to do; he had measured the depth of black anger and its violent potential. Cities like Chicago were not accelerating the assimilation of black people into American society; they were producing totally alienated, dangerous individuals. Bigger Thomas represented the ultimate negation of the optimism of sociologists like Frazier.

The anger which Wright dramatized in its extreme antisocial form was expressive of the anger felt in varying degrees by black Americans all over the country as World War II approached.[6] During the war years some of this anger would find release in the violence of race riots, but most of it, for a few years at least, would be channeled into militant protest by such organizations as A. Philip Randolph's March on Washington Movement and the new Congress of Racial Equality.[7] Randolph represented a new breed of race men who were not afraid to organize the black masses for the purpose of mass picketing and direct confrontation.

6. Sitkoff, "Racial Militancy and Interracial Violence in the Second World War," 661–63, 666–75; Richard M. Dalfiume, *Desegregation of the U.S. Armed Forces: Fighting on Two Fronts, 1939–1953* (Columbia: University of Missouri Press, 1969), 105–31; these pages were published in slightly different form under the title "The 'Forgotten Years' of the Negro Revolution," *Journal of American History,* 55 (June, 1968), 90–106; Garfinkel, *When Negroes March,* 21–27.

7. Dalfiume, *Desegregation of the U.S. Armed Forces,* 64–81; Sitkoff, "Racial Militancy and Interracial Violence in the Second World War," 661–68; August Meier and Elliott M. Rudwick, *From Plantation to Ghetto: An Interpretive History of American Negroes* (New York: Hill and Wang, 1966), 218–19, 222–23.

Bibliographical Essay

A list of all the sources for this study would essentially be a repetition of the footnotes. Instead, the following essay evaluates the more important sources for the study of Negro writers in the 1930s.

Because this study was limited to the public expressions of Negro intellectuals, the bulk of the primary source material was conveniently available at a single depository, the Arthur Schomburg Collection of Negro Literature and History, a branch of the New York Public Library. Particularly useful was the rich collection of scrapbooks which bring together newspaper clippings relating to many of the prominent individuals of the 1930s. Of less value were the vertical files, containing clippings, pamphlets, and articles, which the staff at the Schomburg maintains on each of the figures considered in this study. The most important of the many Negro newspapers on microfilm were the Pittsburgh *Courier*, the Norfolk *Journal and Guide*, the New York *Amsterdam News*, the New York *Age*, the Chicago *Defender*, the Washington *Tribune*, the St. Louis *Argus*, and the Baltimore *Afro-American*. Also on microfilm was A. Philip Randolph's monthly union newspaper. *The Black Worker: Official Organ of the Brotherhood of Sleeping Car Porters and Mouthpiece of the Negro Workers of America.* Of considerable interest, but of relatively little value was the complete microfilm file of Communist party newspapers in Harlem during the 1930s: *The Liberator* (1920–32), *The Harlem Liberator* (1933–34), and *The Negro Liberator* (1934–35). A careful perusal of the editorials and articles by men such as Cyril Briggs, Otto Hall, Richard Moore, and several others confirmed this writer's opinion that black Communist intellectuals abandoned their intellectual independence when writing for the Party.

Among the most valuable sources for the study of Negro intellectuals during the 1920s and 1930s is the series of unpublished research memoranda which Ralph Bunche prepared in 1940 for the famous Carnegie-Myrdal study of Negroes in the United States (published in 1944 as *An American Dilemma*). These memoranda, now in the Schomburg Collection, constitute the most detailed examination of recent Afro-American intellectual history undertaken up to that time. The most important volumes for the present study were: "Conceptions and Ideologies of the Negro Problem," "The Programs, Ideologies, Tactics and Achievements of Negro Betterment and Interracial Organizations" (4 vols.), and "A Brief and Tentative Analysis of Negro Leadership."

A number of journals and periodicals contained important articles by and about Negro intellectuals. The *Crisis* (organ of the National Association for the Advancement of Colored People) and *Opportunity: Journal of Negro Life* (organ of the Urban League) carried a wide diversity of articles on current events, culture, and literature. The *Journal of Negro History* and the *Negro History Bulletin* (1938–) were almost the only publications specifically concerned with Negro history. The *Journal of Negro Education* (1932–), published at Howard University, was most important for its concentration on contemporary affairs. It was essentially an organ of the young radical academicians who dominated Howard during the 1930s. Of less value was the *Quarterly Review of Higher Education Among Negroes* (1933–) because of its narrower focus on specific problems of education. Of critical significance was the short-lived *Race* (1935–36, only 2 issues), which aspired to be a voice for the young radical intellectuals. The younger writers also made brief attempts to publish a literary journal, *Challenge* (1934–37), and the more ambitious, but shorter-lived *New Challenge* (1937, single issue published). *Phylon*, a very important journal, was founded by W. E. B. Du Bois at Atlanta University in 1940.

Important "white" periodicals occasionally concerned with Negroes were *The Nation, New Republic, Survey Graphic, Atlantic Monthly, American Mercury, Current History, The World Tomorrow* and the *Saturday Review of Literature*. Young radicals and Communists published frequently in the Communist party organ, *New Masses,* and occasionally in *International Literature,* a Soviet journal published in Moscow. Another leftist journal which displayed some interest in Negro writers was *Partisan Review.*

While the emphasis in this study has been on thought, rather than biography, a certain amount of biographical information was necessary. Richard Bardolph's *The Negro Vanguard* (New York: Rinehart Inc., 1959) provided brief biographical sketches of nearly all of the individuals considered in this analysis. Also useful was Sterling A. Brown, Arthur P. Davis, and Ulysses Lee (eds.), *The Negro Caravan* (New York: The Dryden Press, 1941); and James A. Emanuel and Theodore L. Gross (eds.), *Dark Symphony: Negro Literature in America* (New York: The Free Press, 1968).

Several figures wrote important autobiographies during the 1930s. W. E. B. Du Bois's *Dusk of Dawn: An Essay toward an Autobiography of a Race Concept* (New York: Harcourt, Brace & Co., 1940), synthesized much that Du Bois had written during the depression years. His later book, *The Autobiography of W. E. B. Du Bois: A Soliloquy on Viewing My Life from the Last Decade of Its First Century*, edited by Herbert Aptheker (New York: International Publishers, 1968), was less useful for the purposes of this study. Du Bois is one of few leading black figures who has received much attention from biographers. The best study is Francis L. Broderick, *W. E. B. Du Bois: Negro Leader in a Time of Crisis* (Stanford: Stanford University Press, 1959). Also useful was Elliott M. Rudwick's *W. E. B. Du Bois: A Study in Minority Group Leadership* (Philadelphia: University of Pennsylvania Press, 1961). The W. E. B. Du Bois Memorial Issue of *Freedomways* (Winter, 1965), contains several suggestive essays.

James Weldon Johnson's autobiography, *Along This Way* (New York: The Viking Press, 1933), offers some good insights into the clash between the older leadership and the young radicals. This should be supplemented by a reading of Bernard Eisenberg, "James Weldon Johnson and the National Association for the Advancement of Colored People, 1916–1934" (Ph.D. dissertation, Columbia University, 1968). Claude McKay's *A Long Way from Home* (New York: Lee Furman, Inc., 1937) documents his romantic Negro nationalism and his bitter isolation. Langston Hughes's two autobiographical volumes, *The Big Sea* (New York: Alfred A. Knopf, 1940), covering his life up to about 1930, and *I Wonder As I Wander* (New York: Rinehart, 1956), which begins at that date, generally offer more insight into the times than the man. Two biographical studies have recently been published: Donald C. Dickinson, *A Bio-Bibliography of Langston Hughes: 1902–1967* (Hamden, Connecticut: Archon Books, 1967); and James A. Emanuel, *Langston*

Hughes, Twayne's United States Authors Series (New York: Twayne Publishers, 1967), which contains a useful annotated bibliography. Arthur P. Davis has written a suggestive essay on Hughes's poetry, "The Harlem of Langston Hughes' Poetry," *Phylon*, XIII (Winter, 1952), 276–83.

Although he never wrote a full autobiography of his mature years, Richard Wright's essay, "I Tried to Be a Communist," *Atlantic Monthly* (August, 1944), 61–70, and (September, 1944), 48–56, and since reprinted in Richard H. S. Crossman, ed., *The God That Failed* (New York: Harper & Row Publishers, Inc., 1949), gave important insight into the stifling influence of the Communist party on black intellectuals. A number of biographies of Wright have appeared in recent years, the most comprehensive of which is Constance Webb's *Richard Wright, A Biography* (New York: G. P. Putnam's Sons, 1968). Webb's book includes a complete bibliography of Wright's published works. Other useful studies of Wright include: Edward Margolies, *The Art of Richard Wright* (Carbondale: Southern Illinois University Press, 1969); and Russell Carl Brignano, *Richard Wright: An Introduction to the Man and His Works* (Pittsburgh: University of Pittsburgh Press, 1970). There has been a flood of critical articles on Wright's fiction. The most important are Nathan A. Scott, "Search for Beliefs: The Fiction of Richard Wright," *University of Kansas City Review*, XXIII (October, 1956), 19–24, and (December, 1956), 131–38; and Ralph Ellison, "Richard Wright's Blues," in *Shadow and Act* (New York: Random House, 1964), 89–104. Robert Bone's discussion of *Native Son* in *The Negro Novel in America* (2nd ed. rev.; New Haven: Yale University Press, 1966), and Herbert Margolies' in *Native Sons: A Critical Study of Twentieth-Century Negro American Authors* (Philadelphia and New York: J. B. Lippincott Company, 1968), were the most helpful.

Other autobiographies, published after the 1930s, were generally less helpful. Zora Neale Hurston's *Dust Tracks on a Road* (Philadelphia, New York, and London: J. B. Lippincott Co., 1942), lacks the penetrating insight which was so evident in her one outstanding novel. George S. Schuyler's *Black and Conservative: The Autobiography of George S. Schuyler* (New Rochelle, N.Y.: Arlington House, 1966), often shows a remarkable lack of memory. Although he was not given much consideration in this study, Horace Cayton's *Long Old Road* (New York: Trident

Press, 1965), is incisive and has considerable value for its comment on the times.

Several fine doctoral dissertations have recently been completed which deal with major figures of the twentieth century. The most important for this study were: Sheldon Bernard Avery, "Up from Washington: William Pickens and the Negro Struggle for Equality, 1900–1954" (Ph.D. dissertation, University of Oregon, 1970); Clare Bloodgood Crane, "Alain Locke and the Negro Renaissance" (Ph.D. dissertation, University of California, San Diego, 1971); and Raymond Gavins, "Gordon Blaine Hancock: Southern Black Leader in a Time of Crisis, 1920–1954" (Ph.D. dissertation, University of Virginia, 1970). The latter, though it focuses on a figure who is not analyzed in this study, provides good insight into the thinking of men like Kelly Miller, Carter Woodson, and William Pickens.

Several useful bibliographic guides for works by and about Negroes have been compiled in recent years, among them *Bibliographic Survey: The Negro in Print*, vols. 1–3 (Washington, D.C.: The Negro Bibliographic and Research Center, Inc., 1965–); Mary L. Fisher, *The Negro in America: A Bibliography* (2nd ed. rev.; Cambridge, Mass.: Harvard University Press, 1970); *The Negro in the United States: A List of Significant Books* (9th ed. rev.; New York: New York Public Library, 1965); and Erwin K. Welsch, *The Negro in the United States: A Research Guide* (Bloomington: Indiana University Press, 1965).

There is no intellectual history of black America which focuses specifically on the 1930s. There are a few excellent syntheses which cover wider periods of time and include the depression era within their scope. S. P. Fullinwider's *The Mind and Mood of Black America: Twentieth-Century Thought* (Homewood, Illinois: Dorsey Press, 1969) is an intelligent and highly imaginative interpretation of Afro-American intellectuals. Robert Bone's *The Negro Novel in America* combines perceptive literary criticism with historical analysis. Two earlier studies of Negro novelists, Hugh M. Gloster's *Negro Voices in American Fiction* (Chapel Hill: University of North Carolina Press, 1948, reprinted in 1965); and Carl Milton Hughes's *The Negro Novelist* (New York: Citadel, 1953) are generally less useful. Edward Margolies, *Native Sons: A Critical Study of Twentieth-Century Negro American Authors*, offers especially useful analyses of Richard Wright and William Attaway. The only major study of black poetry is Jean Wagner's *Les poetes negres des États-Unis: Le sentiment racial et religieux dans la poesie de P. L. Dunbar a L. Hughes* (Paris: Librairie Istra, 1962), the English translation of which, *Black Poets of the United States: From Paul Dunbar to Langston Hughes*, Kenneth Douglas, trans. (Urbana, Chicago, London: University of Illinois Press, 1973), did not appear until the present study was being prepared for the press. David Littlejohn's *Black on White: A Critical Survey of Writing by American Negroes* (New York: Grossman, 1966) is often superficial. Also superficial in its analysis, but helpful as a source of factual material was Earl E. Thorpe, *The Mind of the Negro: An Intellectual History of Afro-Americans* (Baton Rouge: Fraternal Press, 1961). Thorpe's study of Afro-American historians, *Black Historians: A Critique* (New York: William Morrow and Co., Inc., 1971; revision of his earlier *Negro Historians in the United States*), is better written and is one of the few studies on the subject. Any study of Negro or black history should begin with Vincent Harding's provocative essay, "Beyond Chaos: Black History and the Search for the New Land," Black Paper No. 2 (Atlanta, Georgia: Institute of the Black World, 1970). Margaret Just Butcher's *The Negro in American Culture* (New York: Alfred A. Knopf, Inc., 1956), based upon materials left by Alain Locke at his death, offered some useful observations pertinent to the 1930s. *The American Negro Writer and His Roots: Selected Papers from the First Conference of Negro Writers, March, 1959* (New York: American Society of African Culture, 1960), and Herbert Hill (ed.), *Anger and Beyond: The Negro Writer in the United States* (New York: Harper & Row, Publishers, Inc., 1966), are two important collections of essays.

Finally, there is Harold Cruse's polemic, *The Crisis of the Negro Intellectual* (New York: William Morrow & Co., 1967), which is often provocative, sometimes farfetched. While making no pretense at objective scholarship, Cruse has posed many important questions which scholars will not be able to ignore.

Several books have treated Negroes during the years before the depression. August Meier's valuable *Negro Thought in America, 1880–1915* (Ann Arbor: University of Michigan Press, 1963) was indispensible for understanding the basis for many of the deliberations of the 1930s. The major study of the Harlem Renaissance is now Nathan Huggins' *Harlem Renaissance* (London, Oxford, New York: Oxford University Press, 1971). Gilbert Osofsky offers a brief discussion of the Renaissance in *Harlem: The Making of a Ghetto* (New York: Harper & Row, Publishers, Inc., 1966). Stephen H. Bronz focuses on James Weldon Johnson, Claude McKay, and Countee Cullen in his study of the Renaissance, *Roots of Negro Racial Consciousness—The 1920s: Three Harlem Renaissance Authors* (New York: Libra, 1964). Edmund David Cronon gives insight into black nationalism during the 1920s in *Black Moses: The Story of Marcus Garvey and the Universal-Negro Improvement Association* (Madison: University of Wisconsin Press, 1955). Both E. U. Essien-Udom, *Black Nationalism: A Search for Identity in America* (Chicago: University of Chicago Press, 1962), and Theodore Draper, *The Rediscovery of Black Nationalism* (New York: The Viking Press, 1970), discuss black nationalism in a broad context. An excellent documentary collection and comprehensive bibliography on black nationalism is John H. Bracey, Jr., August Meier, and Elliott Rudwick (eds.), *Black Nationalism in America* (Indianapolis: The Bobbs-Merrill Co., Inc., 1970).

Several books treat Negro history in the 1930s. An early study, especially helpful in its emphasis on A. Philip Randolph, was Herbert Garfinkel, *When Negroes March: The March on Washington Movement in the Organizational Politics for FEPC* (Glencoe, Illinois: The Free Press, 1959). Richard M. Dalfiume, *Desegregation of the United States Armed Forces: Fighting on Two Fronts, 1939–1953* (Columbia: University of Missouri Press, 1969), is a model study of a problem which Negro intellectuals finally united in opposing toward the end of the depression. Dan T. Carter, *Scottsboro: A Tragedy of the American South* (Baton Rouge: Louisiana State University Press, 1969), is a superb study of an event which captured the attention of black intellectuals throughout much of the depression era. John Hammond Moore, "The Angelo Herndon Case, 1932–1937," *Phylon*, XXXII (Spring, 1971), 60–71, deals briefly with another cause célèbre of the decade. The two most important works on the relationship between Negro intellectuals and the Communist party are *The Negro and the Communist Party* (Chapel Hill: University of North Carolina Press, 1951), and *Race and Radicalism: The NAACP and the Communist Party in Conflict* (Ithaca, New York: Cornell University Press, 1964), both by Wilson Record. Daniel Aaron's *Writers on the Left: Episodes in American Literary Communism* (New York: Harcourt, Brace and Co., 1961) provides a good introduction to the influence of radical left-wing politics on intellectuals of all backgrounds.

The impact of the New Deal on black Americans is analyzed in greatest detail by Raymond Wolters, *Negroes and the Great Depression: The Problem of Economic Recovery* (Westport, Connecticut: The Greenwood Publishing Corporation, 1970), which should be supplemented by Richard Sterner's *The Negro's Share* (New York: Harper and Brothers, 1943); Donald H. Grubbs, *Cry from the Cotton: The Southern Tenant Farmers' Union and the New Deal* (Chapel Hill: University of North Carolina Press, 1971); and Allen Kifer, "The Negro and the New Deal" (Ph.D. dissertation, University of Wisconsin, 1961), which includes a discussion of Negroes in the Federal Writers' Project. Several articles have also been published which probe the relationship between the New Deal and Afro-Americans, including: Leslie Fishel, Jr., "The Negro in the New Deal Era," *Wisconsin Magazine of History*, XLVIII (Winter, 1964–65), which is generous in its assessment of the effects of the New Deal; John B. Kirby, "The Roosevelt Administration and Blacks: An Ambivalent Legacy," in Barton J. Bernstein and Allen J. Matusow (eds.), *Twentieth-Century America: Recent Interpretations* (2nd ed. rev.; New York: Harcourt Brace Jovanovich, Inc., 1972), is a more critical evaluation which also analyzes the thinking of some of the black writers examined in this study. Kirby offers a much more detailed analysis in "The New Deal Era and Blacks: A Study of Black and White Race Thought, 1933–1945" (Ph.D. dissertation, University of Illinois, 1971). More specialized analyses include: John Salmond, "The Civilian Conservation Corps and the Negro," *Journal of American History*, LII (June, 1965); James A. Harrell, "Negro Leadership in the Election Year, 1936," *Journal of Southern History*, XXXIV (November, 1968); Charles M. Martin, "Negro Leaders, the Republican Party, and the Election of 1932," *Phylon*, XXXII (Spring, 1971); Michael S. Holmes, "The Blue Eagle as 'Jim Crow Bird': The NRA and Georgia's Black Workers," *Journal of Negro History*, LVII (July, 1972); and Holmes, "The New Deal and Georgia's Black Youth," *Journal of Southern History*, XXXVIII (August, 1972); and Christopher G. Wye, "The New Deal and the Negro Community: Toward a Broader Conceptualization," *Journal of American History*, LIX (December, 1972). Finally, Peter J. Kellogg, "Northern Liberals and Black America: A History of White Attitudes, 1936–1952" (Ph.D. dissertation, Northwestern University, 1971), analyzes the attitudes of white liberals, both within and outside of the New Deal, as they appeared in *New Republic* and *The Nation*.

A useful popular history of Negroes during the 1930s was Roi Ottley's

New World A-Coming: Inside Black America (Boston: Houghton Mifflin Co., 1943). Bernard Sternsher (ed.), *The Negro in Depression and War: Prelude to Revolution, 1930–1945* (Chicago: Quadrangle Books, 1969), offers a substantial collection of essays but is most valuable for its comprehensive bibliography.

Several wide-ranging studies provided insight into the intellectuals of the period or the problems they confronted. Gunnar Myrdal's *An American Dilemma: The Negro Problem and Modern Democracy* (New York: Harper & Row, Publishers, Inc., 1944), though now dated in its conception of racial problems in this country, was nevertheless valuable because it delved into almost every aspect of Negro life during the 1930s. Much of the research for this book was conducted by some of the leading young black intellectuals considered in the present study. For a critique of Myrdal's conception of racial problems in the United States, see Carl N. Degler, "The Negro in America—Where Myrdal Went Wrong," *New York Times Magazine* (December 7, 1969). August Meier and Elliott M. Rudwick, *From Plantation to Ghetto: An Interpretive History of American Negroes* (New York: Hill and Wang, 1966), offers a sound historical analysis. John Hope Franklin provides an even more detailed account in his now classic text, *From Slavery to Freedom: A History of American Negroes* (3rd ed., rev. and enl.; New York: Alfred A. Knopf, Inc., 1967). Also useful are E. Franklin Frazier, *The Negro in the United States* (rev. ed.; New York: The Macmillan Co., 1957), and Charles E. Silberman, *Crisis in Black and White* (New York: Random House, Inc., 1964). An imaginative treatment of most of the themes developed in this study can be found in Ralph Ellison's magnificent novel, *Invisible Man* (New York: Random House, 1952).

Index